AD HOC GOVERNMENTS

Special Purpose Transportation Authorities in Britain and the United States

Volume 10, Sage Library of Social Research

SAGE LIBRARY OF SOCIAL RESEARCH

Also in this series:

Ad Hoc Governments

Special Purpose Transportation Authorities in
Britain and the United States

Robert G. Smith

Volume 10
SAGE LIBRARY OF
SOCIAL RESEARCH

 SAGE PUBLICATIONS   Beverly Hills   London

To
Lois

For information address:

SAGE PUBLICATIONS, INC.
275 South Beverly Drive
Beverly Hills, California 90212

SAGE PUBLICATIONS LTD
St George's House / 44 Hatton Garden
London EC1N 8ER

Printed in the United States of America

International Standard Book Number 0-8039-0332-4 (C)
0-8039-0331-6 (P)
Library of Congress Catalog Card No. 73-88910

FIRST PRINTING

TABLE OF CONTENTS

PREFACE

Expressions of "autonomy" and "independence from control" are not claims generally associated with agencies of democratic government. Yet, these very words have been used as self-descriptive for a great many years by a considerable number of units of government that have been playing major roles in two of the largest representative countries in the world—the United Kingdom and the United States. The Port of London Authority, for example, has described itself as "a corporation established by Statute practically independent of Government . . . and . . . broadly speaking, conducting its own affairs without interference" (Port of London Authority, 1958: 4). The former Executive Director of the counterpart of the Port of London Authority in the United States, the Port Authority of New York and New Jersey, declared: "If the task doesn't require the independence and autonomy of the corporate form, there is really no need to create an authority" (Tobin, 1953: 29). Countless units of government in the two countries, performing the most vital public functions, particularly those in the British conurbations and the American metropolitan areas, have been operating under these apparently paradoxical assumptions.

In the United Kingdom, such agencies have been known since the fifteenth century, and have numbered several thousand. They are referred to there, collectively, as ad hoc governments. In the United States, the generic classification

of these semiautonomous units, numbering 23,886, has come
to be that of "special districts." That is the official designation of them in the *Census of Governments* published every
five years by the Bureau of the Census. Americans do know
the words "ad hoc," but they confine them usually to committees of legislative bodies that are not permanent, in
contradistinction to the so-called "standing committees." A
cursory examination of five standard dictionaries of politics
and government in the United States turns up no mention,
whatever, of these two Latin words. The Random House
Dictionary (1967: 18), published in New York, however,
does define "ad hoc" as "for this (special purpose)." This
suggestion of "special purpose" seems to identify them most
clearly, as each is formed to accomplish one particular function, or closely related functions, and, therefore, they, as a
whole, are to be contrasted to the more conventional elected
governments that are in existence to meet all the normal
expectations of the citizens. The characterization of the
widespread proliferation of these special units as "ad-hoc-
ery" by Dr. William A. Robson, Professor Emeritus of Public
Administration of the London School of Economics and
Political Science, could not be misunderstood, however, by
either British or Americans.

On the surface, the establishment of these special governments by the thousands would seem to have been expected
least in the two democratic countries, and, yet, Britain has
had them for some 500 years and America for more than 180
years, and their use today in both countries is increasing.
Furthermore, the most unique British version of them—the
public corporation—and America's distinctive contribution to
them—the special public authority—have been exported to
other nations, and both the public corporation and the
special public authority are found widespread throughout
developing as well as developed governments.

In the light of their common experiences, particularly
those of the past 40 years in which Britain and America
turned to the special-purpose governments to meet pressing
needs of the worldwide depression, those growing from

World War II and urban concerns today, it seems strange that there has not been a lively exchange of information and ideas about these agencies among officials and scholars of the respective countries. The lack of such intercommunication certainly has deprived both the United Kingdom and the United States of cross-fertilization of ideas concerning these units, which is especially serious when one considers that it has been two English-speaking countries, with mutual concerns in the past, that have been pioneering in this unusual kind of agency. The fact is that there have been relatively few studies of special governments even within either of the two countries, regardless of any attempts to study them across national lines, and the only saving factor in this realization of neglect lies in the fact that, although few in number, those that we do have generally are of excellent quality. The United Kingdom, for instance, has been fortunate to have had two internationally recognized urban experts devote their attention to them: William A. Robson and the late A. H. Hanson, Professor of Politics of the University of Leeds. In the United States, such scholars as Victor Jones, of the University of California at Berkeley, and John C. Bollens, of the University of California, at Los Angeles, early identified this area of special governments as one of growing concern. Also, in the United Kingdom and the United States, practitioners deeply involved personally in the functions of these agencies, have written about them from a practical and theoretical viewpoint. Herbert Morrison, later Lord Morrison of Lambeth, who became minister of transport in the second minority Labour government, after the General Election of 1929, gives us, in his book, *Socialisation and Transport* (1933), his own account of his efforts to push through Parliament the London Passenger Transport Bill and to establish therein a public corporation, and, as well, his philosophical and practical thoughts on the nature of such a public corporation. In the United States, Dr. William J. Ronan, who now is chairman of the Metropolitan Transportation Authority in New York, and one of the most influential exponents of the authority district device in America, prepared an official *Staff Report on Public Authorities Under New York State* (1956), still considered to be one of the most balanced analyses in the United States, declaring the public authority to be "one of the most significant developments in modern governmental administration" (Temporary State Commission on Coordination of State Activities, 1956: 3). Other studies of value within each country are mentioned throughout the book.

These few works on special governments are titillating. The subject, obviously, by no means is exhausted. Dr. John M. Gaus, then Professor at Harvard University, tried to explain their sense of anticipation, in the foreword that he wrote for one of the first comprehensive books on *Special District Governments in the United States,* by John C. Bollens. Special districts tell us, he said, "that there are some underlying fault lines where the pressure needs in certain areas has led to the fracturing of the old strata, or levels, of government." It may be, he explained, that "some volcanic energies, deep below, have here and there forced new structures up." There is "so much to learn from the superficial about what lies below it" (Bollens, 1957: vii).

A curiously severe handicap to comparative studies of these "new structures" between the United Kingdom and the United States has arisen in the fact of the centralized government of the former, as against the federal form, in the latter. Ad hoc governments in Britain are created by parliamentary legislation. The Congress of the United States has formed, by its laws, national public corporations, but the fact is that the predominant number of them have come from actions of the state legislatures. John Thurston, of Northwestern University, could not have caught the distinction, in his *Government Proprietary Corporations in the English-Speaking Countries,* published as early as 1937, for the proliferation of the special public authorities in the United States, spawned by the lure of federal monies but created by the states then was just getting under way. Thurston wrote effectively of six British ad hoc agencies, but he centered his attention on the United States on 31 national corporations; one regional (the Port of

New York Authority); and one local (the Boston Elevated Railway Company) to which he made only two passing references. Probably because of his limited selection in America he was able to conclude that "(a)ll the defects of the government department . . . are remedied by the creation of a government corporation" (1937: 7). Subsequent events would serve to challenge the extent of his conclusion.

It is understandable, of course, but regrettable, that international symposia on public corporations years later should have continued to attempt to use the national government corporation of the United States as the base for comparison to special governments of other countries, when, actually, the significant movement in America was occurring on the state level. It is to the credit of such scholars as Albert S. Abel, Professor of Law at West Virginia University, writing on behalf of the United States in the comparative symposium edited by Wolfgang Friedmann, in 1954, that he actually recognized the distinction, even though not its full import. He accurately caught the fact that at that time, the use of the national government corporation in America had been "waning." "That trend will probably continue in the near future," he prophesied. He sensed the fact that "state government corporations are increasingly frequent," and recognized that "use by the States . . . has not been insignificant." He drew back a bit, however, pointing out that state movement in this direction "remains . . . occasional and unsystematic." "Perhaps even more than the United States," he summarized in disbelief, "the States have found in it only an extraordinary and ad hoc response to particular circumstances without ever developing it as a regular instrument of government" (Friedmann, 1954: 345, 351).

In that same year, 1954, a United Nations Seminar on "Public Enterprise, A Study of its Organisation and Management in various Countries" was held in Rangoon. Harold Seidman, of the United States Bureau of the Budget, presented a paper on "The Government Corporation: Its Place in the Federal Structure," by which he meant the national government corporation. Two large interstate authorities, the

Port of New York Authority and the Tennessee Valley
Authority, were covered in separate papers, but there was no
discussion of these units down in the states. No paper on
British corporations was offered, although Professor Friedmann referred to them in his opening comments.

A third symposium, this time entitled "Public Authorities"
was published in 1961 by the School of Law of Duke
University. It contained a thorough presentation of special
agencies in the United States and of interstate authorities.
This time, however, as luck would have it, the British side
was not given. The editor of the published report apologized
for the lack, but blamed it on "circumstances beyond the
Editor's control" (1961: 590).

The national government corporation would appear, at a
glance, to be apposite for comparison to the public corporation established by Parliament. The fact is, however, that
these national corporations in the United States had begun to
lose their significance in American government in the 1940s,
after an extension of their numbers and power under the
early New Deal administration. Concomitantly, those special
agencies created by the states were increasing out of all
proportion, often with the encouragement of the federal
government. By 1954, when two of the international symposia were being published, there were only 78 active national government corporations, but already some 14,400
special districts in the United States. As early as 1941,
C. Herman Pritchett wrote that the characteristics of the
federal public corporation in the United States "have been
disappearing before our eyes, like the Cheshire cat. Soon
there may be nothing left but a smile to mark the spot where
the government corporation once stood." Five years later, he
was to conclude that "for good or ill, American experience
with autonomous public corporations is substantially at an
end" (as cited in White, 1955: 136). The final ax had fallen
with the passage by Congress of the Government Corporation
Control Act of 1945, by which Congress declared it to be its
policy "to bring Government corporations and their transactions and operations under annual scrutiny by the Congress

and provide current financial control thereof." They were required to come under the annual budget process of government departments, as well as audit by the comptroller general. Several existing corporations were discontinued. New national corporations could be established only by the Congress, thus pointing again to the complexities of the federal system in which, in fact, a number of the national corporations had been organized in the states in order to take advantage of the more favorable corporation laws on the lower level. The United States Housing Corporation, for example, had been chartered in New York State in 1918; the Spruce Production Corporation in the State of Washington, the same year, and the United States Sugar Equalization Board, and the United States Grain Corporation, both in the State of Delaware in 1917. It is no wonder that scholars have been confused as to the locale of special units. A spate of recently organized national public corporations have appeared, such as the Corporation for Public Broadcast, in 1967; National Railroad Passenger Corporation (Amtrak) 1971; the United States Postal Service, 1971; and a mixed-enterprise type organization, the Communications Satellite Corporation (Comsat), 1962. State creations continue, however, with unabated numbers.

The author of this book proposes to trace the development of the concept of the special public authority in the United States through the creation of these agencies by the state governments, rather than through those relatively few that were established by the national government, and to set that state proliferation of special public authorities against the development of the concept of the public corporation in the United Kingdom. The study explores the respective movements to special governments comprehensively in the two countries in order to catch similarities and divergencies. Then, in deference to the confusion that could well arise through the fact of the thousands of units involved, the book directs its attention to one major function, transportation, in which special agencies have been playing the predominant role in both the United Kingdom and the United States. It was in that function that both the British public corporation and the American special public authority first emerged in their modern forms. And it is there that the greatest degree of experimentation with special units of government still is taking place. These modifications, or innovations, are being followed by metropolitan officials throughout the world, as all are caught up in the same need to balance automobile traffic with various modes of mass transportation. Not only do the British and the Americans have something to say to each other about their common experiences in this regard over the years, but they may just have therein a dialogue with much wider implications for other countries.

It is the hope of the author that this book will encourage comparative studies of these common special progenies of the United Kingdom and the United States. It may help do so by its identification of points of similarities and divergencies in the course of the evolution of the special transportation units in the two countries. The account is presented chronologically, as that seems to be the perspective necessary to the beginning of such studies, prerequisite to stopping at any point for comparisons in depth.

Professor William A. Robson consented to read the manuscript and made comments of great help to the accuracy of the final account.

—Robert G. Smith

Chapter 1

AD HOC DURABILITY

ENDURANCE IN THE UNITED KINGDOM

In speculating on the possibility that a new global outlook, or "international city" concept, might arise through the use of recently developed techniques of human understanding and communication, Arnold Toynbee (interview, *Illustrated London News,* 1972: 53) warned, however, that as a result, people could come to lose all interest in political matters. National governments, he explained, might be reduced to the role of "public utilities," "like the North Thames Gas Board." If "Britain, Nicaragua, the USA, Honduras, the Soviet Union and all the rest" were to be considered mere operating agencies, "it is possible that people will lose their zest for running the government of those states." Sensing no identification with the "gas boards," they would become bored with government.

Toynbee's use of the analogy of one of London's public utilities, the North Thames Gas Board, serves to point up his understanding of the difference between the public's conception of such an ad hoc unit, and that of its elected general-purpose government. This board was one of twelve area gas boards covering Great Britain in 1972, three of which served Greater London, all under a central Gas Council. Each area board had a considerable degree of independence in performing the essential functions of the manufacture and distribution of gas. Not only were its clients "unwilling to lay down their lives for the North Thames Gas Board," as the interview reported Toynbee to have commented, but, as a matter of fact, that agency had become the butt of public complaints in letters to the editors of the London newspapers. Such letters appeared so frequently in the London *Times* in 1972 that the letter heading in an October issue was entitled, "Gas board again" (1972b). The British Gas Corporation replaced the Gas Council on January 1, 1973, but "North Thames Gas" continued as one of its reorganized subunits.

The persistence of ad hoc government in Greater London raises questions of propriety, especially when one considers that it had survived the rather thorough reorganization of governmental responsibilities in the London Government Act of 1963, which had allocated functions either to the new borough tier, or to the regional tier, known as Greater London. The area gas boards, of course, were integrated into neither tier, but trisected the Greater London area, operating with the degree of autonomy that enabled each to devise its own subordinate structure, under general supervision of the central Gas Council. The supplying of gas, moreover, was but one of a number of vital functions that remained under ad hoc arrangements after the reforms of the governments of London in the 1960s. The Royal Commission on Local Government in Greater London that had been appointed in 1957 to examine the systems of government in Greater London and make recommendations had not overlooked the significance of the omission of these independent units from the integration of governmental responsibilities, and, indeed, had deplored its lack of jurisdiction to look into them:

> The point relevant to our purpose is that the needs of services have forced the creation of special "metropolitan" bodies for police, water, the Port of London, traffic, public passenger transport, gas, electricity, hospitals and advanced technical education. All these are services which have been provided in England by local authorities at one time or another. It is not for us to enquire whether this is still possible in Greater London, since police and water supply are specifically placed outside our terms of reference, and since most of the other services are outside local government and each raises difficult technical issues of its own. But it should be noted that the requirements of these services have led to the creation of specialised "regional" authorities, covering the Review Area and more ... [Royal Commission, 1960: 41].

Exempted from inclusion in the two-tier structure, therefore, were such essential functions as those affecting water, electricity, gas, port, railways, airports, transport, hospitals, police, land drainage, sewerage, postal service, and the development of satellite new towns surrounding the London area. Reasons for their exclusion varied with the nature of the function. In regard to water supply, expressly ruled outside the Royal Commission's review area, the Metropolitan Water Board had argued, in 1957, that "the function of water supply, as one which was necessarily governed by special, particularly hydrogeological, factors ... should be excluded from the terms of reference of the Royal Commission" (Metropolitan Water Board, 1963: 14).

The Royal Commission had not avoided the problem, despite its lack of warrant to include these agencies within its purview. At one point in its *Report* it blamed their proliferation on the "imperfections" of the standard governments of London. In response to a suggestion that the commission recommend the formation of additional special governments of this kind for certain purposes, it stated bluntly that the idea "need not detain us long." Recognition of two "fatal objections" lay behind the dismissal of the proposal by the commission: "these bodies are either the creatures of central government or they are responsible to no one"; and that, inasmuch as "so many of London's problems are interlinked," it "is no solution to separate them still further by giving each to some specially designed *ad hoc* body" (Royal Commission, 1960: 39-41, 182, 188).

There were echoes here of the earlier warnings against the widespread employment of special-purpose units made by William A. Robson, then Professor of Public Administration at the London School of Economics and Political Science. "Sometimes the more pressing technical difficulties may be assuaged for a time," he had written as early as 1939. "But ultimately the *ad hoc* body gives rise to as many problems as it solves. The most serious drawback of the *ad hoc* body [and here the Commission's *Report* some twenty years later came to the same conclusion] is that there is no method of co-ordinating its work with related activities carried out by other bodies. . . . Yet the services of a great modern city are becoming more interrelated every day" (1948: 334).

Rather than undergoing reductions in number, there are indications that there actually may be increases in the uses and functions of special-purpose governments. In 1972, for example, when the government announced that it proposed to develop a third airport for London at Maplin Sands at the estuary of the Thames River, it explained that five ad hoc agencies would shoulder the responsibilities for the undertaking—two new ones to be created for the purpose and three existing ones. The under-secretary of state for the environment stated that, in view of the fact that

> its long time-scale and the crucial issues of Government policy that it raises require substantial public sector involvement . . . (t)he Government have . . . decided to seek powers to establish a Development Authority to undertake the task of land reclamation; secondly, to make land available to the British Airports Authority for the airport and to the Port of London Authority for any seaport development . . . [and] to designate a substantial area for development by a New Town Development Corporation [British Airports Authority, 1972: 67].

The British Railway Board would provide rail links to this outlying area. Later, after rough going in the House of Commons, the bill to effect the Maplin Development went to the House of Lords with a clause attached that would require the Civil Aviation Authority to keep reviewing technical matters involving aircraft noise, and to prevent the development of Maplin airport if its continuing studies so indicate this as desirable.

The Department of the Environment was to serve in a coordinating role, at least in the planning stages, as Maplin was to be, in the words of the British Airports Authority, "the world's first environmental airport" (The British Airports Authority *Report and Accounts 1971-72:* 15). In light of the division of responsibilities for its construction under at least six special-purpose governments, however, the expectations of the government that this venture into urban planning, if ultimately approved, "will present over the next decade a great opportunity for imaginative integrated development," were to face a severe testing (British Airports Authority, 1972: 66). Whether or not approved, the proposal illustrates graphically the continuing importance of ad hoc agencies.

Similar strains of durability are to be found in the other ad hoc governments that dot the United Kingdom, in addition to those in the London region. Under the Local Government Act of 1972, which provides for the reorganization of governments in England and Wales, to be consummated by 1974, and in Scotland by 1975, a number of key functions are not to be included under either the county tier or the district tier, in England and Wales, or the regional or district tiers, in Scotland. "Water, sewage disposal and some sewerage functions are to be removed from local government and put into new regional water authorities, and existing local authority health services are to be allocated to the new regional hospital authorities and area health boards. Social services and the health services will be quite separately administered" (G. W. Jones, 1973: 162-163).

The confusion that could occur in the functioning of these

ad hoc units side-by-side with the newly organized counties and districts has been anticipated by the Study Group on Local Authority Management Structures, set up by the Secretary of State for the Environment to advise on such concerns. Avowing, however, that this so-called Bains Committee (after M. A. Bains, who chaired its working group) wanted to leave to the new governments considerable initiative in methods of local cooperation, its report merely assumed that coordination could be achieved. The committee saw less of a problem in this regard concerning the area health authorities, as their boundaries would be contiguous with those of the local governments. It "will be a simple matter structurally to involve the area health authorities in those services of mutual concern both in the day to day operation and in the forward planning and policy making of local authorities." It foresaw more difficulties with the regional water authorities whose boundaries were not to be contiguous with those of the new local governments. The county joint committees were singled out as one possible solution, although the report suggested that there "might also be a need for some separate coordinative body comprising the regional water authority and representatives of all local authorities within its area" (Department of the Environment, 1972: 92, 96-97).

This continuing justification of ad hoc governments gives credence to Professor A. H. Hanson's contention that "they are unlikely to disappear, either by a process of withering away or by one of absorption." Because of the increasing interpenetration of the public and private sectors, he concluded, "further institutional innovation . . . will almost certainly be required" (Hanson and Walles, 1970: 167-168). Past history also seems to bear him out. Hanson, himself, has traced special agencies to two long-past eras, "the Tudor period [1485-1603] and that of the Industrial Revolution [beginning in 1760]" (Hanson and Walles, 1970: 167). Robson finds them associated with the government of London "from 1839, when the Commissioners of Police for the Metropolis were first set up" (1948: 333). The *Report of the Commissioner of Police of the Metropolis for the year 1971,* some 132 years later, caught up the sense of continuity: "Commissioners come and go, but the enduring stability of the Metropolitan Police is there for all to see" (1972: 9).

ENDURANCE IN THE UNITED STATES

Although the history of the United States Government, as such, does not trace back to the fifteenth century, there never has been a time in its existence, from 1789 to the present, that ad hoc agencies have not played a significant role. Where the United Kingdom can refer to its early "turnpike trusts" as illustrations of special units that collected tolls, America can cite its "turnpike corporate companies" of its first years under a united government. Albert Gallatin, secretary of the treasury in George Washington's first cabinet, made it clear that he favored the "mixed corporation" for the financing of banks, canals, turnpikes, river improvements, and bridges, by both the federal and state governments, and he encouraged its use (White, 1951: 493).

While Professor Robson was warning of the disadvantages of the resort to ad hoc governments, on one side of the Atlantic, such American scholars as Victor Jones, then a professor at Wesleyan University, were issuing strikingly similar admonitions, independently, on the other. "There is no let-up," Jones wrote in the 1950s, "in the pressure to shift responsibility for governmental activities from the general city or county government to special authorities and independent boards. It does not follow, however," he countered, "that each function of government should be separately organized over a distinctive area." He drew a comparison to the trend in Britain by supporting a point first made by Dr. Luther Gulick (V. Jones, 1953: 580), of the United States, to the effect that

the distribution of authority between the central and constituent units should not be based on "guild" autonomy. Persistently in this country and in England as government has undertaken new activities or as crises have arisen in the administration of established functions, the professionalism of one group of specialists after another has shown itself in the demand for preferential position.

The growth pattern had continued, however, almost in mathematical progression. A special report to the President's National Resources Committee, in 1939, began to visualize "a puzzling maze of local government never before duplicated in the history of political institutions," with some 259 special districts in Chicago, alone, and another 212 in Los Angeles (Supplementary Report of the Urbanism Committee, 1939: 27). As census reporting of governments became more sophisticated, national figures revealed 8,299 special districts in 1942; 14,405 ten years later; 14,424 in 1957; (with 1,700 of the increase attributable to redefined classifications) 18,323 were included in the 1962 listing; (with 1,900 attributable to similar changes) 21,264 appeared in the 1967 census of governments; and, finally, 23,886 special units in 1972. None of these totals included school districts, which, because of their numbers (15,780 in 1972), were listed separately. Leading the list, numerically, were special districts for fire protection, followed, in priority, by those for soil conservation, water supply, and housing and urban renewal. In transportation, highway special districts or authorities accounted for 698. On the other hand, the number of special units for mass transit had increased from 14, in the 1967 census, to 33 in the 1972 count, and, if dependent as well as independent districts were included, special agencies for mass transit would number some 150. This constitutes one of the greatest increases in types of government in the history of the country. When turnpikes, mass transit districts, parking authorities, airports, port authorities, and the like, all are added together, there are today some 4,000 special units in the United States involved with transportation.

As was the case in London, cities in the United States felt their impact, particularly as services began to expand beyond the cities' fixed boundaries. One of the first real confrontations between a city government, on the one hand, and special public authorities, on the other, was waged in New York City during the 1960s and 1970s. There, the opening shot was fired by John V. Lindsay in his first campaign for the office of mayor. He pledged that, if elected, he would "speedily place before the people of this City a comprehensive but practical plan for the reorganization, integration and coordination of the various elements of the City's transportation system." This plan would be designed to "blast the encrusted layers of distrust, misunderstanding, non-communication and non-cooperation which have grown and have prevented progress," and which had resulted from the "hydra-headed and fragmented monstrosity" which characterized the city's transportation structure (Lindsay, 1965: 3). The fact that a major portion of the responsibility for transportation in New York City was in the hands of four large special public authorities and a subsidiary authority of one of them presented these ad hoc units·with an open challenge to their powers by the mayor of America's biggest city. The coordination of this functional complex, according to the chairman of a task force Lindsay named to work out the details, "requires that ultimate responsibility be lodged in one spot—the office of the Mayor" (Letter to Editor, *New York Times*, 1966). Even while the task force was meeting, Mayor Lindsay created a transportation administration within his office and an administrator "who shall be appointed by and shall serve at the pleasure of the Mayor" (Lindsay, 1966). Included within the scope of the administration were "subway, bus, truck, automobile, taxi, air, waterborne and pedestrian movement" and, to some extent "movement by rail." Inasmuch as most of these activities were the concern of the four special public authorities and the subsidiary, the issue between the ad hoc agencies and the mayor, just elected by a plurality of a little more than 125,000 votes, clearly was joined.

The resolution of the struggle is discussed later in this book, and its day-to-day skirmishes in another source (Smith, 1969). The relevance of the outcome here lies in its further witness to the permanency of ad hoc government. Mayor Lindsay's transportation administration, which he had set up by Executive Order on January 17, 1966, was not finally approved (for funding) by the City Council until December 11, 1969, almost *four* years later. By that time, however, Mayor Lindsay's plan for bringing the various transportation agencies of the city under his coordinative power as mayor, long since had come from the task force, and had been rejected soundly by the state legislature. (It would have placed the mayor's transportation administrator as chairman of both the New York City Transit Authority and the Triborough Bridge and Tunnel Authority, the two large special authorities wholly within the borders of the City; and would have given the mayor veto powers over the actions of the boards of both.) Instead, the power of coordination of the activities of the New York City Transit Authority, the Triborough Bridge and Tunnel Authority, and the Metropolitan Commuter Transportation Authority had passed almost totally out of the control of the mayor to a newly established, state-oriented special public authority, known as the Metropolitan Transportation Authority. The Transit Authority and the Triborough Authority remained as legal entities, and the Metropolitan Commuter Transportation Authority was subsumed by the much larger special unit that took the same name, but with the word "commuter" eliminated. The separate Port of New York Authority, which bridged the two states of New York and New Jersey, remained essentially untouched. In other words, after a most vigorous confrontation of the mayor of New York City with the special transportation authorities, ad hoc agencies still dominated this significant function, both within the city and regionally. Toward the end of his second term, Lindsay tried once again, and proposed that "vital transportation decisions" be placed "in the hands of an elected body directly responsible to the citizens of the entire region" (*New York Times,* 1973b)—but to no avail.

For purposes other than transportation, special public

authorities in New York City also had fared well. Added to the already long list of such ad hoc agencies within, or directly affecting, the City during Mayor Lindsay's two terms were the Health and Hospitals Corporation, Public Development Corporation, Offtrack Betting Corporation, Battery Park City Authority, Urban Development Corporation, New York City Exhibition Center Development Corporation, Rehabilitation Mortgage Insurance Corporation, and the United Nations Development Corporation. All special public authorities in New York are chartered by the state, but for most of these additional ones, the mayor, himself, had sponsored or defended them.

Concomitant with the debate in England over the development of the Maplin Airport, there was occurring in the United States a similar effort to get approval for another major jetport in the New York metropolitan area. The site finally agreed on was that of Stewart Airport, at Newburgh, New York, just about the same distance from New York City that Maplin is from London. Here, as in the case of Maplin, ad hoc agencies were assigned the principal responsibilities. Stewart Air Force Base was purchased by the Metropolitan Transportation Authority; that authority then created a special land development authority, known as the Stewart Airport Land Authority, "to acquire, hold and administer newly acquired lands until such time as they are used for aviation purposes" (Metropolitan Transportation Authority, 1972: 44). Railroad connections to New York, some 50 miles to the southeast, are to be undertaken by the Port Authority Trans-Hudson Corporation, a subsidiary of the Port Authority of New York and New Jersey, in order to connect the Erie-Lackawanna Railroad with the main line of the Penn Central, for direct service under the Hudson River into Pennsylvania Station in New York City. Passenger and freight service, then, between Stewart and New York City would be available. Automobile traffic for the new airport would be handled by the existing Thomas E. Dewey Thruway, under the aegis of the New York State Thruway Authority, which serves the Newburgh area. The Federal Aviation Administration would report on the environmental impact and hold public hearings.

The similarities in the dependence on ad hoc units of government for both Maplin and Stewart are apparent. Both Maplin, if approved, and Stewart, already agreed to, are to be developed largely by special-purpose governmental agencies. One principal difference must not be overlooked, however: the ultimate decision as to the project in England had to be made by the Parliament; in the United States, the states of New York and New Jersey bore the brunt of the policy-approval, with New York State having to pass on the plans of the Metropolitan Transportation Authority, and both New York and New Jersey being required to endorse the activities of the Port Authority of New York and New Jersey, and of its subsidiary, the Port Authority Trans-Hudson Corporation.

One metropolitan area after another in the United States would show the plethora of special public authorities. Even in the case of those cities that have consolidated their functions with those of the counties in which they are located, the ad hoc units have retained their role. The new city of Jacksonville, which became operational in 1968, after having consolidated the government of the former city with that of Duval County, Florida, illustrates the point. Its first mayor,
* Hans Tanzler, Jr., proclaimed "a single government and a single opportunity to prepare for the future and to take advantage of the whole 844 square miles of the county" (*American County*, 1970: 17). Yet, still remaining fully functional there were the Jacksonville Electric Authority, Jacksonville Port Authority, Duval Hospital Authority, and a housing authority.

Evidence is readily available that even the present crop of 23,886 special districts does not represent the ultimate peak that they will reach. The most probable functions for which they now may proliferate are those of mass transit and pollution control. Dr. William J. Ronan, chairman of the New York Metropolitan Transportation Authority, predicted, as president of the Institute for Rapid Transit, in 1970, that the decade then starting would see the greatest construction of mass transit facilities in the history of the country, with at least $17.7 billion to be spent (*National Civic Review,* 1970: 158). Most transit construction in the United States is directed by special-purpose districts for mass transit.

In September 1973, the Federal Aviation Administration announced that 700 new airports would be needed over the next 10 years. Airport construction very commonly is undertaken by special public authorities (Smith, 1965).

Even the older functions of transportation, such as that of highway traffic, bid to increase their use of the ad hoc agencies in years to come. The International Bridge, Tunnel and Turnpike Association predicted that "U.S. toll facilities will spend more than $1.6 billion for new construction in the three-year period from 1973 through 1975." The Association explained this meant "that the dollar investment in new toll facilities will increase about 25 percent annually, compared with the last six years." The great majority of toll facilities are under the jurisdiction of special-purpose governments (International Bridge, Tunnel and Turnpike Association, Tollways, 1972).

For pollution control, the *Money Manager,* an investment journal focusing on bonds, estimated in July 1973 that at least a quarter of the $4.5 billion on pollution control that American business might spend for the entire year would be paid for by tax exempt bonds. Such financing is used extensively by special public authorities, many of which are being formed for this purpose in the pollution field (Winders, 1973: back page and 42).

COMMON BRITISH AND AMERICAN CONCERNS

Recognition

The proliferation and permanency of ad hoc governments, therefore, characterize public administration in both the

United Kingdom and the United States. The prevalence of
these agencies throughout history in England, Ireland, Scotland, and Wales and in all 50 states of the United States, in
the provision of the most intimate kind of services, such as
health, transportation, utilities, sewerage, and other everyday
needs would seem to assure that, by now at least, they would
have gained popular identification. The curious fact is, however, that there is precious little awareness of their essential
role in either country. The very promiscuity of their use into
widespread functions, often in default of action by the more
conventional governments, has served to blur any conception
of them, collectively, as a functional level of government.
They commonly are accepted on both sides of the Atlantic as
additional extensions of bureaucratic government, one step
further removed from the people than standard departments.
The *Scotsman,* of Edinburgh, (1972a), reflected the remoteness of special governments:

> (D)o we not . . . need a body to collect opinion about local policy
> decisions of the area health boards and all the other ad hoc, often
> unrepresentative bodies whose decisions so often affect us vi-
> tally? . . . The decision to close a hospital or turn local schools
> into a comprehensive or build a ring road calls into being an
> ad hoc "community" which is often vociferous and usually
> hostile.

The *New York Times* (1971b), through an experience of its
former drama critic, Brooks Atkinson, mirrored similar
apprehension in America, in this instance over a plan of the
New York State Power Authority to run a "massive power
transmission line" through Atkinson's community and attempts of the citizens to prevent that action:

> The inequality of the power authority's resources and ours is
> frightening. . . . Although we have threatened no one and have
> taken no hostile action, we are expected to defend ourselves
> against a huge political and technological organization that can
> pay the salaries of executives, engineers, attorneys and public
> relations specialists. . . . They are not interested in our problems.

Even British and American scholars have been deterred from studies in this field by an uneasy feeling that perhaps their work is not worth the considerable time and energy required, as these units, so diverse in nature, may represent nothing more than expediencies for the meeting of problems not otherwise cared for by the general-purpose governments. Terence O'Brien, for one, who wrote one of the first books on public corporations in Britain (1937: 13), admitted that he had been bothered by this uncertainty:

> Do they represent the emergence of a new type of public organisation the imitation of which for other purposes is practicable and desirable? Or is it more accurate and profitable to regard them as isolated empirical responses to widely different sets of problems, which have functioned since their creation for purposes and under conditions so varied that collective study of their past performances and future significance can offer little that is of value?

Indeed, one year before that, another British author, Lord Allen of Hurtwood, had described the public corporation as "an accepted expression of the British commonsense way of doing a technical job efficiently and with general consent" (as cited in Gordon, 1938: 3).

At just about the same time, American writers were considering the value of studying the growing number of special public authorities in their country. They, too, were wondering about the meaning of this movement, in general. Horace Davis (1935: 331), for instance, asked whether the new agencies were not merely "the lazy man's answer to more or less embarrassing questions?" There could be no doubt that, in the United States in the 1930s they were being created in a totally unsystematic way to meet one contingency after another during those depression years. In the late 1930s municipal authorities were chartered in Pennsylvania simply under the title, "No Known Purpose Authorities," apparently as a hedge against their possible need for some, as then, unanticipated function. The Pennsylvania Department of Internal Affairs, listing 49 such authorities, under that category by 1960 said that it was "unable to list an objective" for them, but that no bonds had been issued by them over the years. One such "No Known Purpose Authority" for urban Philadelphia County had been formed in 1938 (Sause, 1962: 37-38; Pennsylvania Commonwealth, 1960: 59).

The late A. H. Hanson, Professor of Politics at the University of Leeds, who devoted much of his time to their study in the United Kingdom and in developing countries, referred to them as "constitutional anomalies" (Hanson and Walles, 1970: 167).

The sheer numbers of them, which would seem to serve to call the attention of the public and scholars to their significance, actually militated against such recognition. "It would be futile," concluded William Anderson, an American scholar whose interest in counting governments had anteceded that of the Bureau of the Census, in regard to his statistics for 1942, "to try to discuss the relative areas, populations, and activities of the special units enumerated. The facts are simply not available" (1942: 5, 36). And even Professor Robson (1937: 10-11), who later was to publish the most comprehensive urban analysis, the *Great Cities of the World*, complained in a book he edited on *Public Enterprise* in 1937 that "anyone who has attempted to master the vast material necessary to study even one of the [ad hoc] institutions . . . can have no illusions as to the magnitude of the task. . . . I doubt whether, with the present rate of change and flux, it would be practicable for a single author to deal with the various special organs."

Robson was one of the first to sense their importance, however. He declared, in that same book, that the commissions and boards "form the most significant development in the field of political institutions which has taken place in Great Britain during the present century" (1937: 9). Twenty-five years later, he was to conclude (1962: 493): "Allowing for some teething troubles which are still not entirely cured, the public corporation which we have evolved is an outstanding contribution to public administration in a new and vitally important sphere."

Causes

A measure of their importance could be taken if reasons for their being formed, and in such numbers, could be determined. If they do represent something more than "isolated empirical responses," in Britain, and "the lazy man's answer," in America, their meaning might be found in causes for their creation. Greater help here then could be given if such reasons could be grouped together in categories, and if a typology could emerge. This would have to be attempted first for each country, independently, but then might provide a basis for comparing reasons for their establishment from one country to the other. If common denominators appeared in such a process, they would be indicative, as, of course, would be differences.

The first clue to reasons for the evolution of them possibly could be detected through names, or titles, that have been assigned to them from time to time and from place to place. Such a lead, however, is unrewarding. In view of the fact that in both countries ad hoc government has emerged in an extraconstitutional realm, no standard terminology commonly assigned governmental levels, has been applied. Rather, wholly unimaginative labels were attached without emphasis on continuity or consistency. The Local Act of Parliament that spawned some 1,800 ad hoc governments over the seventeenth, eighteenth, and early nineteenth centuries, burdened these units with titles certainly not designed to elicit public identification with them: "Courts of Sewers, Incorporated Guardians of the Poor, Turnpike Trusts, and Improvement Commissioners" (Webb, 1922: v). The lack of attention to imagery, here, which could have served to encourage political identity by persons involved with these agencies, is reaffirmed by other labels for special governments in the United Kingdom, which have included: "public boards," "semi-public bodies," "services," "authorities," "conservancies," "transport," "public corporations," and "executives." As a whole, they do not conjure up, in the mind of the public, pictures of the nature of the particular ad hoc unit and of what its role in the government constitutes. The word, "authority," which is so closely identified with special-purpose governments that depend on self-financing in the United States, does not have this same connotation in the United Kingdom, as there the word means government, of a general-purpose nature. In the United States, the word, "authority," indicates a special-purpose unit; in Britain, on the other hand, it usually signifies the more conventional, elected bodies. A story, current in the United States, that the Port of London Authority, the prototype for the Port of New York Authority, received its designation as an "Authority" because David Lloyd George, one of its sponsors, noted that its statute read repeatedly, "Authority is hereby given" appears to be apochryphal. The word "Authority" in Britain means "government," and the Port agency was considered a governmental unit.

As early as 1922, Sidney and Beatrice Webb picked the title, "Statutory Authorities for Special Purposes," which, now in retrospect, seems to serve rather well to define them collectively (Webb, 1922: book title). Dr. L. James Sharpe, Fellow of Nuffield College, Oxford, and University Lecturer in Public Administration at Oxford University, has pared this title down to "special-purpose authorities" (Sharpe, 1966: 92) and that seems to suggest terminology that would be understood both in the United Kingdom and the United States.

American designations for special governments are no improvement over the meaningless terminology adopted in Britain. Some trace back to the American's early association with the British proprietary corporations, in the colonial days, and others are original additions. They include: "commissions," "boards," "instrumentalities of the state," "trusts," "quasi-governments," "trust authorities," "public corporations," "public benefit corporations," "special districts," and "public authorities." Not only do these not evoke political identity among their "constituencies," but they do not, by the same token, help denote the reasons for their adoption.

The nomenclature, therefore, gives no indication of the nature of the ad hoc agency, and, accordingly, offers no assistance in efforts to classify them. Other avenues toward groupings must be pursued. Although A. H. Hanson did warn against such an endeavor, in view of the fact that the ad hoc units in the United Kingdom were so many and "so variously constituted and so heterogeneous in purpose that one has the utmost difficulty in classifying them functionally or typographically" (Hanson and Walles, 1970: 167), he did make a try at so doing for those established since the early 1960s. He suggested the following categories (Hanson and Walles, 1970: 170-172):

1. Those "purely commercial in character"
2. Those that "while engaged in the performance of certain commercial functions, might most appropriately be classified as promotional"
3. Those that are "purely regulatory"
4. Those "concerned with what might be described as the distribution of uncovenanted social benefits"
5. Those others, "some of them of great importance, [that] perform a mixture of functions"

Wolfgang Friedmann, Professor of Law of the University of Toronto (1954: 165-166), had employed, also, categories according to *kinds* of units, comparable to Hanson's later approach, but had limited his list to those concerning one type of these agencies, the public corporation, with which Britain had become identified. He suggested three kinds of public corporations:

1. The industrial or commercial corporation
2. The social service corporation
3. The supervisory public corporation

In the United States, the problem of drawing up a typology for the many more special governments has been, of course, even more precarious. American scholars, rather than shoot for this advanced stage of classification, have had to content themselves with listings of the reasons for which the

23,886 special districts have been formed. A compendium of reasons that had been made by a number of students of the subject in the United States was presented in 1964 by the Advisory Commission on Intergovernmental Relations, which represents all levels of government in the country, and which was set up by Congress "to give continuing attention to intergovernmental problems" (1964b: 53-63). The summary contained the following groupings of reasons:

1. Financial Reasons
    a. "debt and tax limitations," imposed on states and local governments by constitutional and statutory restrictions, and the exemption of special governments from these provisions;
    b. the reliance of local governments traditionally on property taxation, with the special units' ability to broaden this tax base and relieve the overburdened property owner, through resort to user charges;
2. Limitations on Powers of Local Government and the Need for Services
    a. "inability of local governments to establish differential taxing areas within their boundaries," of particular concern to counties, where persons living in a section of a county often could not have a particular service, even though they, themselves, were willing to pay for it, without all persons in the county being taxed for it;
    b. "lack of authority for local governments to contract with each other or to undertake joint responsibility for providing services";
3. Limitations Imposed by Existing Boundaries of Local Government
    a. "strict construction of powers granted local government," which made it difficult for local governments to follow functions beyond their borders, as those functions expanded, and the capability of special governments to adjust to conditions "where the geographic features of the area dictate the territorial scope for the function";
4. Political Factors
    a. inability, or unwillingness, of county governments to assume responsibility for providing a service to small incorporated areas, or unincorporated areas surrounding a city;

5. Business Management—"No Politics"
   a. fear of the intrusion of partisan politics into the operation of functions that must be self-supporting, and, therefore, "must be conducted in a business manner";
6. Public Acceptance of Special Districts
   a. continuing increases in the costs of local government, which has resulted in the public's acceptance of the special unit, as it "permits the service to be provided without its appearing to be a specific burden on the taxpayer";
7. Programs of Higher Levels of Government
   a. the failure of the federal government to encourage general-purpose governments in the performance of certain functions, but, rather, its stimulation of special-unit activity through preferential treatment on grants.

This extensive list of reasons tends to underscore the conclusion of Charles R. Adrian, Professor of Political Science at the University of California (1967: 228), that the "pattern of use for the special district seems to depend upon local customs and perhaps upon the accident of the gradual accumulation of rigid constitutional and statutory restrictions controlling general governments and discouraging the use of the existing units for newer services."

The author of this book (Smith, 1964: 13-14) has culled from numerous sources a summary of the five claims most frequently made on behalf of the special public authority, the ad hoc type of government with which the United States has become most clearly identified. They follow:

1. They make possible the financing of desperately needed capital construction which otherwise would be impossible under the present restrictive ceilings on debt and taxation, set by the states. They do so by floating bonds in the name of the authority, usually without obligation to existing governments, which will be self-liquidating through the collection of charges for the use of the facilities. After the bonded indebtedness has been paid, the facilities and functions are to revert to the parent government.
2. As agencies each engaged in one particular function of importance to the community, they have a greater attraction to professional persons who think in terms of specialization.

3. They must be "business-like" by the very fact that they do not rely on direct taxation, but must finance themselves through the selling of their bonds and the maintenance of a bond rating.
4. They take "out of politics" enterprises that are somewhere in between the private and the public sectors, permitting their operation in the public interest but with the motivations of private business.
5. They make possible, through their flexibility, the formation of more logical lines of jurisdiction, no longer tied to boundaries established centuries ago. . . . In this way they adjust much better administration to area for the effecting of functional needs.

Common Denominators

Four of these five advantages claimed for the special public authority, in the United States, commonly are advanced on behalf of the public corporation, in the United Kingdom. The first claim, involving, as it does, perplexities of finance peculiar to the federal system of government, of course is foreign to the central-governmental structure of Britain. As will be discussed in more detail, later in the book, this difference may prove to be of far more consequence, however, than merely that of differentiating the two governmental systems. In it may lie, in part, suggestions for the future development of ad hoc government in democracies.

The second claim, that special public authorities are more attractive to professional persons, is offered also for the British public corporation. Herbert Morrison, who, as Labour minister of transport, was one of the first to articulate the principles of the public corporation for transportation (1933: 157-159, 165), stressed the role of the board, and the staff:

The Public Corporation . . . must have a different atmosphere at its Board table from that of a shareholders' meeting; its Board and its officers must regard themselves as the high custodians of the public interest.

> To obtain service of the right kind for particular positions . . . the
> Public Corporation may find it expedient to pay salaries substan-
> tially above Civil Service scales, though it should certainly have
> regard to general conditions.

The third claim, that special public authorities must be
"business-like" because they have to finance themselves, also
is one of the most often repeated benefits asserted for the
British public corporation. Morrison (1933: 149, 171)
sought, as he said, "a combination of public ownership,
public accountability, and business management for public
ends." To these ends, he added, "the Board must have
autonomy and freedom of business management. It must not
only be allowed to enjoy responsibility: it must even have
responsibility thrust down its throat." Professor A. H. Hanson (Hanson and Walles, 1970: 174) supported this viewpoint: "The aim of the public corporation is to provide an
organizational form through which the reconciliation of commercial freedom with public control may best be facilitated."
Professor Robson (1937: 363) stressed "the need for a spirit
of boldness and enterprise" as an attribute. Ernest Davies
(1946: 23), then Labour Member of Parliament from Enfield,
wrote of the public corporation's ability "to escape the
dangers of bureaucracy by embracing the flexibility of commercial operation."

The fourth claim, that of taking matters of public enterprise "out of politics," has gained almost equal attention in
the United Kingdom, in association with ad hoc governments.
It was accepted there, however, less naively than in the
United States. Professor Robson once said that the thought
that public policy decisions could be considered "out of
politics" would be tantamount to asserting that one could
"take politics out of politics." Terence O'Brien (1937: 24),
in his early work on the British public corporation, repeated
the claim, but hedged on it:

> Some indication has already been given of the leading characteris-
> tics of these three bodies [public corporations] regarded as

political institutions; and it has been seen that the phrase often used with reference to them—that they have been taken out of "politics"—is, though based (as few members of academic institutions will need to be reminded) on a narrow definition of "politics," a useful description of the essence of the matter.

Professor Hanson (Hanson and Walles, 1970: 170), as well, has expressed certain doubts of this claim, without dismissing it altogether. "Today," he demurred, "there is less stress on the relative absence of 'political interference,' and more on the need for the use of administrative or managerial techniques."

Claim number five, that ad hoc government has come, in order to adjust administration to area, or to "economy of scale," so that an entire function could be handled by one agency to the extent that the area were not so large as to be unmanageable, also has been a cause in Britain. The Royal Commission on Local Government in Greater London, in its Report of 1960 (34-35) acknowledged the fact that a major role of special governments from the early nineteenth century forward has been that of handling functions that had outgrown the delimitations of the designated area of the city of London. The Report makes a point of saying that "at the end of the eighteenth century . . . men began commonly to write of the 'metropolis' as something bigger than but including the City, and with this vogue went new-fangled proposals for reforming London government, then generally referred to as 'the police of the metropolis.' " The first regional response, then, to the expansion of functions beyond the borders of the City of London, had come through the employment of ad hoc government, starting with the Metropolitan Police District, in 1829, and subsequently including the Metropolitan Sanitary Commission, in 1847; the Metropolitan Board of Works, in 1855; and the like. The commission, with some element of pride, points to the fact that it had chosen to use as the center of its Review Area, from 1957-1960, Charing Cross, within fifteen miles of which hub, in any direction, the Metropolitan Police District of 1829 had extended to include the whole of any parish.

There is a similarity, therefore, in the reasons proposed for the reliance on special-purpose governments in the United Kingdom and the United States. General agreement is reached on the following reasons for the formation of special-purpose authorities in the two countries:

1. In their daily operations, they are expected to meet at least their operational expenses through the charges that they levy on those who use their facilities, thus providing a broader tax base through the employment of the user-tax.
2. They do attract professional persons and businessmen, who, for the most part, would not campaign for public elective office, and do, accordingly, draw into public service, a group of citizens with capabilities in highly specialized areas who otherwise would not engage in the give-and-take of normal political campaigns.
3. Special agencies do introduce into the public sector the need for efficiency of operations through the fact that they are required to finance themselves wherever possible from their own resources, as they do not have available to them the unlimited prospects of tax sources.
4. Special public authority board members are not subject to election, as a rule, and, therefore, do not depend on the same kind of political influences that elected officials do for general-purpose governments. Therefore, special government reframes politics around groups of specialists.
5. The fluid-boundaries concept of government jurisdictions is made possible by the resort to special governments that rely on user charges, which, in turn, can be collected anywhere along the route of the facilities they provide for their specialized functions. They do not require fixed boundaries necessary to the collection of property taxes through proportionate assessment within the stable delimitations of the normal local governments. Special jurisdictions may breach those lines for the special function concerned, without, at the same time, destroying them for the other normal functions of general-purpose government.

These are the very considerable roles that special-purpose governments have come to fill in both the United Kingdom and the United States. They inject into the rather rigid mold of intergovernmental relationships in local government in Britain and America a kind of flexibility that enables the whole representative system to adjust to changing conditions. A consideration of these similarities of reasons for their establishment, from the United Kingdom to the United States, may help in understanding why it is that they have come into the world first in the democratic representative types of government, where, on casual attention, they would seem least appropriate. Why should autonomous, semi-independent agencies be raised up to handle the most significant new functions of government right in two of the most representative governments in the world? Closer scrutiny may serve to suggest that it is the democratic countries that, indeed, most lend themselves to this kind of almost para-doxically positive agency that can run through restrictions and get action. They come to cut through, for specific purposes, nebulous areas in which no one clearly has been authorized to act. Such "in-between" zones are inevitable in a system of shared, or delegated powers, which characterizes both the British and American democratic systems. "Gray" areas have appeared, in both countries, for example, in regard to the divisions of responsibilities between the central and local governments. They also have resulted from carefully guarded separations of public and private rights. In each of these instances—that involving the powers of the central versus the local governments, and that between public and private rights—special-purpose governments have arisen to fill in the cracks in between the two sectors, or to connect the one with the other. They have provided for the interstices that have resulted from the fact that respective concerns have been recognized, but that not in all circumstances could a sharp division be maintained between the two segments.

The very persistent respect for relative responsibilities has brought on the establishment of agencies to take care of the exceptions that occur, so as not to interfere with the long-standing tradition of delegations of rights. In still another way, democratic systems lend themselves to the need for special agencies. The insistence in both the United Kingdom and the United States that popularly elected persons, screened by political campaigns, serve as officials of government in the decision-making roles has tended to alienate from governments, particularly on the local levels, certain professional experts, who, increasingly are needed to help with the technologies of modern public functions. Professor Edward C. Banfield of Harvard University, has described the special public authority as the "natural habitat" for the "impartial expert," without whose protection from the electorate he "could not survive." "Perhaps in the next twenty or thirty years," he speculated, "municipal affairs will pass entirely into the hands of honest, impartial, and nonpolitical 'experts'; at any rate, this seems to be the logical fulfillment of the middle-class ideal." If this were to happen, he added, "(w)e may see in . . . the exalted position of Robert Moses of New York, portents of what is to come" (Banfield, 1961: 72, 74). Moses headed four powerful special public authorities in New York State at one time and was their acknowledged spokesman. There is evidence today, however, of growing suspicion of these havens for the experts. Professor Stefan Dupre of the University of Toronto warns (Dupre, 1967: 23) that the "special purpose district poses a delicate trade-off between the values of efficiency and participation." And Peter Self, Lecturer in Public Administration in the London School of Economics, flatly berates them as "so overwhelmingly engineering minded that their activities often aggravate rather than ease the problems of metropolitan areas" (Self, 1955: 278). Presages of public reaction against their lack of responsiveness may be gleaned from two humorous works, one published in Britain in 1972: Antony Jay's *The Householder's Guide to Community Defence Against Bureaucratic Aggression,* in which he includes among "the most formidable of enemies: a ministry, a nationalized industry, a local authority" (p. 7); the other, published in New York, in 1971, as a modification of the popular game of Monopoly, in which participants were to become players in "a piece of broken-field running against an enemy backfield made up of the Triborough Bridge and/or Port Authority, the

Penn Central and/or LIRR (Long Island Railroad), the Team-
sters and . . . [the Metropolitan Transportation Authority]"
(New York Magazine, 1971: insert).

The place of the special-purpose unit of government, in a
democratic system, calls for special consideration in both
countries today, when Britain is putting into effect her
sweeping reorganizations of governments on the local level,
and when America is undergoing an attempt at decentralization of governmental power to the local governments, under
President Nixon's symbol of "The New Federalism." The
United Kingdom and the United States have years of experience in the employment of special governments that could be
shared to mutual advantage.

The Public Corporation/The Public Authority

From the welter of ad hoc agencies, two principal organizational forms have emerged: the public corporation, in the
United Kingdom, and the special public authority, in the
United States. Both the corporation and the authority have
been broken down into subclassifications.

The public corporation, of Britain, is distinguished, first of
all, from the joint stock company, more commonly characteristic of ad hoc governments found on the continent of
Europe where socialism has not prevailed. The joint stock
company is defined as "a form of public enterprise in which
the State itself, or a public authority on behalf of the State,
exercises control through the ownership of a majority of the
shares, reinforced sometimes by the reservation of special
privileges in the bylaws of the company" (Hanson, 1955: 18,
in a chapter by Wolfgang Friedmann). The concept was used
in the early days in Britain and in the American colonies, but
gave way to the public corporation in more recent years. The
public corporation, itself, breaks down into two types, dependent on the method for composing the board. One kind,
known as the representative public corporation, centers on
the fact that the board is elected from among the interests

vitally concerned with the facilities under the control of the corporation. The second type of public corporation, on the other hand, centers on the fact that the board members are to be appointed, by the appropriate minister, on the basis of their wide experience and proven capacity in the function for which the corporation was established. The distinctions here will be considered critically in regard to the evolution of transport special governments in the United Kingdom over the years.

The public authority, in the United States, has to be separated from the generic category of "special districts," under which the ad hoc units throughout the nation are classified. Whereas the British scholars place their reliance on differentiation in the composition of the boards, the author of this book has argued that in the United States, the distinguishing characteristic must be considered to be the source of financial support for these varied units. He identifies from among the 23,886 agencies, grouped together by the Bureau of the Census as "special districts," three types of special-purpose governments: (1) special districts; (2) public authorities; and (3) authority-districts. He suggests that terminology be disregarded, as labels simply have been attached to units as they arose, extraconstitutionally. Rather, he recommends that the differentiation among the three categories, regardless of what they are called, be thought of as the financial sources of income for their capital and operational needs, which has determined their degree of independence. The special district is understood to be a unit of government, operating outside the normal scope of conventional government, to accomplish a single function, or closely related functions, relying primarily on a special tax levy, often on property. The public authority, again is a special purpose government, but differs from the special district in that it must finance itself without taxation, which it does primarily by the issuance of revenue bonds (which will be amortized by the tolls and other charges imposed for the use of the facilities of the authority), in its own name, usually without the support of the "full faith and credit" of any general-purpose government. The authority-

district is the newest type of ad hoc government just beginning to appear in metropolitan centers of America. It
combines certain features of the special district and the
special public authority. The authority-district, designed as it
is for the coordination of various modes of a function, relies,
where possible, on the collection of user charges, but, in
order to incorporate deficit modes with profitable ones, the
powers of the authority-district extend as well to the use of
special means of taxation. This typology, including special
districts, special public authorities, and authority-districts, is
based on the respective sources of income of the three. Much
more will be said of these types in the course of the book.

The public authority, which has dominated the special
government scene in the United States during the past 40
years, as has the public corporation in Britain during that
same period of time grew, in large part, out of the latter.
Definitions of the two show the dependence of the public
authority on the public corporation. The United Nations (as
quoted in Hanson, 1958: 343) has defined—or, perhaps,
explained—the public corporation this way:

(i) It is wholly owned by the state.

(ii) It is generally created by, or pursuant to, a special law
defining its powers, duties and immunities and prescribing the
form of management and its relationship to established departments and ministries.

(iii) As a body corporate, it is a separate entity for legal purposes
and can sue and be sued, enter into contracts, and acquire
property in its own name. Corporations conducting business in
their own name have been generally given greater freedom in
making contracts and acquiring and disposing of property than
ordinary government departments.

(iv) Except for appropriations to provide capital or to cover
losses, a public corporation is usually independently financed. It
obtains its funds from borrowing, either from the Treasury or the
public, and from revenues derived from the sale of its goods and
services. It is authorised to use and re-use its revenues.

(v) It is generally exempted from most regulatory and prohibitory statutes applicable to expenditure of public funds.

(vi) It is ordinarily not subject to the budget, accounting and audit laws and procedures applicable to non-corporate agencies.

(vii) In the majority of cases, employees of public corporations are not civil servants, and are recruited and remunerated under terms and conditions which the corporation itself determines.

The most generally accepted American definition of the special public authority, is one proposed by the Council of State Governments (1953: 3):

Public Authorities generally are corporate bodies authorized by legislative action to function outside of the regular structure of state government in order to finance and construct and usually to operate revenue-producing public enterprises. Their organizational structures and powers are of the type usually associated with public corporations and like the latter they have relative administrative autonomy. Public Authorities are authorized to issue their own revenue bonds, which ordinarily do not constitute debt limitations, since they are required to meet their obligations from their own resources. They lack the power to levy taxes, but are empowered to collect fees or other charges for use of their facilities, devoting the resulting revenue to payment of operational expenses and of interest and principal on their debts.

Worthy of note, again, is the emphasis of the public-authority description on its method of finance, through the revenue-bond-user-charge complex. The explanation of the British public corporation also provides for borrowing and for the use of "revenues derived from the sale of its goods and services." The reliance on these borrowing provisions, however, has been subordinated in the case of the British corporation far more than in that of the American public authority. Whereas the primary emphasis of the special public authority in the United States has been on its revenue-bonding capabilities, to the extent that one writer has termed them "borrowing machines" (Davis, 1935: 330), the focus of the public corporation in the United Kingdom has turned increasingly more toward managerial potentialities. The reasons for this distinction will be examined throughout this book, as they seem to the author to hold the key to the appropriate role for the special-purpose government in democracies.

Chapter 2

BRITISH EXPORT TO AMERICA

There may be little solace for the now defunct Mersey Docks and Harbour Board to recall that it is credited with having been the most important single influence on the creation of the Port of London Authority, its successful competitor. In 1971, as this Board of the Liverpool port area was being replaced by the Mersey Docks and Harbour Company, the Port of London Authority was reporting its first profit since the fiscal year of 1966 (Port of London Authority, 1972: 4). Greater satisfaction for Liverpool could be gleaned from the knowledge that its Harbour Board, established as early as 1858, had been the prototype for the Port Authority of New York and New Jersey, known until 1972 as the Port of New York Authority, the first ad hoc government in the United States to use the word, "Authority." Although the American Port Authority generally credits the Port of London Authority as its precursor, its most famous Executive Director, Austin J. Tobin, has said (1953: 3n):

Despite the accepted role of The Port of London Authority as the first modern public corporation, the writer is inclined to regard the Mersey Docks and Harbor Board, the port agency in Liverpool . . . as the real prototype of the modern public corporation. However the London corporation was the first one to be called an "Authority."

He explained that Julius Henry Cohen, counsel, who was drawing up the interstate compact for the Port of New York Authority in 1921, had gone to England "and studied the organization of the Port of London Authority, as well as its predecessor, the Mersey Docks and Harbor Board" (Tobin, 1953: 3).

The physical setting for the port trust of Mersey was more apposite for the New York metropolitan area, in that friction had broken out, before the trust had been organized, between local governments across the Mersey River–Liverpool, as against Birkenhead, directly across the River, or between Liverpool and Runcorn, on the opposite side of the River but a little further upstream. In New York's case, the aggravations among municipalities, such as Newark, Hoboken, Jersey City, and Elizabeth, were complicated further by the fact that those not only were separated from New York City by the Hudson River, but by a state boundary line between New York State and New Jersey, which ran down the center of the River. Still a further parallel to the pretrust situation in the Liverpool area lay in the fact that the marine pier facilities were municipally owned, for the most part, in the New York region as they had been in Mersey. When the Port of London Authority was organized, it was faced with the different kind of problem wherein the marine facilities were owned privately, for the most part, along with the long-standing right of wharfingers and lightermen "to enter and leave the docks without payment of dues" (Port of London Authority, 1971: 2). One of the principal difficulties of the Port of New York Authority from the beginning was this municipal ownership of the piers and New York City's reluctance to deed them to the Authority.

As a matter of fact, by the time of the passage by Parliament of the Port of London Bill, in 1908, representative port trusts were well known throughout Britain. Four of the ten principal ports there were managed by representative trusts: the Belfast Harbour Commissioners, 1847; Tyne Improvement Commissioners (Newcastle-upon-Tyne), 1850; Clyde Navigation Trust (Glasgow), 1858; and the Mersey Docks and Harbour Board (Liverpool), 1858. Other types of administration of ports consisted of management by railways (today the British Railways Board has control of certain ports "which are largely used for the cross-Channel services of the railways" (Central Office of Information, 1972: 293); management by a mixed company, of municipal and private ownership; and direct ownership by the municipality itself. The Royal Commission on Transport in its report of 1931 found that more than 100 of Britain's ports were being managed by the local port trust (Gordon, 1938: 7-8).

Even in the United States, the idea of the port trust was not entirely new when it was introduced for the Port of New York Authority in 1921. Three years before, the *American Political Science Review* (Guild, 1918: 681-682) had reported:

> As an example of the extraordinary development of a special municipal corporation and its possibilities as a new and flexible agency in the development of a community, the port of Portland stands preeminent under the powers conferred in 1917. Organized in 1891 under act of 1890, the "port" was created to improve the Columbia River, and its territory consisted of an area about that river, including the city of Portland. To its original purpose, similar to that of river and navigation districts in other states, there was added in 1901 authority to provide a dry-dock. The extraordinary extension of powers granted by the legislature of 1917 gives evidence of the utility of this special municipal corporation and the popular confidence in it.

In view of the dissolution of the Mersey Docks and Harbour Board in 1971, however, it would seem more appropriate to cite the Port of London Authority for comparisons to the Port Authority of New York and New Jersey, particularly in light of the hope that such comparisons from this point on will be continued by scholars. The Port of London Authority exists today as a strong ad hoc agency, with its powers even extended under the Port of London Act of 1968, enacted so that the changes made over the years in its regard should be "unified, consolidated and amended" and that "other powers be conferred on the Port Authority." The London Authority is used in this book, therefore, but always with the tacit understanding that its role is that of a kind of intermediary between the former Mersey Docks and Harbour Board and the Port Authority of New York and New Jersey. One point of additional interest here lies in the fact that one of the early studies of the Port of London Authority was conducted and reported by an American, Lincoln Gordon, when he was a candidate for the degree of doctor of philosophy at Oxford as a Rhodes scholar, in the 1930s. His thesis was published in book form in 1938 under the title, *The Public Corporation in Great Britain.* He did not draw comparisons in any depth to public authorities in the United States, although he later, when a professor at Harvard University, published a text on *Government and the American Economy* with two other American authors in which he explored the theory of public enterprise and made some references to the Port of New York Authority, as well as to special districts in general (Fainsod, 1941). He was named United States ambassador to Brazil in 1961.

From the perspective of the 1970s, when the Mersey Docks and Harbour Board has been turned into a public company, and when the Port Authority of New York and New Jersey is embroiled in constant controversy over its role in mass transit, Gordon's findings that the Royal Commission, appointed to examine the plight of the port of London, torn as it was by internecine struggles among private owners, "had no hesitation in recommending the establishment of a non-profit making public corporation" is somewhat startling. He credited "the examples of Liverpool and other great British ports" (Gordon, 1938: 22). He cited, too, the Commission's conclusions in 1902 as to the intolerable conditions of the port. (The London County Council in 1905, during prolonged debates on the nature of the public corporation's board structure, and other controversial details, tried to push through Parliament a bill for municipal ownership or management of the port, but it failed of a second reading.) Special public authorities often come into existence in just this way: through a sense of inevitability brought on by default of successful action by the general-purpose government. The evolvement of the Port of New York Authority had come from a similar feeling of despair (Bird, 1949: 7-8):

> But by the early 1900's growth had produced congestion in the port and renewed friction between the States. Hard feelings were intensified, moreover, because the bulk of the maritime commerce of the port had developed on the New York side of the harbor although most of the trunk railroads had entered the area and located their terminals on the New Jersey side. The railroads developed an extensive carfloat, lighterage and ferry service to take advantage of the waterfront facilities which New York City had repossessed and constructed at great expense, while on the New Jersey side no attempt had been made at unified development of the waterfront and the greater part of it had passed into the ownership of the railroads on a costly and wastefully competitive basis.

What else but a single special authority with a high degree of autonomy and power to bring the warring factions together? That thinking in itself reflects both the strengths and the weaknesses of the resort to this kind of ad hoc government.

In breaking up the little "empires" that had dominated elements of the port trade in both London and New York and in imposing the new special public authority over them, concessions had to be made to fit the peculiar complex of such interests found in each port. The Port of London Authority, as finally constituted after some five years of debates in the Parliament, represented a compromise, with several of its features changed from those of the Mersey Docks and Harbour Board. The compact for the Port of New York Authority compromised even further the provisions of the Port of London Authority, inasmuch as this compact, in the American federal system, had to be approved by the legislatures of two states, New York and New Jersey, over whose metropolitan areas the bi-state agency would function, but also had to be ratified by the Congress of the United States. Structures of government of course are not exportable as prefabricated entities but as concepts of organization that must then be adapted to local conditions and traditions. The asset of the special public authority is just that—that it adjusts readily through the lack of rigidity which characterizes the more conventional governments. The public corporation thereby lends an element of fluidity to government. No full-blown theory of the public corporation attended the acceptance of the port trust for London or for New York. In fact, many scholars question that the port trust should be classified as a corporation. Professor Robson brushes aside this esoteric dispute, however, and suggests that we consider port trusts as "public corporations of a special type" (1962: 27). The complete articulation of the public corporation was not to come until the 1930s, the decade after the approval of the Port of New York Authority. The United States, therefore, adopted from Britain an ad hoc type of agency still in its experimental stages. But that special public authority thereby became the model for the explosion of the special-purpose movement in the United States, under the exigencies of the great depression of the 1930s, without ever a respite for even an intellectual discussion of its proper role. Special public authorities remain to this day, in the States, as expediences. Britain, on the other hand, was encouraged to stop and take a sober look at their proliferation by the need for a vehicle for her nationalized industries, and this debate, led by Herbert Morrison and others in the 1930s, helped to set these agencies in the context of a more theoretical base. More consideration will be given this factor in the succeeding chapters.

As both the Port of London Authority and the Port of New York Authority represent milestones along the path of special governmental acceptance, without the benefit of a comprehensive philosophy, an analysis of their different applications in the two metropolitan areas should prove fruitful.

AUTHORITY
ORIENTATION

One of the advantages of the special public authority is that it is enabled to operate with fluid boundaries so that the authority can leap-frog conventional jurisdictional lines to encompass its particular function wherever it may lead, without, at the same time, erasing those older bounds for their other functions. The marked differences in the geographic delimitations of the two port authorities, therefore, are suggestive of their anticipated roles.

The Port of London Authority

A narrow, elongated stretch of territory, 94 miles in length from the estuary of the Thames River to the limit of the tidal waters westward at Teddington, covering some 4,000 acres, more than 700 of which are water, represents the province of the Port of London Authority. Huddled along the river, usually no more than three miles inland, are the authority's facilities, centering on three large groups of enclosed docks: the India and Millwall Docks in the Greenwich Reach (or continuous stretch of the River); the Royal Victoria & Albert & King George V Docks, at the Woolwich Reach; and the Tilbury Docks, at Gravesend Reach. Its two categories of responsibilities dictate this confinement to the river through (1) its charge "to provide, maintain, operate and improve such port and harbour services and facilities in, or in the vicinity of, the Thames" and (2) "to take such action as they consider necessary or desirable for or incidental to the improvement and conservancy of the Thames." There is one escape clause that empowers the Authority "either themselves or by arrangement between themselves and another person to take such action as the Port Authority consider necessary or desirable whether or not in, or in the vicinity of, the Thames," but only for certain specified purposes (Port of London Act 1968, III, 5 [1] and [2]). "The principal business of the P.L.A.," by its own acknowledgement (Port of London Authority, 1972: 6) "is to provide and run a first-class port with first-class dock capacity and first-class cargo-handling equipment and operations." This Port of London was defined in the Port of London (Various Powers) Act of 1932 in narrow terms, as to its width:

> The limits of the Port of London shall commence at an imaginary straight line . . . drawn from high-water mark on the bank of the Thames River at the boundary line between the parishes of Teddington and Twickenham in the county of Middlesex to high-water mark on the Surrey bank of the river immediately opposite the first-mentioned point and extend down both sides of the River Thames [The Port of London Act, 1968: 5].

By the Port of London (Extension of Seaward Limit) Act, 1964, the Port of London Authority's eastern boundary out to sea was redrawn so as to add under its aegis some 300 square miles of water. This annexation now looms of particular importance, as it extends the new line to Foulness Point, located on Foulness Island, where the Port of London Authority has proposed its construction of a seaport as a major oil terminal and container and other unit-load complex. It is of peripheral interest to note, in regard to the total numbers of ad hoc units in Britain, that on the south side of the estuary of the Thames, which is, of course, under the control of the Port of London Authority, is the estuary to the River Medway, which is under the control of the Medway Ports Authority. "As vessels, in particular the oil tankers destined for the Medway pass through the Port of London Authority's area close cooperation in radar surveillance is maintained between both authorities" (Port of London Authority, 1971: 5).

The Port of London Authority's face is to the river, at times almost to the extent of giving the impression that the Authority is somewhat detached from London. "We have a particular responsibility for London's river," observed its chairman in 1972. "Does London care enough for her river?" "These opportunities for environmental improvement of the River," he rationalized, "exciting and far reaching, belong to the P.L.A. because of our responsibility for London's river" (Port of London Authority, 1972: 8).

No one would propose, as so many have for the Port Authority of New York and New Jersey, that the Port of London Authority be the organization responsible for the coordination of the various modes of transportation in the metropolitan area. The Port of London Authority, to be sure, has expressed concern for the development of roads to the docks, and, as its journal has pointed out on occasion, its action has consisted of "taking a vigorous part," along with shippers, the Chambers of Commerce and the Ministry of Transport, in urging lorry routes to and from the docks. Better approaches in the inward areas of the docks have been a part of the Authority's concerns (*P.L.A. Monthly,* 1962: 199-202). However, one criticism of the Port of London Authority made by the Rochdale Committee of Inquiry into the Major Ports of Great Britain in its 1962 *Report* was that not enough consideration had been given to the improvement of roads to the ports and the planning of routes that would serve to connect ports with their principal markets. The tenor of this *Report* was to the effect that a National Ports Authority should be established for better coordination of development and capital expenditure, and other functions. The Port of London Authority opposed this latter suggestion, but said, of the matter of roads to and from the ports, that the recommendation was "particularly welcome" (*P.L.A. Monthly,* 1963: 18-20). More often than to this inward look, however, the Port Authority's periodical articles gaze at the Thames, under headings such as "Sweet Thames Run Softly," or, more practically, "The Gateway to Anglo-German Trade" (*P.L.A. Monthly,* 1962: 199ff; *Port of London,* Magazine of

the London Port Authority, 1972: 164ff). The epitome may
well have been reflected in a two-part series in the Port of
London Authority's magazine, in 1964, titled, "Port of London—Source of Metropolitan Life-blood" (1964: 311-315;
347-352).

The Port Authority of New York and New Jersey

The configuration of the boundaries of the Port Authority
of New York and New Jersey presents an almost opposite
image from that of the Port of London Authority. "The port
district," as the legislation defined the area encompassed
within the jurisdictional lines of the New York Authority, is
almost octagonal, in a radius roughly equal to 25 miles
around the Statue of Liberty, at the entrance to the New
York Harbor. Instead of the Port of London Authority's
extension of 94 miles along the Thames River, the Port
Authority of New York and New Jersey runs for only some
30 miles along the Hudson River. The Port of London
Authority's enclosure of a little more than 4,000 acres,
however, palls in the face of the New York Authority's
jurisdiction over 960,000 acres. Instead of a band of territory, clustering on the river banks, as is reflected by the Port
of London Authority, an oblique circle of 50 miles diameter
about the center of the Port, enclosing 1,500 square miles,
delimits the responsibility of the Port Authority of New
York and New Jersey.

London does not refer to a "district" in connection with
its Port Authority. Definitions in the Preliminary section of
the Port of London Act 1968 employ a number of other
terms, such as "the former seaward limit," "the limits,"
"mean high water level," "port premises," "the seaward
limit," and "specified premises." The Port Authority of New
York and New Jersey emphasizes the image of a district,
probably to establish an interstate posture, not commonly
understood in the United States, where the federal system is
recognized as only the national government, and the states.

The Port Authority of New York and New Jersey had been furnished, in its original compact, the designation of the "Port of New York District." It was delimited by "boundary lines located by connecting points of known latitude and longitude." The compact defines the district in such terminology:

Thence, due east twenty-five and forty-eight-hundredths miles more or less, crossing the county of Monmouth, state of New Jersey, and passing about one and four-tenths miles south of the pier of the Central Railroad of New Jersey at Atlantic Highlands to a point J of latitude forty degrees and twenty-four minutes north and longitude seventy-three degrees and forty-seven minutes west, said point being in the Atlantic Ocean; thence north eleven degrees fifty-eight minutes east twenty-one and sixteen-hundredths miles more or less to a point K, said point being about five miles east of the passenger station of the Long Island railroad at Jamaica and about one and three-tenths miles east of the boundary line of the city of New York, in the county of Nassau, state of New York [N.J.S.A.: 32: 1-3].

The Port Authority of New York and New Jersey, in its promotional literature, has laid stress on the expansiveness of the district beyond the Hudson River, or the piers of the port. "The Port itself," the authority points out, "might be called nature's supreme effort to provide man with magnificent avenues for the free flow of commerce. It is a great juncture of ocean, rivers, bays and harbors reaching deeply into the surrounding 1,500 square miles of upland within the neighbor States of New York and New Jersey" (The Port of New York Authority, 1961: 2). This Authority's attention has been diverted, accordingly, "upland" or inward to a far greater extent than has that of the Port of London Authority. "The New York-New Jersey Port District," according to the Port of New York Authority, "is a transportation 'hub' with spokes reaching out to the entire world."

Within the United States, the roads and rails that extend outward from the Port to the north, west, and south, are highly important spokes of the "wheel." And within the Port District, 40,400 people, earning $172,700,000 a year, owe their livelihood to the fact that great volumes of ocean cargoes must be transported to the Port from every part of this country. Similarly, such cargo frequently has completed only one phase of its journey when it reaches the Port from foreign shores.

The Port Authority of New York and New Jersey, accordingly, has taken direct responsibility for tunnels, bridges, and the like leading to and from its piers and airports. Its facilities include the George Washington Bridge and Bus Station, Bayonne Bridge, Goethals Bridge, Outerbridge Crossing, Holland Tunnel, Lincoln Tunnel, Port Authority Bus Terminal, New York Union Motor Truck Terminal, and the Newark Union Motor Truck Terminal. Indeed, such an authorization for concerns other than those in the River, or on its immediate banks, was enclosed in the original compact, when the new Port Authority was directed to relate its activities to "a plan or plans for the comprehensive development of the port of New York" that the two States were to draw up, and to "make plans for the development of said district, supplementary to or amendatory of any plan theretofore adopted" (N.J.S.A.: 32: 1-11).

The pivot of controversy of the Port Authority of New York and New Jersey does not revolve about the lack of the full development of the piers of the harbor, resulting from the failure of New York City to deed the Authority its main marine facilities, but, rather, it revolves about the reluctance of the Port Authority to move into the arena of mass transit, throughout its district of 2 states, sections of 17 counties, 350 municipalities, 330 school districts, and more than 200 special districts. This is a far different orientation than that of the Port of London Authority, which focuses on the river.

REPRESENTATION

The boards of the Port of London Authority and the Port Authority of New York and New Jersey are selected on two systems of representation diametrically opposed in principle.

Each reflects the peculiar orientation of its Authority, the members of the Port of London Authority being chosen for their immediate interest in the functions of the Port, and the commissioners of the Port Authority of New York and New Jersey being appointed as generalists to support the overall concerns of the total Port of New York District. The first attempts to place the users of the port in a controlling position on the board; the second tries to create a broad district concept. The London method is known as "functional representation"; the New York system, is that of the "generalist."

The opportunities for ad hoc governments to experiment with various kinds of representation are of special importance in the United States today when the Supreme Court has been insisting on the principle of one-man-one-vote for elections to legislative bodies, on all levels of federalism, with the exception of the United States Senate, whose members must be based on the principle of two per each state. This theory of population-per-area has been carried by the Court from elections to the United States House of Representatives down through those for both houses of the state legislatures, including both the lower house and the state senate, and to include the councils of local counties and municipal governments. In 1970, even local school district boards were included under the one-one ruling. Most recently, however, in March of 1973, the Supreme Court exempted from its decisions in this vein, elected officials of special-purpose governmental bodies, leaving them free to experiment. The specific case concerned the fact that elections for the board of directors of the Tulare Water District, in California, were predicated on the value of property holdings by voters, so that individual or corporations holding land in the district gained one vote for each $100 of property values. Obviously, this method clashed openly with the principle of population and area, or one-for-one voting. The Supreme Court sustained the procedure, however, refusing to press its one-one policy down to that level. Justice Douglas, in a dissent, joined by Justices Brennan and Marshall, contended that the special district is performing "vital governmental functions," and that, to allow control of the voting process by large landowners within the district was to produce "a corporate political kingdom undreamed of by those who wrote our Constitution." Apparently, the majority opinion permits the 23,000 special districts to experiment with various systems of representation (United States Supreme Court, 1973).

The method of functional representation, as undertaken over the years by the Port of London Authority, through its efforts to represent the interests primarily affected by port operations, is one that readily comes to mind in regard to special-purpose governments. After all, the ad hoc unit is formed in order to perform one function, or closely related functions. Functional representation, designed to give participation in the decision-making process of the functional agency to those most involved in that function, would seem perfectly natural and appropriate.

On the other hand, for a port authority, with the broad expectations of the Port of New York Authority, as directed in the compact of 1921, looking at transportation and commerce broadly over a wide geographic district (as the regional agency to be operational on a bi-state plane), persons able to grasp the general interests of the interstate area might seem more in keeping.

The Port of London Authority

The Board devised by the Mersey Docks and Harbour Act of 1857 had been based on functional representation, but with a very narrow understanding of those dependent on the Liverpool Port. The board had 28 members, with 24 of them elected by payers of the dock rates, and the 4 others chosen by the Conservancy Commissioners of the River Mersey. Three ministers served in an ex officio capacity. In practice, this method had resulted in the composition of the board by the Liverpool and Birkenhead shipowners and merchants (Gordon, 1938: 10). The legislation by Parliament for the

Port of London Authority had benefited from this experience, and tried to broaden the base of its functional representation. The allocations per interests were as follows (Gordon, 1938: 25):

Elected (18)
    By payers of dues, wharfingers, and owners of river craft   17
    By wharfingers   1
Appointed (10)
    By the Admiralty   1
    By the Ministry of Transport (before 1920 the Board of
        Trade)   2
    By the London County Council (being members of the
        Council)   2
    By the London County Council (not being members of
        the Council)   2
    By the City Corporation (being a member of the
        Corporation)   1
    By the City Corporation (not being a member of the
        Corporation)   1
    By the Trinity House   1
    TOTAL   28

This membership of the board was pared down by the Port of London Revision Order 1967, cutting back on the representation of the payers of dues, wharfingers, and owners of river craft, which had numbered seventeen or eighteen. The new allocations among interests were as follows:

The Secretary of State for the Environment is to make appointments after consultation with (Port of London Act 1968 Sched. 2, part I, 3):

Chamber of Shipping of the United Kingdom and the   3
    London General Shipowners Society
London Chamber of Commerce and the British Shippers
    Council   3
London Wharfingers Association   1
Association of Master Lightermen and Barge Owners in
    London   1
Greater London Council   1

Corporation of the City of London	1
Corporation of Trinity House	1
National Ports Council	2
Organised Labor	2
The Director-General	1
TOTAL	16

Members, under both the original, and the revised lists, have served for three-year terms.

This disposition of functional representatives illustrates both the advantages and the disadvantages of such a system. The first problem is that of the number of votes to allocate to each interest. The question, in the case of the first board of the Port of London Authority, was that of the numbers to be assigned to labor representatives, or, indeed, as to whether labor was a functional interest that should be listed at all. Labor was given a voice through the requirement that the two members to be selected by the minister of transport and the London County Council were to be recommended "after consultation with such organisations representative of labour as [they] think best qualified to advise them on the matter" (1920 Act). Winston Churchill confronted this question of the functional inclusion of labor, and argued:

> Although I am quite ready to admit that the representation of Labour on a port authority is introduced in this Bill for the first time, I am perfectly certain it is defensible, because, although it is an interest of a particular class, that class is so large, and its interests are so interwoven that it cannot be dismissed as wholly sectional; it is a human, moral, and national interest of a large and responsible character [Gordon, 1938: 29].

Even if the proportions could be worked out for the varied interests involved in the functions of the special authority, the more basic question of the method of functional representation would not be resolved. That problem arises through the fact that the democratic theory is that the person, as a whole, is entitled to one vote. The individual is the unit for voting purposes. Functional representation breaks into that theorem by the thought that an interest, in regard to a function of government, should be the accepted unit. This means that a person's vote, heretofore considered *the* voting unit, could be fragmented, through the fact that one person might be involved in interest groups on various sides of the one issue. An individual thereby may become fractionated for voting rights, if he should happen to belong to associations favoring differing sides of the debate. One functional group of which he is a member may be voting in favor of the topic, another, of which he also is a member, may be opposing that contention. The individual, belonging to both organizations on opposing sides of the issue, becomes less than a unit in the voting. Group or functional concerns may prove of more significance on certain current complex matters, but the shift from the individual to the group represents a departure in voting patterns for citizens of the United Kingdom and the United States.

The Port Authority of New York and New Jersey

The problem of selecting the generalist for appointment to a special public authority is easier to resolve, mechanically, but is just as difficult in principle. The burden is to determine who those individuals are who best are capable of reflecting the welfare of the district at large. From its inception in 1921, the Port Authority of New York and New Jersey has made use of the generalist approach for the composition of its board of commissioners. Six of the commissioners are appointed by the governor of New York State, and six by the governor of New Jersey. The law requires that, of these twelve commissioners, there be "six resident voters from the state of New York, at least four of whom shall be resident voters of the city of New York, and six resident voters from the state of New Jersey, at least four of whom shall be resident voters within the New Jersey portion of the district" (N.J.S.A. 32: 1-5, par. 1). In other words, two-thirds of the commissioners must be residents of the Port District.

For years, in its annual reports, the Port Authority described the commissioners as including "leaders in business, finance, and industry," but more recently as "(l)eaders in business, finance, law and civic affairs." In 1961, the Port of New York Authority prepared a list of the commissioners' backgrounds, under the heading, "Highlights of Commissioners' Experience in Public Affairs and Industry," for a congressional committee. It included the names of those members who had served from January 1, 1946, through 1960, the period of particular concern, in other matters, to the committee. The authority summarized the personal histories as indicating that all 30 of the commissioners so listed "have been honored and have distinguished themselves in both their chosen career fields (in the professions, commerce, and industry) and in public affairs activities or offices." Listed first were those of the current board, showing their career patterns :

1. chairman of an investment fund; chairman of the board and president of a bank
2. partner in an investment brokerage firm
3. president of a cigar leaf tobacco company
4. member of a law firm
5. chairman of the board and president of an industries corporation
6. partner of a law firm
7. chairman of the executive committee and director of a bank
8. president of a paper company
9. president of a lead company
10. city attorney
11. chairman of the board and executive vice president of a bank
12. chairman of the board of a bank

The data for the former commissioners revealed a bit more flexibility:

13. member of a law firm; vice president, treasurer, and director of a bolt and nut company
14. chairman of the board of a towing company

15. president of a bank; president of a manufacturing company
16. state superintendent of works
17. president of the American Merchant Marine Institute; comptroller, New York City
18. senior partner in a concern; assistant corporation counsel of New York City
19. chairman of the board of a bank
20. president and director of a bank; treasurer of a theatre company
21. chairman of the board and publisher of a newspaper; president of a zinc-lead company
22. commissioner of the City of Newark; chairman of a company; president of an insurance company
23. president and honorary chairman of a bank
24. counsel and vice president of a title guaranty and trust company
25. trustee and president of Stevens Institute of Technology
26. vice president and publisher of a newspaper
27. United States attorney
28. professor of politics, Princeton University
29. New Jersey state senator
30. United States senator

[United States Congress, 1960, I: 671-675].

All 30 had been involved in many other activities and employment, but the one chosen above for each is among the best known of the commissioner's positions. These, in summary, include the following career fields:

1. banking (9 commissioners)
2. law (6)
3. industry (4)
4. government service (4)
5. education (3)
6. journalism (2)
7. transportation (1)
8. investment (1)

A more detailed analysis of the other activities given in this report would have to be made to say, with any degree of confidence, that the method of selection had sifted out those best qualified to represent the Port District. It is worthy of passing note, however, that more than half of the 30 commissioners had backgrounds in banking, law, and industry. Omitted areas are evident—such as that of labor. The point illustrated is that the definition of the generalist poses problems perhaps as serious as those raised by the method of functional representation. The larger conclusion may be that in both the United Kingdom and the United States, continuing studies of these aspects and all others associated with special-purpose government are needed desperately. These units should be accepted as permanent elements of democratic government, and their proper roles should be spelled out. No longer will it suffice in either country to brush them off as ephemeral expediencies to meet immediate problems; they are here to stay. It may well be that other systems of representation, or new ones as yet not proposed, for example, should be considered. New York City, in January of 1970, returned to the use of proportional representation for the elections of its school boards. This plan, invented by Thomas Hare of England in 1857, had been used for the election of the City Council of New York City in 1937 and for ten years thereafter, but had been voted out for that purpose in 1947. Having been the system for election to municipal councils in many American towns, beginning in 1915, it all but ceased to exist during the 1940s (largely under the fear of overrepresentation of Communists). Its reintroduction in America's largest city for special-purpose district school boards, whether any more successful than it had been before for general-purpose government, is witness to the need being felt for means toward more responsiveness in the ad hoc area.

CHECKS

Another aspect for further exploration with regard to ad hoc governments is found in ways in which they may be held accountable, without, at the same time, denying them the flexibility that distinguishes them from general governments and enables them to operate to loosen up rigidities for certain functions.

The Port of London Authority

On the face of the statutory provisions, the Port of London Authority is one of the most closely controlled of such agencies. The Port of London Act 1968 contains the following relevant sections:

Part III, 8. – (1) The Port Authority shall as soon as possible after the end of the financial year report to the Minister on the exercise and performance of their functions during the preceding financial year and the Minister shall lay a copy of every such report before each House of Parliament.

(2) The report shall include—

(a) a statement of the audited accounts of the Port Authority for that year; and

(b) any report made by the auditor on those accounts.

(3) A summary of the statement of the audited accounts, together with any report of the auditor thereon included in the report to the Minister, shall within fourteen days of the presentation of the report to the Minister be published by the Port Authority in one or more national daily morning newspapers.

(4) Copies of the report shall for a reasonable period after its presentation to the Minister be on sale to the public at the Port Authority's head office at a reasonable price.

9. The Port Authority shall give the Minister such returns, statistics and information with respect to the exercise of their powers as he may require.

* * *

11. – (2) The Minister may authorize the Port Authority
to purchase compulsory any land which they
require for the purposes of the undertaking.

*   *   *

48. – (3) Moneys borrowed or raised by the Port Authority under this section shall be applied
only –
(a) to purposes to which capital is properly
applicable;
(b) to the repayment of moneys borrowed or
raised by the Port Authority for any purpose; and
(c) with the consent of the Minister, for any
other purpose not covered above.

*   *   *

49. – (2) The total amount of moneys raised by the Port
Authority . . . outstanding at any one time shall
not exceed twelve million pounds or such larger
amount not exceeding twenty million pounds
as the Minister may sanction.

*   *   *

Part IV, 55. – (1) Bonds of the Port Authority shall be issued,
transferred, dealt with and redeemed upon such
terms and in accordance with such provisions as
the Minister with the approval of the Treasury
may by order prescribe.

*   *   *

59. – (2) The accounts for each financial year shall be
audited by an auditor or firm of accountants
appointed by the Minister.

*   *   *

Part VI, – 101. The Minister may give to the Port Authority or
to the council such directions as he considers
expedient in relation to [pollution control] . . .
and the Port Authority or the council, as the
case may be, shall be under a duty to comply
with any directions so given.

Despite these potential controls, however, testimony
through the years has been rather consistently given to the
fact that, as the *Report of the Committee of Inquiry into the
Major Ports of Great Britain* (the Rochdale Report), concluded in 1962 (p. 50) such powers over the Port Authority
are more apparent than real. Gordon had reported, as early as
1938, that "in form the P.L.A. is less independent than any
other public corporation," but that in "practice . . . they [the
restrictions] are rarely called into operation," "initiative
usually rests with the Authority," as his studies had shown,
"and where the Minister's prior approval is required it is
never extended beyond the safeguarding of other interests"
(37). The Port Authority declared in 1958 that it is "practically independent of Government" and functions by
"broadly speaking, conducting its own affairs without interference" (Port of London Authority, 1958: 4).

The Port Authority of New York and New Jersey

The Port Authority of the New York metropolitan area is
subject to some of the same checks. The chief fiscal officer of
New York State and New Jersey is authorized to conduct an
audit of the Authority's books and accounts; the Port Authority is required to submit an annual report to the
governor and each member of the legislatures of the two
states; and new major Port Authority construction of facilities require prior approval by concurrent legislation of the
two states. Its most unique control, however, is that of the
veto, resting in the hands of either governor over "any action
of any commissioner appointed therefrom," which he may

invoke against any provision in the minutes of the commissioners of the Port Authority, within ten days of the issuance of those minutes.

The fact that that veto power has been used in only nine instances in the 47 years since it was implemented by the two states in 1927, need not detract from its potential. The states' failure to resort to the veto may reflect either of two possible extreme conclusions. It could mean that the Port Authority is operating along the line of the desires of the two states, with close and frequent contact among the three governments (the Port Authority and the two states). Or, it could indicate, on the other hand, that the Port Authority has been carrying out its functions in an almost autonomous manner, and that the limited period of ten days given the governors to invoke the veto after the submission of the Authority board minutes has proved inadequate for the governors to offer alternative plans for any disfavored project. A description of the vetoes, made by the author on the strength of a record given him by the Port Authority (1968), reveals that, as a whole, they have not concerned the most important actions taken by the commissioners:

(1) June, 1941—Perhaps the most important issue that has drawn a veto was this first one in which the Board of the Port of New York Authority passed a resolution opposing a Congressional bill concerning the development of the St. Lawrence Seaway project. This was an interesting situation in which the proposed creation of a public authority, the St. Lawrence Seaway Development Corporation, was being objected to by the Port of New York Authority, one of the oldest and most successful public authorities in the country. The fear of New York was that the Seaway project would divert traffic away from the New York port through the St. Lawrence River. Both Governors vetoed the minutes containing the protest, and, thereby, raised a controversy as to whether the Port Authority is in a position to take a stand, as an expression of opinion, which varies from that of official policy of the two States involved in its compact. In this instance, of course, New York State was torn between two Authorities, in view of the value of the Port of New York Authority to New

York City's metropolitan area, and the anticipated benefits, on the other hand, to upstate New York from the development of the St. Lawrence River as a major ocean-connected artery and as a source of inexpensive power through the hydro-electric potential of the rapids of the River near Massena, New York, that would be dammed as part of the project. Subsequently, the two Governors withdrew their vetoes when the Commissioners changed the resolution to one by which the Port of New York Authority staff was to be permitted to submit data to, and to make appearances before, the House of Representatives Committee responsible for the bill.

(2) December, 1949—Both Governors again vetoed a Board resolution, relating to the construction contract for the Port Authority Bus Terminal. The Board readopted the same resolution later that same month, giving their reasons for so doing, and neither Governor vetoed it.

(3) March, 1950—Governor Alfred Driscoll of New Jersey vetoed resolutions of the Board which consisted merely of reports received from the Board's committees. The Governor charged that the delegation of the power in this way to committees made it much more difficult for the Governor to follow the matter, particularly when the full committee reports were not forwarded with the Board minutes.

(4) April, 1951—Governor Driscoll complained about a resolution of the Board which injected the Authority into policy-making beyond what he considered to be its proper role. This veto concerned the recommendation of the Port Authority of a Federal constitutional amendment which would clarify the right of the States to land lying under coastal waters. The Governor's objection was to substance, similar to that of the very first veto of 1941, in regard to the declaration of public policy by the Authority, on matters he considered beyond its purview.

(5) October, 1953—Governor Driscoll again took advantage of the veto power, this time against a resolution of the Authority Board to bar jet aircraft from Port Authority airports.

(6) August, 1961—In the midst of the controversy occasioned by the Port Authority's interest in the location of a jetport in the "Great Swamp" in Northern New Jersey, Governor Robert

Meyner, who also looked favorably toward that site for the jetport, vetoed sections of the minutes of the Board of April, 1961. He questioned two provisions:

(a) The increase in salary for the new Director of the Community Relations Department of the Port Authority;

(b) The increase in charges for bus companies using the Eighth Avenue Bus Terminal of the Authority in New York City.

The salary proposal for the Director of Community Relations was resubmitted by the Board, with a report of the Authority's public information program, and was not vetoed. The resolution relating to the Bus Terminal was rescinded, and a new one substituted. This one was not vetoed.

In short, as this record shows, the two governors, together, have vetoed two resolutions of the board of the Port Authority; and one governor, alone, from New Jersey, has vetoed five actions. These negative reactions have been 9, in number, out of hundreds of board actions. Not one involved the rejection of a project planned by the Authority, although it is true that the major plans had to be approved in legislation individually by the two state legislatures. Its most important effect has been to object to policy statements by the board. The Port Authority's assessment of the infrequency of the exercise of the veto is that it testifies to a close interrelationship between the Authority and the governors in the planning stages: "The mere existence of the veto power has necessitated that before any major policy decision is taken by the Commissioners, it is reviewed with the offices of the Governors to ensure its concordance with state policy. To do otherwise would run the irresponsible course of courting a veto" (Port of New York Authority, 1968). At its best, however, the veto's threat, which serves as a deterrent to precipitate action by the Authority, is negative in nature and not conducive to the kind of positive cooperation needed today in metropolitan areas. It is after-the-fact, in that the two states may be faced with an action of the Port Authority that has taken months to prepare, and have only ten days to accept or turn down the undertaking. Such a short period is totally inadequate for the consideration of alternatives, so important to the planning process. It comes down almost to a confrontation in which the governors are told to take this suggestion, or nothing. One of the governors of New York, Alfred E. Smith, who also had served as a commissioner of the Port of New York Authority, objected strongly to the veto proviso: "The Port Authority should be regarded as independent and not subject to constant supervision by the Governors of the two States. Moreover, it puts a burden and a responsibility upon the Governors which I am reluctant myself to assume" (Tobin, 1953: 30n). Here, again, studies are needed to fashion a more positive means of interrelationship between special-purpose and general-purpose governments, without destroying their respective advantages.

British citizens have turned to their Parliament for control over ad hoc governments; they have not conceived them as further extensions of pluralism whereby functions will be decentralized to local control. Americans, to the contrary, would like to visualize the special districts as mechanisms for bringing the control of everyday functions closer to them, locally. In either case, there is need for a new kind of check—whether at the national level or the local or state level. It might involve a new concept of operation for a governmental agency in a democracy. It might be considered a theory of action-reaction, in which a special government, performing highly technological functions difficult for the average citizen to comprehend under plans approved by the general-purpose governments might well be given freedom to implement that policy, without day-by-day interference by the general public. This would be in an operating capacity, not in a planning or policy-making role. What, then, is required and what we now lack is some kind of way of reacting periodically to the operations of the special government. Britains and Americans are more conditioned to approval through an elected forum, or legislative body, before action by governments, with that general-government's implementation of the legislation spelled out step-by-step. The special agencies, on the other hand, might be understood as highly professional groups of experts, operating under policies determined by elected bodies, but free to put such policies into effect in any way that they, in their technological wisdom, agree to be most effective. They would anticipate no interference in so doing, but they would know that at certain points they would be called to account through some kind of device as yet not invented.

The British have experimented since the 1940s with consumer groups—known as consultative councils or consumer councils—in the nationalized field industries. The first of these came in connection with the coal industry in 1947, and was known as the National Industrial and Domestic Coal Consumers' Councils. These were followed in the next two years by Area Electricity and Gas Consultative Councils, which included district committees. They are set up by the Secretary of State for Trade and Industry in England and in Wales, and for Scottish electricity by the Secretary of State for Scotland. They have 20 to 30 members, appointed by the minister, who are not paid, and who are nominated by interested groups—mainly local authorities (Central Office of Information, 1972: 216). They are used also in areas of transport. Herbert Morrison had foreseen their role as that of providing "an avenue of rectifying errors, of promoting good policy pleasing to the public and the users . . . and of exposing foolish or unsound criticisms" (1933: 175). Their importance varies, as might be expected, from one council to another, and still is being changed through organizational alterations. The latest shift has been to an arm's length relationship between councils and the nationalized industries, with recommendations to this effect made by a select committee and accepted by the government in a White Paper entitled, *Nationalized Industries Relations with the Public.* In practice, the change has been put into effect with the reorganization of the state gas industry into the new British Gas Corporation, as of January 1, 1973. No longer is the chairman of the National Gas Consumers' Council to be a member, ex-officio of the National Gas Board (Treasury and Department of Trade and Industry, 1972).

Professor Robson reported, in 1962, "general agreement

among a considerable number of investigators and competent observers that the Councils have fulfilled their purpose to a limited extent, but that in general the results have so far been less far reaching than might have been expected" (Robson: 257).

As of October 1, 1973, the ad hoc National Health Service began to employ an ombudsman to "look into complaints against hospital authorities, executive councils and the public health laboratory service board." Sir Alan Marre, the parliamentary commissioner (ombudsman) since 1971, had his duties extended to include this position as health service commissioner (ombudsman) under provisions of the National Health Service Reorganization Act 1973, and the National Health Service (Scotland) Act 1972 (*Times,* London, 1973; *Glasgow Herald,* 1973).

The action-reaction formula is not easily adapted to the more traditional democratic concepts, but it seems to become increasingly necessary, especially for the large metropolitan areas where concentrations of expertise are required.

FINANCES

The statutory provisions relating to finance for the Port of London Authority and the Port Authority of New York and New Jersey are more similar in their overall content than are those for any other aspect of the two special Authorities. It is obvious that the New York Port Authority was strongly indebted to its prototype in London for these financial arrangements. Yet, in practice, the differences between the two in the application of these regulations, and in their understanding by those concerned, represent the most significant differences of the two. These are subtle distinctions, but of the greatest importance for a determination of the appropriate place of such agencies in democratic governments. The comparison is applicable not only to the two port authorities, but to public corporations versus special public authorities, in general. The differences today, in part, depend on the fact that many of the British public corporations represent nationalized industries, whereas in the United States, the special public authority governs a quasi-public area of functions without the kind of clarity of distinction between public and private that socialization implies. The port authorities, however, are not subject to such influence, as ports in the United Kingdom have not been nationalized. There is a more fundamental perception of the public nature of the public corporation in Britain than there is of the special public authority in the United States. It is a fine line but a very real one.

The distinction, in great part, depends on the fact that the two port authorities have had to invest heavily for the facilities essential to modernized ports. In its annual report for 1971, the Port of London Authority (1972: 28) reported the gross value of its assets, as of the last day of that year, to be £153,132,000. As of that same day, the Port Authority of New York and New Jersey had almost $2.8 billion invested in its facilities (Levitt, 1972: II, 59). Both had had to achieve these results principally on their own, without help from other governments. The two had gone into the open market to borrow money, and both were defraying these obligations by resorting to tolls and other charges made for the use of their facilities. Indeed, the degree of autonomy built up over the years in each instance by these port authorities had been predicated on just such capabilities: the proven abilities to conduct a public function so efficiently that it would pay its own costs, even with the most modern of port buildings and equipment. The word "efficiency" is the most common expression of special public authorities anywhere. The Port of London Authority insists that even its more recent assumption of responsibilities for pollution control will "not distract us from our first duty, to make the Port of London second to no other port in efficiency now and in each year to come." "And we know," its report adds, "that the best test of this efficiency will lie in our ability to make a trading profit year by year" (Port of London Authority, 1972: 8). The New

York counterpart Authority echoes the similar theme: "In order to finance—on a self-supporting basis and without cost to the general taxpayer . . . the . . . facilities essential to that development, it . . . has been necessary . . . to develop sufficient revenue potential and to utilize modern efficient business methods to build a strong credit base and a sound financial structure" (Port of New York Authority, 1967: 49). The results, in terms of physical plants, are similar; both Authorities have facilities that they, quite rightly, are proud to show. One complaint occasionally lodged against the Port Authority of New York and New Jersey is that its structures may be even too elaborate, reminding one of Gordon's warning in 1938 of "the dangerous latent possibility inherent in a public corporation . . . in the temptation to further its prestige by constructing striking monuments to its enthusiasm which place an unwarranted burden on its consumers" (Gordon, 1938: 71).

Obviously, both the Port of London Authority and the Port Authority of New York and New Jersey have established sound credit bases. They have gained the confidence of the investors and the investment system. Neither has defaulted on debt. The two have proved that they can live up to the statutory and legal requirements that they meet their obligations, on their own, and on time. In so doing, however, the Port Authority of New York and New Jersey has become far more influenced by the desire to continue to satisfy its bondholders (its principal form of borrowing being the revenue bond), than has the Port of London for the holders of its port stock (which, bearing fixed rates of interest, has been its long-term public issue). The bondholders, for the New York Authority, have come to be considered one of its most powerful "constituents" if not *the* most powerful one. No such connotation is associated with the stockholders of the Port of London Authority. The reason may well be found in a short section of the Port of London Act 1968 which reads: "It shall not be necessary for a person who lends money to the Port Authority to enquire into the application of that money" (Part IV, 50). The stockholder is fully protected in

his investment, even to the extent of being able to "apply to
the High Court for the appointment of a receiver and manager
of the undertaking [of the Port of London Authority] " if the
Authority has been "in default in the payment of interest on
the stock for not less than three months" if he is joined by
"holders of port stock to an aggregate nominal value of not less
than five hundred thousand pounds" (Part IV, 54.–[1]).
(Many American special authorities have adopted this protection for their bondholders, usually stating the amount of
bondholders concerned necessary to such action as "twenty-
five per centum in aggregate principal amount of the bonds
of such an issue then outstanding.") Even here, nonetheless,
Port of London Stock Regulations as early as 1921 had made
it clear that the receiver and manager, so named, could "only
administer the port in accordance with the Port of London
Acts, and not specifically in the interest of the holders"
(Gordon, 1938: 39-40). Court decisions have determined that
the stock of the Port of London Authority requires of the
Authority only "the obligations of a corporation to preference stockholders with no claims on capital and with no voting
rights" (Gordon, 1938: 40).

The priorities for the use of receipts by the Port of
London Authority indicate that the performance of the
functions for which the Authority was created has first call
and then, the obligations to repay borrowed funds:

47.–(1) the receipts of the Port Authority on revenue account in
each financial year shall be applied for the following purposes in
the following order: —

(a) the payment of working and establishment expenses (including the provision of pensions, or comparable benefits for or
in respect of persons employed or formerly employed by them)
and of any part of the cost of performing the Port Authority's
duties or exercising their powers which is properly chargeable to
revenue account;

(b) the payment of interest on A port stock and on port stock
ranking *pari passu* therewith;

(c) the payment of interest on other port stock and moneys borrowed under . . . [borrowing powers] of this Act;

(d) the payment of interest on moneys borrowed by the Port Authority and raised by other means;

(e) making such provision for depreciation as the Port Authority consider necessary" [Port of London Act 1968, chapter 32, part IV, section 47 (1)].

The different emphasis by which the Port Authority of New York and New Jersey places first priority on its bond-holders is illustrated by its similar provision:

Subject to prior liens and pledges . . . the revenues of the Port Authority from facilities established, constructed, acquired or effectuated through the issuance of sale of bonds of the Port Authority secured by a pledge of its General Reserve Fund may be pledged in whole or in part as security for or applied by it to the repayment with interest of any moneys which it may raise upon bonds issued by it to provide funds for terminal purposes, and said revenues may be applied by the Port Authority to the fulfillment of any other undertakings which it may assume to or for the benefit of the holders of such bonds [N.J.S.A., 32: 1-35.6].

The paramount concern for the current activities of the Port of London Authority, and, only then, for the obligations of the stockholders, is apparent in the ordering of priorities in the quotation from laws applying to it, above. On the other hand, the prior responsibility of the Port Authority of New York and New Jersey to its bondholders is made clear in the laws cited above for the American counterpart.

The British do not cut loose their special-purpose units and force them onto the open market. Rather, through a number of measures, the British control more carefully the borrowing by special-purpose agencies. The Port of London Authority's borrowing is controlled by a parliamentary provision to the effect that it is limited to an amount "outstanding at any one time" of "twelve million pounds or such larger amount not exceeding twenty million pounds as the Minister may sanction" (Port of London Act 1968: Part IV, sec. 49 [2]). The minister's role is not only to check excesses by the Port Authority, but to give an authoritative overview that will result in lower interest rates for the stocks and bonds issued by the Port Authority.

Nearly all the "nationalised industries established by the Labour Governments between 1945 and 1951 issued bonds by way of compensation to the previous owners who were expropriated. Moreover, some or all of the nationalised industries raised further capital on the market by the issue of bonds until 1956, when Harold MacMillan (the then Chancellor of the Exchequer) explained that in future all capital requirements of the corporations would be met by Treasury loans. The reason for this was that the demands were too great for the market and the Treasury had to step in to make up the residue. The bonds were of course at fixed rates of interest, they have always been guaranteed by the Treasury, they are all redeemable and they carry no voting rights of control of any kind" (Robson, 1973). Since 1956, the Exchequer has provided advances for the major projects of the special corporations. The minister has played a key role in the approval, or disapproval, of financial proposals.

The bondholder of the Port Authority of New York and New Jersey, on the other hand, by its statutes, has been written into a very real place in its decision making. This is done individually for projects, as they have been been financed in various ways, as to the degree of state help and the like. Its most extreme expression was found in 1962 in regard to the Port Authority's project for the construction of the World Trade Center and its acquisition of the Hudson and Manhattan Railroad, which connected New Jersey to Manhattan under the Hudson River, and would be extended to the World Trade Center, in downtown New York. The usual American safeguards for investors was provided in a pledge by the states of New York and New Jersey that they would not

> diminish or impair the power of the port authority . . . to establish, levy and collect rentals, tolls, fees or other charges in connection with any facility constituting a portion of the port development project or any other facility owned or operated by the port authority of which the revenues have been or shall be pledged in whole or in part as security for such bonds . . . or to determine the quantity, quality, frequency or nature of the service provided in connection with each such facility [N.J.S.A. 32: 1-35.55].

In addition, however, the legislation contained a clause, which became known as the "Covenant," because the heading of that section of the statute read just that way, "Covenant with bondholders." This was a legally involved statement to the effect that the Port Authority was not to apply any revenues or reserves pledged to bonds for this project for any additional passenger railroad purpose without the consent of the bondholders unless the deficits from such additional service would not exceed an amount equal to one-tenth of the money in the Port Authority's reserve fund at the end of the preceding year. What it meant, in more simple terminology, was that the Port Authority, having undertaken the rejuvenation of the deficit-ridden Hudson and Manhattan Railroad, would not venture into other mass transit rail projects. This clause was enacted at the very time that the public was clamoring for greater attention by the Port Authority to mass transit in the port district, and correspondingly less to facilities for the automobile. The *New York Times* (1973a) caught up these complaints editorially:

> A decade ago, the Port Authority sought and won a restrictive covenant that excused it from further participation in mass transportation. . . . As an agency to provide and coordinate mass transit service, the Port Authority has never left the roundhouse. Its concern has generally been with revenue-producing projects,

not with commuters. But the priorities have to change. The commuter must not be damned; he must be served.

A commissioner of the Authority had spoken for the Port Authority's position:

> (W)hile supporting efforts to solve mass transportation problems, the Commissioners have continued to try to avoid violence to the 1962 pact wherein Port Authority bondholders must be protected. In other words, the Commissioners have a dual responsibility here to advance mass transportation and, at the same time, protect the guaranteed interest of Port Authority bondholders, and they go hand in hand now and will in the future [*New York Times*, 1972a].

The vehicle through which the bondholders would express themselves is a bank, known as the trustee for the Authority. It operates under an indenture, by which it is given responsibilities by the Authority for handling its banking and commercial transactions, and, for its part, the bank agrees to ascertain that the proper reserves are maintained at all times and to protect the rights of the bondholders. It is the trustee, the bank, that will institute suit against the Authority if it feels that these rights are being violated by an action of the Authority, or imposed on the Authority by the states. The Port of London Authority has a bank as trustee, but it does not stand in this strict advocacy position.

The reason for this difference is made the more difficult to ascertain by a realization that both countries accept the obligation of contracts of public agencies. Both countries protect the holders of government obligations. And both include special public authorities under this provision. There is an emphasis on the clause, as claimed by the American special public authorities, however, that is not sought by the British ad hoc units. Britain and the United States are equally insistent on the private rights of individuals against the government, through the common law, and both protect these rights against encroachment by governments, including special-purpose agencies. The British, however, modify this priority just a bit more than do the Americans. A British expert on English Law explains it this way: "In the United States the existence of constitutional safeguards of those rights and the absence of a sovereign legislature (in the English sense) have had the consequence that the conflict between private rights and governmental necessities has been more clear-cut than it can be in this country" (Mitchell, 1954: 23). In other words, the fact that the Port of London Act 1968 had been passed by Parliament and that that sovereign body had inserted the stipulation that it "is not necessary for a person who lends money to the Port Authority to enquire into the application of that money," helps shade the emphasis, in regard to the stockholders of the Port of London Authority, to its public role and to its need to exercise its functions for the public at large, rather than the stockholders. It is a matter of emphasis but a significant one. In speaking of administrative tribunals—and not referring at all to special-purpose units—Professor Robson pointed out that they, being "unfettered by the existing legal tradition," had been "able to break away entirely from the prevailing body of legal doctrine based on private rights." "In short," he explained, with reasoning that does have application to special-purpose authorities, "the tendency towards the social-isation of government has been accompanied by a parallel tendency towards the socialisation of law" (Robson, 1970: 549). The public corporation of Britain is pointing toward its public concept, whereas the special public authority of the United States continues to overemphasize the rights of the bondholder, to an extent that overprotects him at the expense of the public at large. More will be said about this distinction throughout the book.

Its meaning for the development of the special government trend should not be underestimated. In Britain, the special-purpose governments arose out of the "undesirability of the profit motive." They proliferated because "no single concern among the competing groups could be found willing, or could find investors in the money market willing, to undertake the risk of large-scale capital improvement while remaining uncertain of the action of competitors" (Gordon, 1938: 317). In the United States, they came rather for those functions that would be revenue-producing, to the extent that special-authority bonds would have high ratings in the open market, and, as one writer complained, "they picked the plums" of government responsibilities and left the "prunes" for the general-purpose officials.

Chapter 3

THE THEORY OF THE PUBLIC CORPORATION

FOR TRANSPORTATION

The theory of the modern public corporation emerged from the debates and discussions over a parliamentary bill to coordinate transportation in the London area, beginning in 1930, and culminated in the passage of the London Passenger Transport Act of 1933. This was 25 years after the establishment of the Port of London Authority as a modified public corporation, and it was seven years after the creation by Parliament of two national public corporations, the Central Electricity Board and the British Broadcasting Corporation. That the theory evolved from the anticipated use of such an agency for transportation was not by predesign, but "largely an accident of politics" (Davies, in Robson, 1937: 155). From that time on, however, "the public corporation in Britain ceased to be an accidental divagation [digression] from well-tested forms and became conceived as a new agency of public administration, with its own peculiar characteristics, advantages, and requirements" (Gordon, 1938: 245).

In view of the fact that much of the writing on the philosophy of the public corporation had been done by the Fabians, and that Herbert Morrison, one of the more articulate champions of socialism, was to crystallize the arguments for its use as the coordinating agency for London transportation, the theoretical rationale for this special-purpose agency often is construed merely as socialist doctrine. It represents, to be sure, a link in socialist thought. Professor Friedmann has pointed out that "(m)odern moderate socialist theory has . . . used the public corporation as a compromise between the older ideas of socialism [which had been more concerned with the principles of socialization than the technicalities and instrumentalities] and the newer necessities of economic management" (1954: 544, 545). Morrison, of course, was concerned here with the acceptance of a vehicle for transportation coordination to complement the nationalization of that function. But the theory of the public corporation had a much broader base than that; it reflected the outgrowth of consideration of organization over a number of years by three political parties of Britian—Conservative, Liberal, and Labour. As a result, therefore, the theory of the public corporation, born in the parliamentary struggle of the early 1930s, has application not limited to any specific political persuasion.

No such theory has been devolved for the American offspring, the special public authority, probably because the United States has been willing to settle for the social-welfare state, rather than nationalization. This more nebulous understanding of the area between public and private sectors has not forced upon Americans the necessity of defining the mechanisms that bridge the two. The special public authority still is regarded here as a temporary expediency to cope with emergency situations attendant first upon the depression of the 1930s, next those of World War II, and now the explosion of the population to the suburbs. Their significant role in the American governmental process has not been crystallized politically to the point that it could be expressed in terms of a theory. In fact, a good part of their acceptance in the United States is attributable to the anonymity in which they operate. Even in relation to the American's most far-reaching contribution to the special-government movement, the river-valley authority, as represented by the Tennessee Valley Authority, the mechanism of organization has been understated. In his widely known work on the philosophy of the T.V.A., *Democracy on the March,* David E. Lilienthal, one of the fathers of that Authority, minimizes the importance of the corporate form: "It is not ... the fact that the T.V.A. was cast in the mold of a corporation that is distinctive. The corporate device for public undertakings was, of course, neither new nor unique" (1945: 181-182). Indeed, the entire New Deal government, of which the T.V.A. was a part and under which special authorities were spawned, never was expressed in philosophical terms. An eminent historian of American political traditions has explained the New Deal this way (Hofstadter, 1948: 311-312, 313):

> At the heart of the New Deal there was not a philosophy but a temperament.... During his [Franklin Roosevelt's] presidential period the nation was confronted with a completely novel situation for which the traditional, commonly accepted philosophies afforded no guide. An era of fumbling and muddling-through was inevitable. Only a leader with an experimental temper could have made the New Deal possible.

The accident of Herbert Morrison's association of his philosophical exposition of the public corporation with transportation came about through the juxtaposition of his appointment as Minister of Transport in the new Labour government of 1929, with the fact that before Parliament at that time happened to be private bills for the setting up of a common fund and common management for various modes of transportation in London. His first assignment as Minister of

Transport, thus, was to comment on these bills, known as the "Co-ordinating Bills," which had passed two readings and were to come before the House of Commons. His intimate concern with this legislation was heightened by the fact that, just before his appointment in the Labour government, he had been secretary to the London Labour Party and leader of the Labour Party in the London County Council. In these posts, he had been concerned with problems of transport in London for a number of years. Liberal and Labour members from London were in opposition to the Co-ordinating Bills. Confronting him as the New Minister of Transport in the Labour government, therefore, were suggestions for co-ordinating transportation in London which he and his colleagues had been opposing back in the London government. Characterizing the provisions as presaging "a permanent private monopoly in London traffic," he set up an attack on the pending bills and succeeded in having them defeated in 1929, on the promise that he would initiate new measures. At this point, he foresaw some form of public ownership that would, at the same time, "provide for the principle of commercial management of a self-supporting, consolidated transport system, thus ensuring the advantages of vigorous business enterprise" (Gordon, 1938: 256). The bill that he presented to Parliament in 1931 further envisioned the public corporation:

1. a Board of five members appointed by the Minister of Transport, chosen from among those persons who "have had wide experience, and have shown capacity, in industry, commerce, or finance or in the conduct of public affairs"
2. a coordination of passenger transport in the London Traffic Area, with a monopoly over all modes except those of private vehicles and taxicabs
3. ownership of the Underground Group, the Metropolitan Railway, the transport facilities of the London County Council's and the 13 local governments' tramways, and private companies

4. issuance of London Transport Stock as compensation for the private stock holdings
5. financial independence for the Board, and the freedom to organize itself internally
6. jurisdiction of revision of rates by the Railway Rates Tribunal
7. right of the Minister to intervene in the withdrawal of services
8. audit under authority of the Minister, annual report, and other publications [Gordon, 1938: 257-259].

After prolonged debate, the bill came out of the Joint Committee, "modified in many details but substantially unaltered in its main outlines" (Gordon, 1938: 261). Just as it was reported back to the House, however, another general election occurred in 1931, with the first national government, largely Conservative in composition, voted into power. Mr. Morrison was out as Minister of Labour, replaced by Mr. P. J. Pybus, a Liberal. A new bill was drawn up, and was carried over to the 1931-1933 session of Parliament, now with a Conservative Minister of Transport, Mr. Oliver Stanley, as of February 1933. It was passed on July 1, 1933. Ernest Davies, British specialist on finance and transportation, has summed up the enactment of this legislation as follows:

> Before the Bill was passed through all these stages the Labour Government fell, the Labour Minister of Transport was succeeded by a Liberal member of the National Coalition Government who in turn was superseded by another Minister of Transport, also a Liberal. . . . The Bill was launched by a Labour Government, and by pure chance was carried over to a 'National' Government, where it was piloted farther by a Liberal, eventually to become law through the hands of a third Minister of Transport who was a Conservative.

The formation of the London Passenger Transport Board, under this procedure constituted a "unique" experience, he concluded (Davies, in Robson, 1937: 162-163).

It was in this ambience that Herbert Morrison formulated a theory of the public corporation as a structure of government that might serve as a consistent coordinating agency for transportation. This was published in the book, *Socialisation and Transport* that same year, 1933. He visualized the public corporation for transportation as a synthesis of certain public and private characteristics. "We are seeking," he explained, "a combination of public ownership, public accountability, and business management for public ends" (p. 149). The word "public" obviously dominates his definition of the corporation. This was to be an agency of government, however, that was to pay its own way, and, therefore, was to enjoy a degree of freedom in its operations not commonly accorded government departments. Its governance was to reside in a board, but one not influenced by special interests, one oriented to public considerations. Primary requisites for its members were to be those of "suitable grounds of competence." Members of the London Passenger Transport Board, for example, were to be experienced, and to have proved their capacity "in transport, industrial, commercial, or financial matters in the conduct of public affairs" (Morrison, 1933: 159).

Appointments to the board were to be made by the minister of transport, after consultation with the Treasury. They would have a fixed term, and would be removable by the minister. In short, the board was to be accountable to the minister for overall policy, but was to have a high degree of flexibility in its daily operations. The minister was not to interfere in the day-by-day work of the board, but the board would function with a considerable autonomy, within its clearly defined sphere. He suggested the possibility of a "quasi-judicial tribunal" to hear appeals of grievances of the public, particularly in matters of pricing, and a consultative council. Otherwise, he would place reliance on the dedication of the board to the public interest and on informal communication between the board chairman and the minister, so that the latter would be informed sufficiently to defend the public corporation for transportation in parliamentary discussions (Morrison, 1933: 149-191).

LONDON PASSENGER
TRANSPORT ACT 1933

A comparison of the 1933 London Passenger Transport Act that finally became law after its confusing path through parliamentary changes and procedures reveals sections fitting Morrison's standards and others quite at variance. Davies considered it exceptional that not more provisions of Morrison's transport bill had been excluded from the Conservative's measure. It was not, he thought, an "unrecognizable hybrid" (Davies, in Robson, 1937: 163). He did, however, suggest that the Conservative government leaders were "incompetent midwives" for the delivery of legislation that had been conceived by Labour (Davies, 1946: 26). As the first modern special-purpose agency for the coordination of transportation, nonetheless, it deserves consideration, both for its consistencies and inconsistencies, as well as for its first test of Morrison's principles. It was established as a body corporate and public, or a public corporation, and it was authorized to operate on a broad regional scale. And, of greatest significance in comparison to the development of the special public authority at the very same time in the United States, the British public corporation was directed to the problems of *mass* transportation, rather than to those of automobile. The special-purpose authority was being adapted to a coordinative, regional approach for transportation in 1933, on a scale that was not to be attempted in the United States until some 30 years later, and then, too, through the employment of the special public authority. America, therefore, could well look carefully at these British efforts of the 1930s.

Lesser efforts to coordinate individual modes of the transportation function had taken place in England even prior to this enlarged one in 1933. Herbert Morrison testified that his efforts had been preceded by "small and disconnected beginnings, leading up to an increasing degree of consolidation and larger and larger units of operation" (O'Brien, 1937: 203).

These pre-1930s bits and pieces of consolidation had included the following:

(1) mergers of the railway companies, through the Railways Act of 1921, into four amalgamated railway companies, still privately owned: the London, Midland and Scottish; London and North Eastern; Great Western; and Southern.

(2) the merger, by 1913, of most of the number of separate companies that had been underground railway sections in London since the 1870s, by the privately owned Underground Electric Railways Company of London Ltd.

(3) absorption by the London General Omnibus Company, a private company first founded in Paris in 1829, and reformed as an English company in 1858, of most of the holdings of independent proprietors, so that, by 1930, the L.G.O.C., as it commonly was known, owned most of the motor buses of London, as well as control of the Green Lines Coaches, Ltd., which operated on a metropolitan level. This virtual monopoly had been aided by the Government, through its London Traffic Act of 1924, which had set up the London and Home Counties Traffic Advisory Committee, and had given the Minister of Transport, after advice from this Committee, the power to limit the number of omnibuses operating in the streets of the metropolitan area under its jurisdiction. Competitors of the L.G.O.C., which were beginning to arise in large numbers, therefore, were cut off.

(In 1912, the Underground Company and the London General Omnibus Company combined their interests, and added to them three private tramway companies. This became known as the "Omnibus Group," or the "Combine." By a Private Act of Parliament, in 1915, they were permitted to set up a Common Fund, by pooling their receipts. This resulted in economies for all involved, and was a major step toward consolidation of efforts, even from one mode to another, in part, as underground railway facilities as well as those for omnibuses now were operating in certain matters under the Common Fund. The Combine was, however, private, and only a holding company type organization.)

(4) the buying up of tramway services, owned traditionally in England not by private companies, but by local governments, by the London County Council, beginning as early as 1889. By 1932

the London County Council owned most of the tramways, to the extent of some 167 miles of lines, out of the total of 328 miles, over the metropolitan area.

Prior to the passage of the London Passenger Transport Act of 1933, therefore, there had been mergers within the four modes of transportation in the London area: railways, underground, buses, and trams. Two of these (railways and underground) had resulted from the creation of private monopolies; one, for buses, privately also, but with the help of the London Traffic Act of 1924; and the fourth, for the tramways which always had been publicly owned, by direct action by the London County Council. None of these four mergers was complete; there were still pockets of competitors. What was almost totally lacking, moreover, with the slight exception of the Combine, were interrelationships among the four modes. The result, by 1930, were "overlapping of passenger transport services and facilities, failure to use each mode of transport for the purposes for which it was best adapted, poor return on the capital invested in most of the transport undertakings, and the inability of many of the undertakings to extend their plant or create the new facilities of interconnection and speed which conditions demanded" (O'Brien, 1937: 209).

These amalgamated strongholds of the four modes of transportation help to explain why it was that Herbert Morrison's theory of the public corporation first emerged in the struggle to coordinate them, rather than in the less powerful and complex undertakings of the Central Electricity Board or the British Broadcasting Corporation, formed seven years earlier. It is not without meaning that today in the United States the first real test of the special public authority as a regional coordinative agent also is associated with transportation in its many modes. Transportation is visible; it is a hardware function in that its facilities are tangible; it is subdivided into clearly defined modes each with its traditional guilds; it represents, in the aggregate, huge sums of capital investment; and its subdivisions are jealous of one another. Electricity, to be sure, is hardware, when seen in its use in the home or factory, but there is the element of the abstract in its operations, in that its production and transmission are represented in an unseen wave of energy. Broadcasting is clearly software, involving, as it does, cultural, educational, and recreational services. Transportation stands exposed for all to see.

The London Passenger Transport Board (known thereafter as "London Transport,") was the new public corporation assigned the task of transportation coordination in the London area. Although the London Passenger Transport Act of 1933, which raised up this board, has been criticized when compared point-by-point with Herbert Morrison's standards for a public corporation, it still appears quite advanced to this American author, writing in the 1970s when the United States is just beginning to conceive of its special-purpose agencies as intermodal, areawide, and encompassing both deficit and surplus-producing modes of transportation.

Intermodal

On July 1, 1933, the undertakings of three of the four principal modes of transportation in the London area were transferred to the London Passenger Transport Board. That group came into control therefore, of the partly merged, partly separate, modes of the underground railways, buses, and tramways. The railway undertakings were not transferred to the L.P.T.B., as even Mr. Morrison agreed that it was not practicable to attempt to sort out the suburban lines when those lines were integral parts of a railway system extended throughout the country. All four of the private mergers of the railways impinged on London: the London, Midland and Scottish; London and North Eastern; Great Western; and Southern, as British railways radiated out from London to all sections of the country. All four mergers, accordingly, were essential elements in the picture of coordination of transportation for London. This fact of railway regions, following the main lines of the railroads that flow out from London, still plagues attempts at coordination by any metropolitan public corporation in the London area. The structure for handling this complexity in the 1933 act was that of a

Standing Joint Committee comprising four persons to be appointed by the London Passenger Transport Board and one each from the four railway mergers. The eight would elect a chairman from among the membership. This Joint Committee was to draw up plans for cooperation among the five components, and was to plan a pooling of the receipts of the passenger functions under the board and of those under the four railway mergers, between any two stations within the area of the L.P.T.B. This latter looks to the possible balancing of rates and schedules. For the three modes specifically under its control (underground railways, buses, and tramways) the new board was charged with the responsibility for balancing them so that deficits of one would be offset by surpluses of the other. It was to be conceived of as a unified system. Even receipts of the railways' and the board's passenger services were to be pooled, if that could be worked out.

Regional

This board, with its comprehensive coordinative duties, covered a very large geographic area, extending far beyond the boundaries of the present Greater London. It encompassed in whole the administrative County of London and the County of Middlesex and parts of seven other counties. It included 184 local authorities, or governments. Some 9,500,000 people lived within it. It was not drawn totally according to the logic of the transportation needs, as might be expected. "The area was a compromise arrived at as a parliamentary bargain between conflicting parties in the course of the passage of the London Passenger Transport Bill" (Royal Commission on Local Government in Greater London 1957-50, 1960: 110). Its importance is seen, however, in the fact that it was to continue to be used by the various coordinating special governments of the London area until it was abandoned in the London Transport Act of 1969. Also continuing down through 1969 was a "special area" set up under the 1933 act. This was a district of 1,550 square miles, of the total of 1,986 square miles in the London Passenger Transport Board area, within which that board was to have complete powers over road services in regard to bus and coach services. Those two districts, that for the London Passenger Transport Board, and that, within the first, the "special area," continued in effect for 36 years. The delimitations that they established, however, were complicated by the fact of other district lines concerning transportation. Allowed to stand, even under the 1933 Act, were the boundaries of the London Traffic Act of 1924, which approached those of the London Passenger Transport Board area, but at some points were narrower, and at others wider than that new area. A royal commission later reported that the 1924 lines simply had been drawn by the appropriation of the boundaries of the London and Home Counties Joint Electricity Authority and were adopted for traffic purposes in 1924 "because there was no time to think of anything better" (Royal Commission on Local Government in Greater London 1957-60, 1960: 110). These overlapping jurisdictions add to the fears of the fragmenting effects on governments of the special-purpose government proliferation.

Representation

The strongest provision of the London Passenger Transport Act of 1933 was that concerning the composition of its board. It carries to the ultimate the desire to take "out of politics" the management of a technological function such as that of transportation. It illustrates, again, the impossibility of accomplishing that wish for an agency engaged in the making of public policy. The act specified:

> The chairman and other members of the Board shall be persons who have had wide experience, and have shown capacity, in transport, industrial, commercial or financial matters or in the

conduct of public affairs and, in the case of two members, shall be persons who have had not less than six years experience in local government within the London Passenger Transport Area.

The board was to consist of a chairman and six other members. Appointment of these members was to be not by the minister, however, as Morrison had proposed, but by a curious "electoral college" procedure. Six ad hoc appointing trustees were to make the appointments. The trustees were to be:

1. the chairman of the London County Council
2. a representative of the London and Home Counties Traffic Advisory Committee (set up under the London Traffic Act of 1924, and covering a large region, whose boundaries were not coterminous with those of the London Passenger Transport Board's area)
3. the chairman of the Committee of London Clearing Bankers
4. the president of the Law Society
5. the president of the Institute of Chartered Accountants in England and Wales

The design clearly was to take appointments to the board out of the hands of the minister for fear that his choices would be predicated on political considerations. As it happened, two of these five trustees were from Bristol, more than 80 miles from the London Passenger Transport Board area. The three professional representatives were appointed to the presidency of their organizations annually, and, therefore, continuity on the board for them would be impossible, unless they continued to be reelected to the professional positions (Gordon, 1938: 264). The trustees also had the power to determine the length of the term for the members, from three to seven years. The trustees chose for the first board two members representing companies to be taken over by the board; two members of municipalities; one from the trade union movement; one from banking and industry; and one experienced in transport matters (Davies in Robson, 1937: 166). Lord Ashfield was named chairman; he had been the chairman and managing director of the private Combine, which had coordinated underground, omnibus, and certain tramway companies. The vice chairman selected by the trustees also had had broad experience in transport, but again with private companies. He had served in the North Eastern Railway, and ultimately had become director of the Traffic Combine, of which Lord Ashfield had been the chairman. These two obviously had had helpful experience, but there was some objection, especially from the Socialists, as to their "capitalist" indoctrination. Perhaps it is not surprising that the early programs of development, under the London Passenger Transport Board were "largely in completion of programmes initiated by the Combine," but it is perfectly conceivable that that would have been its thrust had not two top officials of the Combine been named to head the new board. The board did subsequently branch out into some other avenues (Gordon, 1938: 311).

The more serious objection to the entire indirect method of appointment, however, hinges on its divorcing of the members of the board from the minister of transport, now that he did not have the power of appointment. Their accountability became confused: if not to the minister, who had not appointed them, how could it be to the trustees who had no other function but to name them in the first instance? With the appointing power dissolved after its act of appointing the board, the members chosen must have felt a lack of responsibility to those to whom they owed the position. The *Economist* declared the trustee device to be "merely a piece of political pedantry, introduced to 'save the face' of Conservative politicians who opposed the measure while in Opposition" (Gordon, 1938: 262).

Significance

Regardless of incongruities, however, the importance of the London Passenger Transport Board of 1933 lies in its constitution as a public agency for the coordination of the various modes of transportation over a broad regional area. The public corporation, with the approval of all three British parties as to its objectives, had been turned to the service of mass transportation. The meaning of that decision can best be appreciated only by an analysis of the special-purpose government development in the United States during the same period of the 1930s and 1940s (the London Passenger Transport Board lasted until 1947). The direction of the special public authorities in America was toward the more profitable modes of transportation, mainly those associated with the automobile, to the neglect of the needs of mass transit.

The introduction of inventions in the field reflected impressive similarities between the United Kingdom and the United States. Horse-drawn streetcars came to New York City, for example, in the 1830s, and, in that same decade, they were appearing in London. City railroads were first used in both cities also in the 1830s. An underground was completed, on a trial basis, in New York in 1863-1865, and in London in 1870. Some city regulation of mass transit was imposed in New York, with the New York City Rapid Transit Board in 1894, and, in London, under the London Passenger Traffic Conference of 1907, although the earlier role of the Metropolitan Board of Works dating back to 1855 should not be overlooked. The New York City subways were purchased by the city in 1940 and placed under a Transportation Board of the city government, where they were neglected, as automobile facilities expanded under the aegis of the special public authorities. In England, as has been described, the London underground in 1933 was placed under the ad hoc London Passenger Transport Board with the design of coordinating its use with those of other mass transportation modes. Subsequent organizational forms of the public corporation have been experimented with in British transportation since 1933. They all have emphasized mass transportation. The agency, itself, may well be only the catalyst in this focus. A great many factors add up to so all-embracing a national concept as this one for mass transportation over the automobile. T. C. Barker and Michael Robbins, (1963: I, xx), who have written a comprehensive history of London transportation, have identified the complexity of the reasons:

> The form these transport developments took was determined by a number of factors: by Parliamentary action, for instance, which was ultimately responsible in the nineteenth century both for linking the mainline termini by means of an underground railway and for keeping the horse tram out of central London; by high site values, greedy railway promoters, and financial crises which all helped to make railway building very costly, thereby keeping railway dividends low and hindering the raising of fresh capital; by reduced omnibus operating costs, made possible by tax reductions and cheaper horse feed, which helped to preserve the profitableness of horse traction in London even in the heyday of the steam locomotive; by able businessmen who were able to gain a growing share of the traffic at the expense of their less resourceful rivals.

The public corporation may have served to crystallize certain of these diverse factors.

There is no mistaking the emphasis in the United Kingdom, however, as against that in the United States during the same period of time from the 1930s until today. Britain had lived through her period of the "Turnpike Trust" for more than 150 years beginning early in the 1700s which had spawned some 1100 of these special agencies and 23,000 miles of roads. With the advent of the automobile, Britain decided not to return to the toll method of financing its roads. Sidney and Beatrice Webb, who wrote the fascinating account of the Turnpike Trust era, simply concluded: "There was . . . no convenient way by which the all-pervading motor car traffic could be taxed locally, in any definite relation to its use of the road. No one suggested a return to the tollgate" (Webb, 1913: 250). The United States, on the other hand, which had experienced the turnpike companies in the late eighteenth and early nineteenth centuries, returned to the toll system when the automobile began to demand attention there. The boast of literally several thousand special authorities (International Bridge, Tunnel, and Turnpike Association, Tollways 1973) in America is that they have served the car interests:

> Name any of the existing major engineering works on which modern life in this country depends, and ponder a frightening thought: Many of them could not be built today. The environmentalists could tie up such projects, indefinitely. . . . Let's face it, we wouldn't have the industrial society we live by. The motor age would have faltered long since with cars and trucks overwhelming the primitive roads of the horse-and-wagon age. Cities would have no freeways, no major bridges spanning rivers and industrial yards. The Golden Gate Bridge or Bay Bridge in San Francisco and all the great bridges in the New York City region would still be just ferry crossings.

British automobile interests, in these years, could but watch with jealousy this American addiction to the automobile. The British Road Federation lamented (Syme, 1959: 15-16):

> More than thirty years ago America decided to build a new kind of road called a "motorway." This would have no sharp corners and no crossroads. Only motor vehicles would be allowed to go along it. . . . Drivers could join or leave the road only at certain points. . . . (In Britain) (m)otorways are not only required in the country; they must be built in towns and cities too.

American limited-access highways of this kind were made possible by the combination of the revenue-bond-user-charge methods of finance in the hands of the special public authorities. The first one of its kind, to which the British Road Federation apparently alludes, was the Pennsylvania Turnpike organized under a commission, or special public authority. After a grant of money from the federal government, under a New Deal program, for feasibility studies, the super highway had been made possible financially by the issuance of revenue bonds, secured solely by the anticipated tolls to be charged drivers for its use. The road became, thereby, an autonomous unit of government, borrowing money through the bonds to build the road, building the highway, and then paying off the debt through charges to those who travel over it. This is the characteristic pattern of the special public authority in the United States. The agency becomes an almost totally self-contained unit:

> The [Pennsylvania] turnpike is virtually a city in itself. It has a rolling daily population of upward of 165,000 (figuring an average of two persons per vehicle); a $3,000,000 radio network and a 170-man state police force to protect travelers as well as the highway itself. There are 1,300 turnpike employees, including 750 assigned to field maintenance and 450 assigned to toll collection. Its accumulated surplus was estimated at $19,000,000 [*New York Times*, 1961].

Not the automobile, but mass public transport has become the characteristic unit of travel in London. By 1907, when New York City was opening its first regular subway, "the main Underground network of Central London was in very much its present shape," wrote John R. Day in 1972 for a book published by London Transport. "All the lines had extensive inter-change facilities, and London had the finest underground railway service that could then be imagined." In December of that year, the London Passenger Traffic Conference, formed in July to coordinate the operations of all the underground companies of London, agreed to use a common symbol for all their stations, which still is a trademark of the London scene: the word, "UndergrounD," written with a capital "U" and "D" (Day, 1972: 103). A travel guide to London, published in America and distributed in part through the compliments of BOAC, again reveals the difference in emphasis on the relative modes of travel: "The Underground . . . bears as little relation to the New York subway system as the bowler to the beret. The seats are padded and plush-covered; the cars are insulated against all but the worst clakety-clack; . . . All lines and stations are so clearly marked that only a child could get lost" (Mayor and Burton, 1969: 48). "London claims to have the best street transport system of any major city in the world," the London *Times* asserted, in advertising its new book, *History in the Streets,* in 1972. "The complex network of routes served by the familiar red double-deckers is widely envied. The vehicles themselves have become synonymous with Great Britain; few British weeks or trade fairs take place abroad without a London bus or two being sent" (1972a). "The Underground keeps London's heart beating," proclaimed a London Transport advertisement that same year.

There are, to be sure, constant criticisms by the British of London Transport, and the sense of pride in the coordinated system well could be overdrawn by a visitor. The very fact of both praise and blame, however, in itself, helps to indicate the lively concern for mass transit in London, and illustrates the identification of the citizen with London Transport. Despite all the frustrations of the commuter in Greater London—and there are many—one could not find the extreme kind of vilification of the Underground and surface mass transit that one finds of the subways and buses in the New York metropolitan area. There is, it is true, a sort of uneasy feeling today that Britain may be getting into the same problems. The chairman of the Nottingham Council's Transport Committee, for instance, recently lamented that, if "America, with its vast spaces, cannot cope with the pollution and urban dereliction which has resulted in giving the motorist his freedom, how can we in this small, densely populated island, hope to do so" [*Times* (London), 1972c], but the comparison, to date, is considered favorable. It still, today, would be difficult to imagine an editorial entitled "Subway Purgatory" being run in the London newspapers. Such an editorial did appear, however, in the *New York Times* in the summer of 1971 about conditions under the New York City Transit Authority, after a fire in the subways. "(W)ith each new incident, the risk grows that exasperation and fear may have disastrous consequences," it concluded (*New York Times,* 1971a). The year before, the *New York Times* (1970) had used its editorial powers to indict the same special public Authority:

The sheer bad graphics and classic confusion, the wrongheaded-
ness of so many "improvements" make it almost seem as if the
whole grotesque thing were put together by vindictive underground gremlins. Well, it's not gremlins; it's the Transit Authority. Even stratified filth (a layer for every administration) and
grim cellar lighting fail to obscure the authority's abysmal
standards of non-planning and antidesign.

British-born author, Anthony Burgess, was quoted by London's *Evening Standard* (1972) as summarizing the differences: "I often feel suicidal in Rome, Paris and London and
there is no antidote there except drink or literature. In New
York, when the desperate mood comes on, all I have to do is
descend to the subway after midnight and observe the omni-
present evidence of violence. Then the urge to go on living
rushes in with the speed of a suburban express train."

Chapter 4

MARRIAGE OF AUTHORITY AND AUTOMOBILE

✦

While the British were developing a theoretical setting for the public corporation, the Americans were busily engaged in testing its empirical potentialities. President Franklin D. Roosevelt adopted the special public authority as a vehicle for implementing his emergency New Deal measures on three levels of government: national, state, and national and state combined. The closest he came to an explanation of its philosophical meaning was in his call to Congress to establish the Tennessee Valley Authority in 1933. It was in that context that he coined the definition of the public corporation as "clothed with the power of government but possessed of the flexibility and initiative of a private enterprise." This description often has been quoted in the United Kingdom. So practically was the use of the special authority considered in the United States, however, that a lawyer for the Federal Surplus Relief Corporation, in justifying the use of the corporate form by the federal government to an inquiring United States senator in 1935 simply explained:

> In organizing Federal owned corporations to perform certain functions, one of the factors considered has been that, where branches of the Government are engaged in numerous activities with business men ... experience indicated that the use of a corporation expedites the work because the business men and their lawyers are more accustomed to dealings with corporations than with ordinary Governmental administrative units [Pressman, 1935].

NATIONAL GOVERNMENT CORPORATION

On the national level, the Government Corporation, as it was called, came to meet three purposes: (1) "to facilitate the extension of credit to hard-pressed banking, insurance, transportation, manufacturing, and other private corporations, and also to the states and their subdivisions"; (2) "to carry on activities of a commercial or business nature"; and (3) "to deal with emergency problems that could be sharply isolated, such as procuring rubber or tin and expanding plant facilities" (White, 1955: 129). President Roosevelt employed it in all three directions. Under the New Deal, the Government Corporation appeared in great numbers, including the Tennessee Valley Authority, 1933; Federal Surplus Commodities Corporation, 1933; Home Owners Loan Corporation, 1933; Federal Deposit Insurance Corporation, 1933; Federal Savings and Loan Insurance Corporation, 1934; Federal Prison Industries, Inc., 1934; Federal Farm Mortgage Corporation, 1934; and many others. Then, still under the Roosevelt administration, those to meet war needs, such as the Defense Homes Corporation, 1940; Defense Plant Corporation, 1940; Defense Supplies Corporation, 1940; Rubber Development Corporation, 1940; the United States Commercial Company, 1942, and the like (Marx, 1959: 226-227). There were some 100 of these government corporations at their height prior to their decline in the later 1940s. Reasons for their fall from prominence have been discussed in the preface, centering on the fears of the Congress that these New Deal agencies were getting too powerful and were not sufficiently under the checks of the iegislative branch. The Government Corporation Control Act, approved December 6, 1945, so achieved this purpose for the Congress that the federal agencies soon came to lose their meaning as special units and began to resemble more closely subdivisions of the departments. Their borrowing capabilities, which give the American special public authority its unique place in government, were sharply curtailed by the Control Act (sec. 303[a]):

> All bonds, notes, debentures, and other similar obligations which are hereafter issued by any wholly owned or mixed-ownership Government corporation and offered to the public shall be in such forms and denominations, shall have such maturities, shall bear such rates of interest, shall be subject to such terms and conditions, shall be issued in such manner and at such times and sold at such prices as have been or may be approved by the Secretary of the Treasury.

Not much room for experimentation there. Other provisions were equally restrictive.

Roosevelt's Encouragement of State Special Authorities

Roosevelt was far more successful in his encouragement of special public authorities in the states. Indeed, the single most effective stimulus for their widespread proliferation was a letter that the president wrote in December of 1934 to the governors of the states, suggesting, as one possible way of making the municipalities in their states "legally able to take full advantage" of contemplated public works programs of the New Deal, the creation by the states of "municipal improvement authorities" and "non-profit public benefit corporations or agencies." He had found in the first eighteen months of attempting to funnel federal funds down to the states, he explained, "the difficulty of gearing the legal machinery which has served municipalities of your States adequately for decades to the speed with which the Federal Government must extend credit to achieve desired results." Revision of the "procedure relative to municipal finance is essential, at least for the duration of the existing emergency," he declared. His letter contained five recommendations for accomplishing this:

1. Simplification of the procedure for the authorization and financing by municipalities of public-works projects, and conferring of additional powers upon municipalities to undertake such projects and issue bonds to finance the same.
2. Creation of municipal improvement authorities without power to tax, but with power to issue bonds payable solely from the income of revenue-producing improvements, such as water, sewer, and electric light and power systems.
3. Authorizing municipalities to engage in slum clearance, including condemnation of necessary lands, and the construction, operation and maintenance of low-cost housing, to make contributions therefor, and to enter into contracts with the Federal Government in connection therewith.
4. Providing for the creation of non-profit benefit corporations or agencies to provide for the electrification of rural communities with the assistance of the Federal Government.
5. Validation of bonds and other obligations heretofore issued by municipalities for public-works projects and sold to the Federal Government.

He even offered the governors the services of the Legal Division of the Public Works Administration for the purpose of suggesting bills "which if enacted into law would enable municipalities of your State to secure the benefits of this phase of the recovery program" (Roosevelt, 1934).

The intent was not disguised but was clear. The president was recommending that the governors use the carrot of federal funds, desperately needed in the states, to encourage the state legislatures to create ad hoc agencies to circumvent the normal restrictions that the states had come over the years to impose on borrowing by local governments. These limitations were in the form of a ceiling on the total amount of debt to be incurred, based on a percentage of the assessed valuation of the taxable property in the municipality; and the approval of the voters for borrowing by specific bond issuances on a referendum. Occasionally, in a few states, there was a limit also on the amount of taxes that the municipality could impose. In the depression years of the 1930s and 1940s, most of the local governments had reached these limits and could borrow no more. In fact, rather than go further in debt, the towns could not meet their current obligations. It is estimated that, from 1929 through 1937, almost $3 billion of state and local debt could not be paid. This amounted to more than 15 percent of the average municipal debt owed at that time (*Bond Buyer*, 1965: 22). Some 3,200 local governments were involved in falling behind "in paying interest or principal on debt" (Advisory Commission on Intergovernmental Relations, 1961: 20). When the Roosevelt administration had attempted to lend money to local governments, it had run up against this financial fact of legal barriers to their accepting it. The federal government was proposing that the states either overlook their constitutional or statutory restrictions, or enable the federal government to run around them and work with new special-purpose units down in the towns and counties that would not be bound by these provisions that apply to the general-purpose governments only, "at least for the duration of the existing emergency." The federal administrator even would furnish the states with the appropriate legislation to be passed. It was a curious commentary on the federal system, from top to bottom. It resulted, as could have been predicted, in the accepfance by all the states of the special public authority device, until they were to number, by the 1970s perhaps 9,000 throughout the country, in addition to some 14,000 special districts. The lure of money proved irresistible.

In fairness to the proposal of the president, it should be

noted that he had offered alternatives to the establishment of these new units of government: the "conferring of additional powers upon municipalities to undertake such projects and issue bonds to finance the same," authorizing "municipalities to engage in slum clearance . . . and to enter into contracts with the Federal Government in connection therewith," and the validation of "bonds and other obligations heretofore issued by municipalities for public-works projects and sold to the Federal Government." There were these options, then, which would have cemented a firm federal-town relationship. Indeed, one of the two major touchstones of the entire New Deal program, the National Industrial Recovery Act (Title II, sec. 203[d]) of the previous year, 1933, had contained a stronger stipulation in this connection:

> The President, in his discretion, and under such terms as he may prescribe, may extend any of the benefits of this title to any State, county, or municipality notwithstanding any constitutional or legal restriction or limitation on the right or power of such State, county, or municipality to borrow money or incur indebtedness.

That entire act was declared unconstitutional by the Supreme Court in 1935. The legal entanglements in each of the states that would have followed attempts to abridge constitutional and statutory financial powers would have tied up any legislation to that effect in the state legislatures, and then in court litigation. The states could not wait; the expediency of the special public authority made delay unnecessary. The country was launched on a federal-special-authority nexus rather than a federal-general-purpose government interrelationship. With the help of the president, and, indeed, the Congress, this new-found partnership continued into, and right through, the 1940s at the very time that the same Congress was suppressing the distinctive qualities of the federal government corporations, culminating in their almost total sublimation under the Government Corporation Control Act of 1945.

Roosevelt was convinced of the need for capital construc-

tion to get the economy moving by priming the pump and to
put vast numbers of the unemployed to work on these kinds
of government projects locally. It is of interest to note that
almost a year before he had written the governors in December of 1934, he had been sent an advance copy of an Open
Letter to him written by John Maynard Keynes, British
economist and writer. The letter, prepared for publication in
the *New York Times,* had commented in part as follows:

> At the moment your sympathisers in England are nervous and
> sometimes despondent. We wonder whether the order of different
> urgencies is rightly understood, whether there is a confusion of
> aim, and whether some of the advice you get is not crack-brained
> and queer. If we are disconcerted when we defend you, this may
> be partly due to the influence of our environment in London.

Among his recommendations to the president was this one,
relevant to the purposes for which the special units of government were being formed, but not making any references to
these vehicles:

> In the field of domestic policy, I put in the forefront, for the
> reasons given above, a large volume of Loan-expenditures under
> Government auspices. It is beyond my province to choose partic-
> ular objects of expenditure. But preference should be given to
> those which can be made to mature quickly on a large scale, as
> for example the rehabilitation of the physical condition of the
> railroads. The object is to start the ball rolling. The United States
> is ready to roll towards prosperity, if a good hard shove can be
> given in the next six months [Letter and enclosure, Frankfurter
> to Roosevelt, 1933b].

Another observation made by Keynes in this letter is perti-
nent to the comparisons being made in this book, to the
effect that almost "everyone here has a wildly distorted view
of what is happening in the United States." This impression is
reflected by others, and may well help to explain why there
was so little recognition in both Britain and the United States
of the resort, simultaneously, in the two countries, to the

unique innovation, the public corporation. One might have expected a lively interchange of viewpoints between officials who were engaged in such far-reaching experiments, at the very same time some 3,000 miles apart, both under democratic philosophies. There apparently was nothing resembling this dialogue, although an awareness throughout by both parties that they were undertaking similar experiments. Felix Frankfurter, constitutional expert who had been responsible for much of the early New Deal legislation, was in England at Oxford in the fall of 1933, in a private capacity, but with letters of recommendation from President Roosevelt, and, indeed, it had been to him that Keynes had passed his letter for showing to the president in advance of its being printed in the American newspaper. He wrote Roosevelt on October 29, 1933, that "(O)n the whole, the press despatches from America are inadequate and misleading." "Partly," he thought, "this is due to the meagerness of the cables—a brevity induced, I suppose, by economy—partly to the usual desire of the press to give polemic aspects of the situation." And Admiral Sir Lewis Bayly wrote from Surrey in 1934: "The ordinary Englishman who is not much acquainted with the USA is simply bewildered with Roosevelt's immense experiments and his long views." "Why," he complained, "is the Atlantic so wide and rough?" (Bayly to Halsey Powell, 1934). Yet, 1933 was the year of Herbert Morrison's crystallization of the theory of the public corporation for transportation, on the one hand, and 1934 was Roosevelt's institutionalization of the special public authority in the American states, on the other.

PROLIFERATION
IN THE STATES

In America, the states were quick to seize the bait on the president's line, and one state after another went about setting up machinery for special governments that would satisfy the New Deal administration. For the most part, this took the shape of state enabling acts by which municipalities and counties could, by action of their councils, establish public authorities for the specified purposes. Such legislation by the states was of two kinds: (1) mandatory, in which the special public authority would be chartered by the state in the act; or, more commonly, (2) permissive, under which the local government retained the option as to whether or not to have the authority. Other action to this end by the states consisted of fitting its special public authorities into a pattern of interrelationships with a national government corporation, each for one particular function. The United States Housing Act, of 1937, for example, created the United States Housing Authority to make loans for dwellings of families of low-income, and the loans were to be made to special local housing authorities that the states would establish. In these various ways, the federal government succeeded in its desire to have on the local level governmental units, apart from the municipalities and counties, with whom it could work in a variety of functions. The Advisory Commission on Inter-governmental Relations (1964a: 15) discovered their extent in a study made in 1964:

> A relatively new type of Federal aid recipient has arisen in recent years—the special purpose units of government with independent or semi-independent status. These new units, actually induced and some times even required by about a quarter of all Federal programs, include public housing and urban renewal authorities, State and local planning agencies, local area redevelopment organizations, industrial development authorities, State and county rural area development committees, irrigation districts, water users associations, soil conservation districts, State and county agricultural stabilization and conservation committees, and State and Local Farmers Home Association committees.

The commission, advisory to the Congress and representing all levels of government in the United States, urged the federal government to take a new hard look at what it had brought about. The federal departments had preferred to work with the special units, the report explained, because of the latters' "professional quality performance" that general-purpose governments could not assure "due to difficulties encountered in staffing problems, local political problems, and State limitations on taxing and borrowing authority." The commission's recommendation was that "the Congress and appropriate executive agencies take legislative and administrative action to remove from Federal aid programs for urban development all organizational limitations which require or promote special-purpose units of local government to the disadvantage of general-purpose units of local government (i.e., municipalities, towns, and counties)" (1964a: 23). Some change of attitude by the federal government has resulted, but the expansion today of the special units for transportation, both mass and private, and for pollution control indicates a continued interest of the federal agencies in special government.

Travelers about the nation encounter special units on all sides. The area of the Great Salt Lake was a special public authority; Kennedy International Airport is a facility of the Port Authority of New York and New Jersey; the Golden Gate Bridge is a special district; the 17.6 miles of combined bridges and tunnels between Maryland and Virginia constitutes the Chesapeake Bay Bridge and Tunnel Commission; public housing authorities are found in most of the towns and cities of America; the Central Oklahoma Transportation and Parking Authority centers on Oklahoma City; the Maryland Port Authority is one of several dozen port authorities in the nation; the Tennessee Valley Authority is the best known of the regional authorities and covers parts of seven states; Mount San Jacinto Winter Park Authority illustrates their use for recreation facilities; Wood's Hole, Martha's Vineyard & Nantucket Steamship Authority is a long title for a short ferry service; county and municipal sewer authorities are very common; the Chicago Transit Authority operates one of the few subways in the United States; the Public Auditorium Authority of Pittsburgh and Allegheny County and the San Diego Stadium Authority are two of such athletic and entertainment units; the Dormitory Authority of the State of New York, the Alabama Trade School and Junior College Authority, and the Indiana Central School Building Authorities reflect their widespread employment for educational construction; the Lower Neches Valley Authority of Texas is one of several in that state for uniting river valleys; the St. Lawrence Seaway Authority is international between the United States and Canada; the Southeastern Michigan Transportation Authority is a six-county authority that focuses on Detroit, whereas the Kansas City Area Transportation Authority encompasses seven counties; the Hillsborough County Airport Authority serves that western Florida area; the Jersey City Incinerator Authority demonstrates still another of their functions; and the State Sanitary Authority of Oregon, the Gulf Coast Waste Disposal Authority of Texas; and the Ohio Water Development Authority predict the expansion of the special authorities into antipollution efforts. Pennsylvania (Pennsylvania Municipal Authorities Association, 1969, sec. 4A) alone has provided by law for special public authorities for:

projects of the following kind and character, buildings to be devoted wholly or partially for public uses, including public school buildings, and for revenue-producing purposes; transportation, marketing, shopping, terminals, bridges, tunnels, flood control projects, highways, parkways, traffic distribution centers, parking spaces, airports and all facilities necessary or incident thereto, parks, recreation grounds and facilities, sewers, sewer systems or parts thereof, sewage treatment works, including works for treating and disposing of industrial waste, facilities and equipment for the collection, removal or disposal of ashes, garbage, rubbish and other refuse materials by incineration, land fill or other methods, steam heating plants and distribution systems, incinerator plants, waterworks, water supply works, water distribution systems, swimming pools, playgrounds, lakes, low head dams, hospitals, motor buses for public use, when such motor buses are to be used within any municipality, subways, and industrial development projects including but not limited to projects to retain or develop existing industries and the development of new industries.

These are for special public authorities. In California, where the more predominant unit is the special district, some 50 categories are permitted including such less obvious ones as: cemetery, pest abatement, citrus pest control, veterans building and memorial, and grade separation (Bigger, et al. 1958: 98).

The Special District

The distinctions between the special district and the special public authority are marked, although both represent ad hoc governments (Smith, 1968: 59-93). The special district is the much older form in the United States. It arose first in unincorporated areas lying around cities and towns. As people pushed beyond the city's fixed boundaries into this area, they needed certain public services; but, in view of the fact that no government was incorporated there, they were ineligible for such functions. Their answer was to incorporate themselves, under state law, as a special district but just for that particular function. Later, special districts were formed as people living within incorporated governments wanted peculiar services that others in the total jurisdiction of the general-purpose government did not care for. They occur now, therefore, throughout the country in both unincorporated and incorporated segments of government. The special district is a unit of government performing one function outside conventional governments and financing that function under a special tax levy, generally on property within the district. It is governed by a board elected by the persons living within the district. This type of special government does not break sharply with, or do violence to, the normal pattern of local government in America. It involves merely a group of citizens who want a government to perform a service for them for which they are willing to pay by a special tax levied on their properties. For this purpose, they elect a board of their peers, which they can hold accountable, to manage the undertaking. In order to make the district legally capable of fulfilling the public function, the district is chartered by the state as one of its subdivisions. Other functions desired by these people are not added to the responsibilities of this district but are assigned to a new special district created in the same way for that function. These districts do not disturb the democratic pattern of local government, except through the fragmentation of efforts, which, of course, is serious. An Assembly Interim Committee on Municipal and County Government (California State, 1961: 11) assessed the problem created by special districts in California (for the 50-odd functions) and came to this conclusion:

> An important facet of the district problem is that nearly 1,700 of the 3,038 special districts in the State are governed by an elected governing board and therefore enjoy a high degree of local autonomy. This local autonomy does not always provide the grass-roots control that it is presumed to, since district government tends to be confusing to the citizen. The citizen is often at a loss to know where to go to register a complaint, which district is providing what service, and what the tax dollar is being spent for. In order to be a conscientious citizen, residents of some areas would have to keep up with activities of as many as 10 or 12 governments. Poor district voting records indicate that the average citizen has little interest in the day-to-day activities of districts, probably due to the large number and their small-scale operation.

The Special Public Authority

An entirely new frame of reference for special government in the United States was introduced by the special public authority of the 1930s. The special public authority lacked all the normal assurances of governments: it could not rely on property taxation; it was not governed by a group of persons elected within its fixed-boundary jurisdiction by citizens living therein; it could not borrow money by pledging the value of the property within its area; and it could take on only selected functions each of which would have to return a surplus to be paid by those persons who were to use its facilities. Nothing like this form of government had been known in America. It clashed with the traditional concepts of fixed boundaries, real-property assessments and tax collections, elected representatives selected by the residents, and allocation of priorities of services so that all the expectations of government could be weighed one against the other and priorities established. The special public authority, then, became an island of experimentation. Because it was blocked from the customary tax sources, it recoiled within the separate function allotted it, and developed into the most self-sustained governmental unit the country had ever experienced. To undertake any of its functional requirements, the special public authority had to gain the support of its bonds in the open market, and to maintain those ratings, it had to continue to induce the users of its facilities, to the utmost, to pay off its bond offerings. "Government by bond resolution" came to identify its method of decision making, with the bondholders as perhaps its most clearly definable constituency. Nothing like this kind of influence of the investment market is known in the United Kingdom where special governments borrow more through the minister than individually in competition in the open market. It must be recognized, however, as the essential ingredient in the special public authority movement in the United States.

The person least aware of his or her peculiar and dominant role in local government in the states is the very bondholder who holds the purse strings. He or she comes into this position of power quite unwittingly. One of the first actions of a special public authority once it is created by a vote of the municipal or county council, under enabling legislation of the state, is to begin to finance itself. This it does by issuing bonds for the particular facility it plans to construct, be it a bridge, a turnpike, a hospital building, or any other. It does so usually in its own name, without any promise by the general-purpose government that created it that its "full-faith-and-credit" will underwrite the bonds. The authority is

on its own in the open market, where it must compete for
the loan of money with all other special and general-purpose
governments attempting at that time to borrow money for
capital construction projects of all sizes. The bonds usually
are purchased by large syndicates, including banks and investment concerns from various parts of the country. The syndi-
cate agrees to buy the bonds from the new authority, and
then it parcels them out to buyers over a period of time as
the market acceptance dictates, both as to the time of sale
and the place of sale of them. The strong possibility is,
therefore, that the bondholders will be found all over the
United States for the issue of any one authority and, indeed,
in other countries. These are good investments as they are
exempted from income taxes on all levels. Coupon bonds
frequently are used by special authorities rather than regis-
tered bonds, and these former do not bear even the name of
the purchaser. When the bearer, or owner, of any of them
wants to turn in the coupon for his bonds, he does so in any
bank in the world, and receives his periodic payment of
interest and principal. That bank from which he received his
money then forwards the coupon to the trustee bank of the
authority, and relies on the trustee bank to recompense the
bank that had paid the couponholder. The impersonal nature
of this kind of "constituency," the bondholders, is in direct
contrast to the registration of voters by name for a general-
purpose government that has come to characterize democratic government. Even though the person is not conscious
of the kind of political power with which his purchase of
special authority bonds has endowed him (or her), without
his knowledge, he has come to have a decisive impact on
decision making, especially in the cities of America. He
epitomizes the "Most influential person in a democracy—the
person who neither knows nor cares." He or she—the unnamed coupon bearer—must be "consulted" for any change
of any importance in the operation of the function of the
special public authority. If, for example, a public authority
for parking wants to close one parking lot in a town and open
another, as business dictates, it may not do so without the

approval of a majority of the bondholders. If that authority has come to the conclusion that a five-cent rise in the tolls for the metered parking is justified, it may not institute this increase without prior permission from the bondholders. The communication between this parking authority and its nebulous, unnamed constituency, is, at best, impersonal. It appears, in its most glaring form, in paid advertisements in which the trustee bank seeks to contact the unregistered bondholders to refund bonds that they hold. They, the bondholders, merely are designated by serial numbers of the bonds they own. When reading such a notice, one cannot escape the thought as to whether such an anonymous group of persons, who know nothing at all about the special public authority, or the municipality in which it is located, should have this kind of veto power over the planning of the community. Is it really a constituency?

A perusal of the kind of functions undertaken by the special public authorities, as indicated, for example, by the listing of those for Pennsylvania, will show that they almost all are ones for functions for which user charges can be collected, in that persons who use facilities of special public authorities for transportation, marketing, shopping, terminals, bridges, tunnels, and the host of other functions can be charged for the privilege. In other words, these functions are revenue-producing and the tolls so extracted can be used to pay off the revenue bonds or the borrowed money that made the construction of the facility possible in the first place. Only such building projects, capable of amortizing themselves through their users, are permitted the special public authority. Others, deficit in nature, are continued under the control of the general-purpose governments. Further examination of the Pennsylvania list will reveal the number of special authority functions related to the automobile: bridges, tunnels, highways, parkways, traffic distribution centers, parking spaces, and motor buses for public use. What better source could be found of persons willing to pay for the privilege of the facilities provided than the car owner? Indeed, the automobile came into its own in America at the very time that the special public authority became recognized. The Pennsylvania Turnpike was completed in 1937, and, as a result, the decade of the 1940s has been described as that of the turnpike authorities. The Maine Turnpike Authority was chartered in 1941; the Elizabeth River Turnpike Commission, by Virginia, the following year; the West Virginia Turnpike Commission, in 1947; the Ohio Turnpike Commission, 1949; and the Highway and Bridge Authority of Pennsylvania, in the same year. The New York Thruway Authority, squeezed in, in 1950, and the Oklahoma Turnpike Authority waited only until 1951 to get underway. Coming in such numbers, the toll roads represented the point at which the special authorities broke away from complete dependency on the federal government for the kinds of loans the New Deal had made available and began to find other sources of their own making. The Pennsylvania Turnpike had started with a grant from the federal government in the amount of $30 million from the Reconstruction Finance Corporation, which had been organized in Washington in 1932 even before Roosevelt had become president. The major trend away from federal-government sponsorship is seen in the case of the New Jersey Turnpike Authority. More than one-half of its $220 million loan, in 1950, was made by the New Jersey insurance and banking institutions rather than by the government. From then on, special public authorities have gone into the investment market, on their own, where they have competed with other governmental units and private businesses in seeking to borrow money--to "float" bonds. This step relieves them further of dependency on conventional elected governments. Alfred E. Smith, Governor of New York and one-time Commissioner of the Port of New York Authority, had foreseen this private investment for special public authorities as early as 1926. "Where is that money coming from?" he had asked of an authority in New York State. "Not from the city of Albany, [in which this particular authority was to be located] or the State of New York, or the Federal Government, but from the people that believe that [the new authority] . . . will yield sufficient money in return to amortize the bonds and pay the interest on them" (Hapgood and Moskowitz, 1927: 267-268).

Most of the early special authorities had been nurtured, at least in their embroyo stages, by federal funds, as President Roosevelt had anticipated. Any of the considerable number could be cited as an illustration. The Buffalo Sewer Authority—to pick one at random—was one such agency. It had been established by a state charter in 1935 to take over the operation of the sewer system of Buffalo, after orders from the New York State Department of Health that the pollution of the Niagara River by city sewage must stop had gone unheeded because of Buffalo's financial plight (shades of the 1970s). The Federal Public Works Administration had granted $6,728,302 to the sewer authority to help finance its sewage disposal plant, and the Federal Works Progress Administration had contributed another $4,480,314 for the construction of over five miles of its sewers for storm water relief. The authority also was to receive repayable advances of $32,675 from the Federal Housing and Home Finance Agency (Temporary State Commission on Coordination of State Activities, 1956: 213-294). "In all, eleven New York State authorities borrowed money from either the R.F.C. (Reconstruction Finance Corporation), the P.W.A. (Public Works Administration), or both, and seven authorities received P.W.A. grants for public works" (Temporary State Commission on Coordination of State Activities, 1956: 51).

The fact that the turnpike authorities had been able to unshackle themselves from the federal government, and had been able to compete in the bond market elevated them to a position of major importance in American federalism. The commensurate movement that had made this independence possible was that of the invention of the automobile. It is not without significance that 34 of the first 53 state special public authorities formed in America were in the area of transportation, and only 19 of the first 53 were for other functions. It was by chance that the special public authority and the automobile came into their own at the same time: the special authority and the automobile formed a natural marriage. It is of interest to recall that the public corporation and the facilities of mass transportation had been brought together in the United Kingdon at almost the same time— 1933—also quite by accident.

In the 1940s, the turnpikes became a way of life for Americans. The United States entered the era of the toll taker with its identifying toll token or coin. The symbolism caught hold. Evidence was found in such imagery as:

contests for "Miss Parkway";

the balloting by riders of buses of the Southeastern Pennsylvania Transportation Authority as to which of the colors, exhibited by buses painted bright red with a blue band, gold tan with maroon band, royal blue with red band, or sky blue with maroon band, they preferred;

the offering for Christmas shoppers by Tiffany's of New York, a sterling silver token holder, priced at $9.75;

publication by the New York State Thruway Authority of a brochure entitled "How to Build Your Own Thruway";

the construction of the "Glass House," a carpeted, candlelit, restaurant that straddled the Will Rogers Turnpike of the Oklahoma Turnpike Authority, so that the 70,000 visitors to it annually could dine while the cars swirled by underneath them;

the opening of a free car-wash at the northernmost service area of the Florida State Turnpike by the Authority as a convenience and a break in the trip;

the designation of titles of "Turnpike Rivals" as applied to high schools along the superhighways;

the selection by the United States government in 1964 of the Verrazano-Narrows Bridge across the New York harbor as the design for a five-cent postage stamp;

the manufacture and sale of a "Turnpike Toll Gun," which was advertised for Father's Day as a "Neat new weapon to shoot your way through the exact change lanes of the countless turnpike pay stations." "It eliminates digging for change," the advertisement continued, and it "holds up to 24 quarters."

The toll takers had become a lively part of American life. The New Jersey Highway Authority, went so far as to pub-

licize the fact that a child had been given the middle name
"Parkway" because he had been the first child to have been
born on its Garden State Parkway, the turnpike that runs the
length of New Jersey along its shoreline. His birth had
occurred outside the Holmdel State Police barracks in the
summer of 1955, just ten days after the super-highway had
been in full operation. The Authority had seized this opportunity to attempt to humanize the image of so technical a
public function as that of a toll road, and had declared the
child a charter member of the "Garden State Parkway Stork
Club" with a certificate. A decade later, he was invited as a
guest of the parkway's anniversary party, along with 31 other
children who had been delivered along the same parkway,
setting, according to the Authority's public relations, a national record for highway births. Fascinating sociological
studies could be made of the effects of the turnpike on the
everyday life of the American public. The same New Jersey
Parkway that had given birth to these 32 youngsters, for
instance, had resulted, also, in the death of between 20 and
30 riders each year, even though it is considered one of the
safety leaders among toll roads in the nation. This parkway is
but one link in a chain of what are known as "limited-access"
highways (because entrances and exits are spaced at some
distances, so as not to interrupt the rapid flow of traffic) that
extend clear from Boston all the way to northern Illinois,
beyond Chicago. They are located, as well, in other states.

Efforts to attract and please riders is unremitting, as the
users constitute the second principal "constituency" of the
special public authority. The bondholder sets the whole
process in motion by making available the capital for the
authority's projects, but it is the user, through his or her
payment of tolls and other charges for the enjoyment of the
facilities built with that borrowed money, who alone will
amortize the authority's debt. The president of the International Bridge, Tunnel and Turnpike Association expressed
the users' importance this way: "If you would like a one-
sentence description of what your Association tries to do for
you, it might read like this: Its aim is to make your facility

the safest, smoothest, most convenient way for the motorist to travel, so that his decision to spend money with you is easy to make and pleasant to remember afterward" (1972: 21). With no tax sources available to it, the authority's existence depends on the continued collection of the tolls. The *Weekly Bond Buyer* (1965: 4) gives further evidence:

> There is nothing quite like the anxiety that follows the opening of a new major toll road facility. No sooner is the ribbon cut than authority officials are besieged with requests for vehicle counts and revenue data. The first fragmentary reports are snatched up, analyzed, measured against the traffic engineers' estimates and projected 10 or more years into the future.

The tolls must be high enough to satisfy the bondholders but not too high as to alienate the users. The amount of the toll is left to the board of the authority, generally, and is not subject to review by any other government. This is contrary to the more common custom of having rates for the use of public facilities of other governmental agencies reviewable by a board, such as a public utilities commission, to protect the public's rights. The authority, however, argues that a review board could not force a change in the rates the authority fixes, for to do so might interfere with promises made to the bondholders that their investment would not be jeopardized in any way, and that tolls would continue to be charged in amounts that would assure regular payments of principal and interest on the bonds. The user may not be residents of the area in which the authority operates, and, as in the case of the turnpike authorities, they generally are not. This is so, also, for authorities' ports, airports, recreation parks, transit, enviornmental control, and others. This fact again introduces an element of absentee control, as in the case of the bond-holders. The two essential "constituencies" of the special public authority, the bondholders and the users, often from places distant from the municipality, come to have the pre-vailing voice in matters directly affecting that community. This leads to a confusing question as to accountability by the

authority board. Does it account to the bondholders, to the
users, to the community, or to persons in the municipality
living in the immediate vicinity of its projects and daily
affected by the authority's activities and buildings? The interrelationships of these four groups never has been resolved.
Daniel L. Kurshan, (1968) director of administration of the
Port Authority of New York and New Jersey, has offered the
following differentiations:

> We owe to the bondholder, the obligation to remain solvent and
> strong enough fiscally to repay our debts. We owe to the facility-
> user, the responsibility of high standards of public service (opera-
> tions and maintenance) and providing such new facilities that are
> needed to improve service levels within the fiscal limitations of
> continued self support. To our neighbors, we owe the responsi-
> bility of minimizing the environmental impact inherent in most
> modern public facilities. Towards this end, we evolve noise abate-
> ment procedures at airports, acquire strips for parks at vehicular
> crossings, etc. To our parents [the two state governments], we
> owe the responsibility of continuous liaison and policy review.
> Obviously, the four are inter-related. A new public service might
> be desirable from the users' point of view, but unacceptable to
> the neighbors, our parents, or financially imprudent. Any one of
> the three coming out negative could result in "No-action." I don't
> see this as a stalemate but rather as a wholesome resolution
> (negative) based on an assessment of all operative factors.

The chairman of the Port of London Authority (1972: 7)
may have meant little by his statement of responsibilities as
to the order of priorities contained in his annual report for
1971, but he stated them in this interesting way:

> The responsibility of the P.L.A. To whom? We have a general
> responsibility to the whole nation for the efficient running of the
> port. We have a more particular responsibility to traders, industry
> and all who live in London for the efficiency of the port, and for
> the proper use and development of the river and of the other
> assets which we own. We are appointed by the Secretary of State
> for the Environment.

There is no mention here of the Port of London Authority's stockholders.

The problem, in its larger setting, is one endemic to the special authority method. It was expressed years ago by Professor Victor Jones, when he warned that the special authority "weakens the general government for its most important function of bringing the complementary and divergent interests of a locality together into a community" (1950: 272). The authority interrupts this function of general government in another way besides that of representation, as Jones also had feared: it exempts large expenditures from the American principle of annual budgets for governments and annual appropriations that insists that all the many interests competing for the public's taxes must come together, through the medium of the budget, and each must present its case for continued support from the common pool of funds available to the community for the coming year. The government, then, after having heard the arguments of all the interested parties, must establish priorities of needs, and divide the total sum accordingly. However, with so many of the vital functions of government today handled outside the general governments, there are removed from the annual budget review powerful interests whose amounts are among the largest in the community. The special authorities do not have to compete. Through the revenue-bond-user-charge complex that they employ, these agencies finance themselves, and do not have to prove the relative values of their projects as against other needs. The authority projects must be revenue-producing, further distorting priorities, and they tend, accordingly, to be for hardware functions of government rather than for software. The result in one local area after another is that special public authorities are responsible for the more dynamic, profitable, modern functions, leaving to the elected council the more prosaic, deficit-ridden, traditional "housekeeping" roles. The budget has been called the greatest instrument for democracy on all levels of government. Its process is made less effective by the deferment of special-authority functions. It is one thing to examine a facility of the special agency and to admire its effectiveness; it is quite another to evaluate that same facility in the light of its service to the community as against other perhaps more pressing needs.

The combination of revenue-bond financing and user-charge reimbursement has served the motoring public well. The International Bridge, Tunnel and Turnpike Association (1971) could report by 1972 that toll facilities in the United States amounted to 95 bridges (77 of which were operated by special authorities) used by 856,835,193 revenue vehicles a year; 48 toll roads (all but 8 of which were under special authorities) serving 1,847,646,000 paying vehicles the past year; and 10 tunnels (all run by special agencies) for 174,047,093 tolled vehicles. Its president claimed that since "1966 in the United States alone, more than two and one half billion dollars has been spent for new construction, replacement and improvement of toll facilities" (IBTTA, 1972: 18). The question of the value of all these services for the automobile, however, was beginning to be asked in the context of their cost vis-a-vis the neglected modes of mass transportation. The IBTTA (1972: 20) president recognized the growing criticism, but countered:

> This leads me to note that the nature of the toll business appears likely to involve us all in more, rather than less, cooperation with the support of other modes of travel. Some of our members are actually running mass transit services, both highway-oriented and rail-oriented. . . . Where else would a government turn than to a well-established, going public corporation which already has the know-how, the manpower, the credit and the authority to go ahead and get the required job done.

The latent desire for the balancing of transportation modes has been felt most in the cities of America. Not only had the special authorities been used to construct superhighways connecting cities and towns, but they had been employed in the cities and suburbs to provide automobile facilities of roads, bridges, tunnels, and parking lots for the daily commuter.

Rare is the city or suburban town that does not have an off-street parking authority. The development of these special agencies for the automobile commuter reached its ultimate peak in New York City, although almost all American cities had shown similar proclivities for the car. New York City had started on this path during the New Deal period, and, as in so many instances, under the spur of federal inducements of money as loans for revenue-producing undertakings. New York State had not waited for President Roosevelt's letter to the governor to gear its legislative process to the accommodation of the special public authority, but had gotten underway with these agencies when Roosevelt had been its governor before he moved up to the White House. New York State, with New Jersey, of course, had introduced the word "Authority" into the United States with the charter for the Port of New York Authority in 1921. Sixteen other special agencies had been chartered by the state before President Roosevelt's bid to the states at the end of 1934. Nine of the sixteen had been for transportation, all for the automobile; one for power; one for a park; two for regional markets; one for an industrial exhibit; one for a spa; and one for the American Museum of Natural History Planetarium. The state already had borrowed for certain of these special-authority projects from the federal government, from the Reconstruction Finance Corporation, which had been founded a year before Roosevelt had been inaugurated. The Reconstruction Finance Corporation was one of the federal government corporations that worked through special authorities in the states in a combined approach. It was used extensively by the new special units throughout the country as the New Deal program got underway. It frankly encouraged the adaptation of the special-government methods:

Title I, Sec. 4. (a) To aid in financing agriculture, commerce, and industry . . . the Corporation . . . is authorized . . . to purchase the securities and obligations of, or make loans to, (A) municipalities and political subdivisions of States, (B) public agencies and instrumentalities of one or more States, municipalities, and political subdivisions of States, and (C) public corporations, boards, and commissions: Provided that no such purchase or loan shall be made for payment of ordinary governmental or non-project operating expenses as distinguished from purchases and loans to aid in financing specific public projects.

This act named the public corporations as eligible for its benefits, and it provided for capital expenditures for their projects. It was ready-made for their expansion.

The Triborough Bridge and Tunnel Authority

In New York City, a series of individual special public Authorities were formed, beginning in 1933, to construct bridges and tunnels across the East River, between the Boroughs of the Bronx and Manhattan, on the one hand, and those of Brooklyn and Queens, on the other. (The fifth Borough of the City, Richmond, is situated on Staten Island.) The basic impetus for their establishment was federal funds. Subsequent mergers of these separate East River Authorities were to produce one of the most powerful units of government in the history of the country—known as the Triborough Bridge and Tunnel Authority. The chain leading to this combination had begun with the creation of the Triborough Bridge Authority in 1933, for the building of the Triborough Bridge, and then the Bronx-Whitestone Bridge. For the first of these ventures, the Triborough Bridge Authority, had received a grant of $9.202 million from the Public Works Administration. The Authority financed the Bronx-Whitestone Bridge through the flotation of a public-revenue bond issue, for which the Authority's original debt to the New Deal was refunded.

In 1935, another Authority, the New York City Tunnel Authority, was chartered to build the Queens Midtown Tunnel, also across the East River. This special-purpose unit took full advantage of federal financing, through the use of a Works Progress Administration Traffic Project, as a feasibility study, followed by a loan from the Public Works Administration in the amount of $47.130 million and a direct grant of $11.235 million.

Both the Triborough Bridge Authority and the New York City Tunnel Authority then had set about to add to their jurisdictions by mergers with other Authorities that had been established for the building of individual bridges, tunnels, and parkways. Finally, in 1946, these two enlarged Authorities, the Triborough Bridge Authority and the New York City Tunnel Authority, themselves merged into the Triborough Bridge and Tunnel Authority. This agency became the consummate illustration of the force of the New Deal's emphasis on special public authorities, as sponsored by federal monies. It represented the merger of six public Authorities: the Triborough Bridge Authority, Henry Hudson Parkway Authority, Marine Parkway Authority, New York City Parkway Authority, the Queens-Midtown Tunnel Authority (which had never really gotten underway), and the New York City Tunnel Authority. Essential seed money had come from the federal government, but the Authority's sound credit base had caused it to come to rely on the strength of its own bonds. They, in turn, reflected the automobile orientation of the Authority, and of its chairman, Robert Moses, as its major structures were designed for the motoring public. Large surpluses were accumulated as the Triborough Bridge and Tunnel Authority continued over the years to grow with the automobile traffic.

On the West Side of New York City, represented by the Hudson River between New York and New Jersey, the Port of New York Authority simultaneously was constructing bridges and tunnels across that river for the automobile. The Port Authority improved the existing Holland Tunnel, and built through the 1930s the Goethals, Outerbridge, George Washington, and Bayonne Bridges; the first tube of the Lincoln Tunnel; and its Inland Terminal between 8th and 9th Avenues. These all made easy access for the car coming in from New Jersey, or leaving the city for trips to the west.

By the 1940s, therefore, New York City was committed to

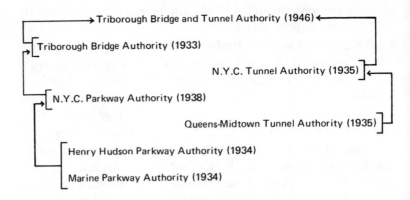

**Figure 1: EVOLUTION OF TRIBOROUGH BRIDGE
AND TUNNEL AUTHORITY**

the automobile, which, through the facilities of the Triborough Bridge and Tunnel Authority on the East River, and the Port of New York Authority on the western Hudson River dominated transportation in and out of the city. Robert Wood compared the jurisdictions of these two large special Authorities to that of the "spheres of influence" doctrine of international relations (1961: 128-129). The orphan in the city, however, was mass transit, which had been proved unable to compete with the kind of advantages that were extended to the special authorities, particularly those of federal funds. The rival automobile, coupled with the effects of the Depression, had made private ownership of the subways, or underground, untenable, and, in 1940, the city of New York had bought the subway system and placed it under a City Transportation Board. The shift in ownership, from private to public had had little meaning, however, as the two large Authorities, on its flanks, continued to build attractive and expensive conveniences for the motorist. The condition of the subways deteriorated even further.

The New York City Transit Authority
When the city sought additional tax sources to help shore up the subways, the state of New York not only refused to

permit these, but imposed on the city, in 1953, the New York City Transit Authority, against the will of the city government. It was a misapplication of the word "Authority," as the new agency lacked any kind of financial independence and had none of the semiautonomous features that had built up the Triborough Bridge and Tunnel Authority and the Port of New York Authority. It was designed, consciously by the state, to give the state control of the subways, or, at least, to prevent dominance of them by the city. In an apparent attempt to force efficiency on the New York City Transit Authority, the state created a kind of hybrid ad hoc government that was hamstrung from its inception. It was given no capital budget of its own, but had to rely on the city government for any improvements or additions to its equipment. The city already had demonstrated, when the subways had been under its own board, an inability to plow capital money into the subways. On the side of operations, those costs were to be borne entirely by the new Transit Authority, from the fares it would charge. This is a common proviso for special authorities and public corporations, and, apparently, is an attempt to place efficiency of operation in a central place in their goals. Without improved cars, stations, and other facilities, however, the subways could not attract the riders necessary to meet operational costs. Increased fares might serve only to drive more of them to the comfort of their own automobiles and into the tunnels, and onto the bridges of the Triborough and Port Authorities. With rapidly rising labor costs, chargeable as they are to the operating budget, and therefore to be paid by the fares, constant haggling over fare increases, which crept up and up, ensued. The Transit "Authority" functioned from 1953 until 1968 with scarcely any capital help from the city, and almost none from its own sources, and with completely inadequate operational budgets. It was kept alive, at all, by the juggling of the bookkeeping listings, by such devices as showing as credits for its operating budget payments by the city for its transporting of school children, transit police costs, profits from the sale of power plants to a private utility, purchases by the city of subway cars from the Authority, and other such subterfuges. The result was a desperate kind of holding operation during the years of critical expanding needs of all sorts.

The board structure of the "Authority" also had been made awkward by the state. The five members consisted of 2 persons appointed by the governor, 2 by the mayor, and the fifth a resident of New York City who was on the Board of the Port of New York Authority. The Port Authority commissioners were appointed by the governor, with the obvious result that the new "Authority" included three of the governor's appointees, and 2 of the mayor's. The state, of course, prevailed, despite the fact that the subways were totally within the city's limits. The *New York Times* of May 17, 1953, commented: "The five authority members are seldom in agreement on anything. Two were appointed by Governor Dewey, two by Mayor Impellitteri, and the fifth is a refugee from the peace and quiet of the Port of New York Authority who skips from one faction to another " (Temporary State Commission on Coordination of State Activities, 1956: 51). This impossible stalemate was changed in 1955, but with a board composition only a degree less confusing. The new board had three members, one appointed by the governor, one by the mayor, and the third, who would be chairman, to be named by the other two. The members had staggered terms of six years each, so that their terms could not correspond to those of either of the appointing powers, the governor or the mayor.

New York City's subways had been plagued by financial worries since their establishment at the turn of the century. These fiscal concerns had existed whether the subways were under the private ownership of the Interborough Rapid Transit Company; or under public control by the New York City Board of Transportation; or the quasi-public direction of the New York City Transit Authority. Public transportation in the city of course had antedated the subways by many years. As early as the 1830s horse-drawn streetcars had been servicing the people of the city, and at a considerable expense to the rider, who had had to pay 37 and one-half cents for a ride of less than one mile, and 50 cents for one to two miles. The city had fixed these fees. As costly as they were, the street-cars had made possible the advent of the commuters, as persons could push northward from the area of Manhattan proper, and travel regularly the additional distances from their homes to work in Manhattan (Ellis, 1966: 258-259). Simultaneously, in the 1830s, New York City's first railroad was constructed with the chartering of the New York and Harlem Railroad in December 1831. It was designed to extend from 23rd Street northward along the Harlem River, and thence into Westchester County, and the line was inaugurated from White Plains, in Westchester, in 1844. It also ran a horse-drawn operation southward in Manhattan, connecting City Hall and 26th Street. Its construction, both north and south, had been made possible by financial assistance of the New York & New Haven Railroad, and thus began the pattern which was to eventuate in the New York, New Haven & Hartford system (Weller, 1969: 35-38).

To the south and east of Manhattan, the Long Island Rail Road, which began operation in 1836, enabled the new "commuters" to live on the Island and ride to work in Manhattan. In fact, between 1831 and 1858, eight City railroads were incorporated, and sixteen omnibus companies ran 544 licensed stages throughout Manhattan and into nearby communities. By the time of the Civil War, citizens of New York were complaining bitterly of traffic congestion. The *New York Times* summarized the attitude with the conclusion that "There is not enough room on the surface of the city to accommodate the traffic which its business requires" (Ellis, 1966: 337-338). Attempts to go underground were suggested by the 1860s but were thwarted by powerful politicians, such as "Boss" Tweed, who were profiting from their interests in surface transit. Governor Reuben E. Fenton vetoed a bill that would have permitted a Michigan railroad man, Hugh B. Wilson, to construct an underground railroad, with a sum of $5,000,000 he had raised for this purpose. Alfred Ely Beach, an inventor, actually did succeed in getting a bill through the state legislature allowing him to dig a "pneumatic mail tube" for one City block, between Murray and Warren Streets, just west of City Hall. Two years later, after surreptitious excavation of the tube area by workers, the "subway" was completed, and in 1870 the waiting room of it was opened for public inspection. That is as far as it got, however. When Beach applied for a new charter, this time for transit in his tube, the governor vetoed it. The measure finally was approved on a second try, in 1873, but the depression of that year made it impossible for Beach to finance his venture, and Governor Dix withdrew the charter (Ellis, 1966: 339-340).

Instead of going underground to relieve the traffic congestion, New York City went to the air, and its elevated trains became known throughout the world. This decision was made by the first of New York City's rapid transit commissions, which had been authorized by the state legislature in 1875. Elevated lines were built first on Third and Sixth Avenues, but were permissible as well on Second and Ninth. The first two Avenue lines were opened in 1878, and passengers rode for only ten cents. By 1886, elevated trains in New York City (which by then had crossed the Brooklyn Bridge) were carrying their absolute capacity load of 1,000,000 passengers a day. Even the newly installed cable cars, which began running on the ground in the City in 1885, could not enable the trolleys to take up the slack of those who could not force their way onto the elevated. In 1898, a study showed that "100,000 commuters arrived by bridge and ferry from Brooklyn, another 100,000 or more came by ferry from New Jersey, and more than 118,000 arrived daily at the overcrowded Grand Central Station from Westchester County and from Connecticut. By 1900 New Yorkers were riding the city's streetcars—a billion times a year" (Ellis, 1966: 464).

In the face of the growing demands that something be done to relieve the untenable situation, the State Legislature finally relented, and, in 1891, passed an act for rapid transit for New York City. That same year, the city board, consisting of the mayor, city comptroller, and the city commissioner of public works, obtained approval from the Board of Aldermen, for plans for a subway, and announced that it would accept bids for its construction. No company would bid, however, as opposition had been announced by certain political and business interests, particularly by the Metropolitan Street Railway Company, which controlled most of the surface transit.

Three years later, the state legislature again established a New York City rapid transit board, and this time New York City held an election at which municipal control of the subways was voted by the citizens. New York City, significantly, therefore, became the first owners of the subways, and hired a contractor to build them, and operate them for the next 50 years. Ground was broken in 1900, and the first branch of the subway opened October 27, 1904. This, the beginning of the Interborough Rapid Transit (IRT), extended from City Hall, along the East Side to Grand Central Station at 42nd Street, turned west to Times Square and then north up Broadway to 145th Street. The City also built the Brooklyn Manhattan Transit (BMT), and leased it out for operation, the first section of which was opened in 1917, but the Independent system (IND) was publicly operated by the City from its inception in 1931 (Tauber and Kaplan, 1966: 133-134).

First proposed in the early 1860s, and consistently defeated by vested interests during the 40-year interval, the New York City subways came, by the time of their opening in the present century, just when the automobile was beginning to capture the interest of the public, and was to become a major competitor for riders. Before ground had been broken in 1900 for the city's first subway line, the city already had more than 100 taxicabs, driven by electric batteries. As the underground was starting, the United States could count 13,824 automobiles, and New York's first automobile show was held that year in Madison Square Garden, with 51 exhibitors (Ellis, 1966: 461).

LINDSAY'S EXECUTIVE-
ORIENTED AUTHORITY

The first serious attempt to right the imbalance among the modes of transportation in New York City was made by Mayor John V. Lindsay, as recently as 1966. The problem by the time he became the chief official was described in chapter one. It will be recalled that the legacy inherited by Mayor Lindsay was that of a complex of transportation authorities each for a different mode of travel and none coordinated with the other. On either side of Manhattan was a large, affluent public authority catering to the automobile, the Port of New York Authority to the west, and the Triborough Bridge and Tunnel Authority, to the east. Running through the center of the city, to all the boroughs except Richmond, was the deficit-ridden New York City Transit Authority, with an impossibly awkward board composition, no capital funds, and operational costs incapable of being met, as they were required to be, from the fare box without inordinate fare increases that would serve only to frighten away riders. Also extending through three boroughs, Manhattan, Brooklyn, and Queens, was another special public authority, this one for the bankrupt Long Island Rail Road, which ran out beyond the city limits on Long Island. The pattern was clear: the two Authorities serving the automobile were piling up surpluses; the two Authorities for mass transit, one for subway and the other for commuter railroad, were going further in debt. Surpluses for the Authorities that were aggravating the transportation problem by bringing cars readily into the city, and the deterioration for the Authorities that could have relieved traffic congestion through their resort to mass transit—that was the practical result of the emphasis on the car and the sublimation of subways and railroads. That was, as well, the inevitable result of reliance on semiautonomous special public authorities, each with its own monopoly. The Triborough Authority and the Port Authority were free to run their own affairs through self-financing, in part by tolls from the automobile. The New York City Transit Authority was a misnomer, as it resembled a special public authority in almost no way; and the Metropolitan Commuter Transportation Authority, which had taken over the deficit-plagued Long Island Rail Road was an agency of the state in that the state was responsible for shoring up its reserves required in support of its bonded indebtedness.

Lindsay's proposal for balancing the modes of private and mass transportation had involved the appointment by the mayor of a transportation administrator, who would then be the chairman of the Triborough Bridge and Tunnel Authority and of the New York City Transit Authority. In addition, the mayor would have a veto over actions of those two Authorities. The plan did not touch the activities of the Metropolitan Commuter Transportation Authority, nor of the Port of New York Authority, as their jurisdictions extended beyond the boundaries of New York City and could not, therefore, come under the province of the city transportation administrator. As was mentioned earlier, the Lindsay plan was defeated soundly by the state legislature, and was replaced by a coordinating suggestion of Governor Nelson Rockefeller, which will be discussed in more detail in chapter six. Of interest here, in a description of the American special authority as compared to the British public corporation, is the fact that one of the principal powers causing the defeat of the Lindsay legislation was the bonding interests. That dependency of the American special authority on the issuance of revenue bonds, and the bondholders that thereby became involved, is a characteristic that sets it apart from its British counterpart. The mayor had tried to reassure the bondholders of the outstanding obligations of the Triborough Bridge and Tunnel Authority in the body of the suggested bill:

> The powers granted to the authority and the mayor by the provisions of this title shall not be exercised in any manner which would violate the contract provisions with respect to, or the contractural rights of the holders of, bonds issued pursuant to the general bond resolution adopted by the authority in nineteen hundred sixty-two and series resolutions in connection therewith [New York State. Intro. 5417, sec. 1222].

Despite this disclaimer, the bondholders' rights were upper-most against the Lindsay bills in the legislative hearings in the state capital, Albany, in March 1966. Bond counsel for the Triborough Bridge and Tunnel Authority (1966: 15) stressed the significance of investor confidence:

> (P)ublic authorities have demonstrated an efficiency both in construction and operation that has not been matched by any other form of governmental organization. Authorities have been able to carry on their functions because of the confidence of prudent investors that they would be managed in a business-like fashion, with small staffs chosen solely on the basis of ability, free from political control, and with political control limited to appointment of the members by the Governor, Mayor or county officials with the power of post audit given to the State, City or County Comptroller.
>
> Public and, more important, investor confidence in public authorities would be irretrievably damaged by the enactment of legislation such as that proposed by the Mayor here.

Samuel I. Rosenman reemphasized the rights of the bond-holders:

> Without such autonomy, without such political freedom, no Authority will ever gain the confidence of investors. Who would buy an Authority bond secured only by anticipated revenues, if he knew in advance that the Chairman certainly, and all the members probably, would be serving at the pleasure of an elected official who needs votes to stay in office [Triborough Bridge and Tunnel Authority, 1966: 21].

Finally, the trustee, the Chase Manhattan Bank, representing both the Triborough Bridge and Tunnel Authority (1966: 38) and its bondholders, advised:

> In view of (1) the seriousness of the questions presented by the . . . Proposed City Acts; (2) the public importance of the questions; and (3) the large amount ($379,300,000) of Bonds of the Authority outstanding, we believe that the Proposed City Acts, if adopted, should be submitted to the courts for a prompt adjudication of whether or not they are unconstitutional.

Chapter 5

ACCOUNTABILITY

American special public governments have evolved from the localized special districts in unincorporated areas outside a city into large organizations within cities, such as the Port Authority of New York and New Jersey and the Triborough Bridge and Tunnel Authority. It now is the sense of remoteness that worries Americans about them.

PLURALISM

If any theory has been accepted in regard to these units in the United States it has rested on the belief that they have reflected merely an extension of control over essential functions to those who want such services. Their continued proliferation, therefore, has been justified on the premise that it fits the principle of pluralism, traditional to America, wherein governmental authority is distributed among various interest groups so that no one would come to dominate. This emphasis, according to Professor James W. Fesler, of Yale University, "has been expressed in the establishment of relatively independent and autonomous commissions, boards, corporations, code authorities, departments and special units of government." They catch up the focus on "specialization, segmentation, functional autonomy, and pluralism" that have been developing throughout American life (1949: 120). The more the giant metropolitan authorities stress the efficiency that their size contributes to their operations, therefore, the more they arouse apprehensions with the public:

> We do not like to pay taxes and we do not associate taxes with services. . . . (T)he typical citizen . . . rather cynically, *expects* government to be relatively inefficient. And since, to him, it is going to be inefficient come reformer or professional administrator, he wants a voice in local government. He wants to be able to reach the decision makers when he has a problem [Adrian, 1961: 150].

Criticisms of the huge special authorities have voiced this fear. The *New York Law Journal* (Mason, 1967: 4) expressed the pluralist philosophy in this way:

> Closely related in principle to the problem of home rule is the problem of the dangerous separation of certain [special] authorities from responsiveness to the people whose lives and welfare are affected by their actions. . . . This is . . . largely the reflection of the dynamics of a structure in which control is too removed and too disproportionately unwieldy for the feed back from the local community most directly affected to be operative. In starting in motion these powerful and possibly too efficient bodies, we may find that we are only Sorcerer's Apprentices.

"In the past, it [The Port of New York Authority] has carried out the wishes of the business and financial community efficiently. Now it needs more application of what the mass of people want—and need" (*New York Times,* 1969). David E. Lilienthal labeled his progeny, the Tennessee

Valley Authority, "Democracy at the Grass Roots." "A man
wants to feel that he is important," he explained. "He wants
to be able not only to express his opinion freely, but to know
that it carries some weight; to know that there are some
things that he decides, or has a part in deciding" (Lilienthal,
1945: 84-85). He was referring to one of the most extensive
multipurpose authorities in the country, covering, in all, parts
of seven states, "an area all told about the size of England
and Scotland, with a population of about 4,500,000 persons." Even there, he argued, citizen participation in decision
making could be meaningful.

MINISTERIAL
RESPONSIBILITY

Nothing resembling this concept of pluralism traditionally
had been associated by the British with their public corporations. When troubled by the unresponsiveness of such units in
the United Kingdom, they have expected to find that there is
something wrong with the interrelationships between the
appropriate minister, representing Parliament, and the ad hoc
agency concerned. This is a quite different understanding of
accountability. The group of specialists constituting the
public corporation have been expected to know more about
its technological functions than do the public, and, especially
in their everyday actions are not to be interfered with by the
people. Only when there was a review of some overall policy
in regard to the function was there to be influence by the
citizens, and then through the minister who serves in a liaison
capacity between them and Parliament, but who, himself,
was expected to make the necessary adjustments. He was the
one to hold them responsible. "The public corporation,"
according to Herbert Morrison, who articulated their philosophy for transportation in 1933, "are, for the most part,
free from direct parliamentary pressure and the indirect pressure of the consituents of the M.P.s [Members of Parlia-

ment]" (1964: 263). He detailed (1964: 274) the fine line relationships that have existed between the minister and the board of the public corporation:

> It may be that in the opinion of the Board the Government is restricting them unduly on matters of development and capital expenditure, or that controlled material of some sort are not being made available to them by the Government. The Minister should never resent them putting their case to him with frankness and vigour, and if he is convinced they are right he should urge their case to the appropriate authorities. . . . On the other hand, the Minister, who has to answer for the general work of the Boards in Parliament, must (without taking over the essential duties of management) have the right to question Boards on aspects of policy or management about which he is apprehensive and to urge appropriate action. These matters involve subtle relationships, for whilst the rights and responsibilities of the Boards have to be respected, their Chairmen must not become arbitrary Emperors of Industry.

The fear of the British critics of the London Passenger Transport Board's composition in 1933—which had led Morrison himself to refer to it as "pitiful" and Professor Robson, with equal despair, as "fantastic"—was not that it prevented control of the board's functions locally, under a concept of pluralism, but, rather, that it interposed an electoral college between the minister and his right to appoint the board. Morrison had proposed, as it will be recalled, a five-man board, appointed by the minister from among those persons who "have had wide experience, and have shown capacity, in industry, commerce, or finance or in the conduct of public affairs." He would have had the sole responsibility for these appointments. Instead, in the act as it finally had emerged, six "appointing trustees" had been required to make the appointments to the transport board. The minister's relationships with the board thus had been disrupted. That was the British concern.

TRANSPORTATION
ACT 1947

An even more severe break with the theory of minister-board relationships came with Transport Act of 1947. The transport board, which had served to integrate the transportation modes of the London area despite its initial handicaps was abolished. In its stead there was created by Parliament an even more complex system of special units than had prevailed with the electoral-college arrangement, caustically described by Robson as "tiers of semi-government bodies superimposed one upon the other" (1962: 96). The basic flaw in the structure, according to the British theory of responsibility for special governments, lay, again, in its provision for an intervention between the minister and operating units of a national commission. The design had been motivated by national concerns inasmuch as this act nationalized the railways and other inland transport facilities, and transferred to the new British Transport Commission all their "undertakings, parts of undertakings, property, rights, obligations and liabilities," as well as those of the London Passenger Transport Board, which had included underground railways, buses, and tramways. The act "embodied the most grandiose scheme of nationalisation so far witnessed in Britain" (Robson, 1962: 95). Functioning under the commission were to be the so-called "Executives," a form of organization not new in Britain but unknown to Americans. These Executives were to be six in number, one each for: railways, road haulage, road passenger transport, hotels and catering (of the railways), docks and inland waterways, and the London passenger transport. (The Road Passenger Executive was abolished in the fall of 1952, and the Road Haulage Executive the following year.) The entire thrust of the act was national: the focal point of power was to be the British Transport Commission, on the national level.

It is, of course, the introduction of the "Executives" as a special unit of government for transportation that most interests those studying special-purpose governments. Each was defined in the Transport Act of 1947 as "a body corporate with perpetual succession and a common seal" (Ch. 49, sec 5, par. 3). They are legally, therefore, public corporations. They were almost totally different, however, from the special public authorities that were sprawling throughout American metropolitan areas at the same time. The high degree of difference is indicated by the 1947 Act's (Part I, 5[8]) delimitation of powers for the Executives:

> No such delegation [of power from the British Transport Commission] shall be so framed as to empower the Executive to borrow any money unless the borrowing is temporary, is for the purpose of carrying on the current business of the Executive and is authorized, either generally or specially by the Commission.

The American special authorities' most precious endowment—that of borrowing money—was denied the British Executive. Other witnesses to the impotence of the Executives were not lacking in the act. They were to have only those powers delegated by the British Transport Commission (Transport Act, 1947: Part I, 5[4]):

> Each Executive shall, as agents for the Commission, exercise such functions of the Commission as are for the time being delegated to them by or under a scheme made by the Commission and approved by the Minister.

In a form of reverse dependency, the act stipulated that, in view of the fact that the Executive was performing merely those delegated duties, "any rights, powers and liabilities of the Commission shall be treated as rights, powers and liabilities of the Executive, and the Executive only" (Part I, 5[9]9a).

The Executives, then, were powerless. They were simply "to assist the Commission in the discharge of their functions in the manner specified." They were to be "agents for the Commission" (Part I, 5[1] and [4]). One of these Executives, the London Transport Executive, certainly must have felt the sting of subordination, after the kind of power its predecessor, the London Passenger Transport Board, had exercised from 1933 until 1947. The role of the minister had been made even more ambivalent. He had the power of appointing the members of the British Transport Commission, and of the six Executives, with the approval of the commission. For the commission, itself, he would name a chairman, and

> not less than four nor more than eight other members, all of whom shall be appointed by the Minister from among persons appearing to him to be persons who have had wide experience and shown capacity in transport, industrial, commercial or financial matters, in administration, or in the organisation of workers [note here the additional categories, over those in former acts], and of whom the Chairman and not less than four other members shall be required to render whole-time service to the Commission [Part I, 5 (2)].

The minister also was empowered to appoint the members of the six Executives. Each Executive was to consist, as did the national commission, of "a chairman and not less than four nor more than eight other members appointed by the Minister," but this time "after consultation with the Commission." They were to be chosen with an eye on the same kind of backgrounds as had been recommended for the members of the commission (Second Schedule, sec. 4[1]). The minister thereby had broad powers of appointment both to the national commission and to each of the six Executives. From that point on, however, he faced the continual frustration of having to sit by and watch the British Transport Commission make decisions to be carried out by the Executives, without much involvement in what should have been his relationships with the local operating groups. It was the British Transport Commission rather than the minister that was "to take such steps as they consider necessary for extending and improving the transport and port facilities within Great Britain in such manner as to provide most efficiently and conveniently for the needs of the public, agriculture, commerce and industry"

(Part I, 3[1]). It was to the commission rather than the minister that fell the major power to "levy such fares, rates, tolls, dues and other charges, as to secure that the revenue of the Commission is not less than sufficient for making provision for the meeting of charges properly chargeable to revenue, taking one year with another" (Part I, 3 [4]).

The minister was given token, after-the-fact power, however, in that he was permitted "after consultation with the Commission, [to] direct the Commission to discontinue any of their activities, dispose of any part of their undertaking, dispose of any securities held by them, call in any loan made by them or exercise any power they may possess to revoke any guarantee given by them" (Part I, 4[5]). It was all negative. The minister held a veto only but no positive role in the minister-public corporation nexus that Morrison had conceived as the proper chain of accountability. Between the minister and this public corporation, the London Transport Executive (and five other Executives) the British Transport Commission had been imposed. These Executives were a far cry from the special public authorities dominating automotive transportation in the United States.

From outside, the idea of the consultative committees, taken over from the 1933 Act, was perpetuated. The minister here had the power of appointment, as he also had with the commission and the Executives. He was to select a central consultative committee for all of Great Britain, to represent the users, and then one for each of the fields of nationalization (railways, docks and inland waterways, roads, hotels, road haulage, and London Transport). For each one of these there were to be two such groups, "a Transport Users Consultative Committee in respect of traffic and a Transport Users Consultative Committee for both passenger and goods traffic" (Part I, 6[1][a][b]). Membership on the consultative committees was to consist of an independent chairman and such members "appointed by the Minister as the Minister may from time to time determine" from among "members appointed, after consultation with such bodies representative of the interest concerned as the Minister thinks fit, to represent agriculture, commerce, industry, shipping, labour and local authorities," and "members appointed from among persons nominated by the Commission" itself (Part I, 6[4]). They were to serve at the pleasure of the minister, who could "at any time, after consultation with the Central Transport Consultative Committee, abolish any Transport Users Consultative Committee" (Part I, 6[20] and [3][a][b]). This negative power for the minister must have seemed, by him, as gratuitous. The Consultative Committees were to be advisory, to "make recommendations in regard to any matter [including charges] affecting the services and facilities provided by the Commission which has been the subject of representation . . . made to the Committee by users of those services or facilities, or which appears to be a matter to which consideration ought to be given, or which the Minister or Commission may refer to them for consideration" (Part I, 6[7]).

In regard to the railways, nationalized by this act of 1947, the British Transport Commission, under an act of 1953, dissolved the Railways Executive and divided Great Britain, instead, into six railway areas, five of which were in England and Wales, and one for Scotland (Robson, 1962: 97-98).

TRANSPORTATION ACT 1962

A closer approach to the American device of the special public authority than the carefully controlled, almost clerical, "Executive" came in the United Kingdom under the Transport Act of 1962. This measure of Parliament represented an abrupt change of direction in the matter of the nationalized industries, and, of importance for this book, in the use of the ad hoc governments. The 1962 act was acknowledged to be a "reorganisation of the nationalised transport undertakings," and, for the purpose "to provide for the establishment of public authorities as successors to the British Transport Commission" and its Executives (Transport Act, 1962, ch. 46, preamble).

Its purpose was to give a policy-making role to the ad hoc agencies but not to decentralize control to the local areas. Decision making was to be shared by the newly created boards, but with the orientation still to the national level. Provided for in the 1962 act were not the kind of almost clerically subservient Executives that had served under the former British Transport Commission, but for four special public authorities to be known officially as the British Railways Board, the London Transport Board, the British Transport Docks Board, and the British Waterways Board. The word "Board" was to replace the term "Executive" as ad hoc units for transportation. Decentralization was contained in the 1962 act to the point that the British Railways Board was subdivided into six "Regional Railway Boards" to be known as: the Eastern Railway Board, the London Midland Railway Board, the North Eastern Railway Board, the Scottish Railway Board, the Southern Railway Board, and the Western Railway Board. These regions tended to follow the lines of the major railroads, and, except for the Scottish board, their geographic regions tended to radiate out from London, as did the major rail trunklines. The symmetry of the "board" structure was broken only by the provision for The Transport Holding Company, which was to coordinate the activities of the bus companies (Transport Act 1962, part 1, 2; and part 1, 29).

The significance of the 1962 act lay in the abolition of the Transport Commission, which had been extremely feeble and ineffective. One factor in regard to the role of the new "boards" which would compare with that of special public authorities in the United States is that of their financial interrelationships with the government. The public authority in the United States gained its extreme degree of autonomy from the simple fact that it was able to finance itself. The "Executive" in the United Kingdom, on the other hand, had had no borrowing capabilities of any kind, but had been totally dependent on the ministry for capital considerations. The boards, under the act of 1962, again, as had been the case with the "Executives" were to be held to the requirement that their revenues would have to cover their costs. Almost the same words appeared in the provision for the boards as had applied to the Executives: "Each of the boards shall so conduct their business as to secure that their revenue is not less than sufficient for making provisions for the meeting of charges properly chargeable to revenue, taking one year with another" (Transport Act 1962, part 1, 18[1]). But, the boards were given leeway in regard to their capital expenses, where the Executives had been closed out of all capital considerations. The boards, contrary to the former Executives, were empowered to borrow for capital expenditures. This made them policy making as well as operational units of government. It allied them much more closely to the American public authorities whose very existence depended on their capabilities for floating revenue bonds, in their own name and equity, in the American bond market. The boards' powers for capital budgeting did not go that far—the British boards were enabled to borrow from the minister for capital improvements in the facilities necessary to their functions. The boards could borrow temporarily from the minister, or from "any other person," or, and of greater signification, they could borrow "otherwise than by way of temporary loan" from the Minister, for varied capital purposes, being, in general, "expenses incurred in connection with the provision of improvement of assets in connection with the business of the board" (Transport Act 1962: part 1, 19, esp. [1] [2]). These capabilities were extended to the boards "for any purpose for which capital moneys were properly applicable" (Transport Act 1962: part 1, 19[2] [h]).

The board, then, was a far different ad hoc agency than had been the Executive. It was to be involved intimately in the policy-making process of government concerning transportation, with both operating and capital funds at its disposal. This was no mere clerical, administrative branch of the central commission. This was a branch with genuine powers in its own right, but with the decided advantage of direct access to the ministry, from which most of the funds for it would come. The board, itself, therefore, was to have major responsibilities. The composition of the board, in the light of these extended powers, became particularly important. Under the 1962 act, the new London board was to "consist of a chairman, a vice chairman and not more than nine nor less than four other members." The minister was to make the appointments, as he had under the 1947 act, but with a degree of difference: he was to do so, in 1962, "after consultation with the chairman of the Board"; in the 1947 arrangements, he did so "after consultation with the Commission" (Transport Act, 1962, part 1, 1[2]; Transport Act, 1947, Schedules, Second Schedule, sec. 5 1). In both acts, the criteria for selection were to be those of functional interests in the concerns of the Executive or board, such as "transport, industrial, commercial, or financial matters, administration, applied science, or the organisation of workers," but in the more recent act, there was added the qualification that "the Minister in appointing them shall have regard to the desirability of having members who are familiar with the special requirements and circumstances of particular regions and areas served by the Board" (Transport Act, 1962, part 1 1[3]).

The London board was charged with the duty of exercising its powers under the act "to provide or secure the provision of an adequate and properly co-ordinated system of passenger transport for the London Passenger Transport Area, and to have due regard to efficiency, economy and safety of operation as respects the services and facilities provided by them" (Transport Act, 1962, part 1 7[1]). Implicit in the assignment of such broad powers to the board is the expectation that both operational and policy-making responsibilities must be assumed by it. Such duties as those of "efficiency, economy and safety" fall under operating responsibilities, but those of coordination go beyond the realm of daily concerns into that of overall policy for the area. The London board would have to "co-operate with the Railways Board for the purpose of ensuring that the services provided by the London Board are properly co-ordinated with the railway services of the Railways Board in the London Passenger

Transport Area" (Transport Act 1962: part 1, 7[2]). This would call for a level of concern beyond the day-by-day functions of the board, especially when one considers that not one of the regional railway boards but four of the six set up by this act in the country impinged on the London area. Indeed, the London board was to be intimately associated with the planning aspects of transportation in the London area, through its involvement in the "South East Study" published in 1964, and the extensive London Traffic Survey of 1961, published in 1964 and 1966. In 1966, the ministry of transport recognized the board's planning interrelationships by setting up the Transport Coordinating Council for London thereby formalizing the former informal contacts among the British railways, the London board, and the newly created Greater London Council (Day, 1972: 164; Rhodes [ed], 1972: 272-273).

In fact, under the restrictive financial obligations of the boards, their planning responsibilities came to give way to the dire necessities of everyday operations. As in the case of the former Executive, the new London board was required to pay its way from revenues. This same requirement applied to the Railways board. This proviso of self-sufficiency came to affect planning in the London area from the standpoints of both the London board and the Railways boards: "under the fragmented regional structure of administration . . . it was difficult for British Railways to concert a policy for . . . improving. For London Transport it became increasingly obvious during the 1960s that their obligation to provide an adequate system of passenger transport was in conflict with their financial obligations, and this inherent conflict of obligations acted to inhibit their forward planning" (Rhodes [ed], 1972: 277).

By 1965, the conflict had become so acute that the minister acknowledged that the matter needed serious consideration. And he postponed the fare increases that the London board had found essential to continue to meet its expenses out of revenue, assuring the London Board that it would not have to make up the losses sustained while the discussion was ensuing. Finally, "at the end of 1965, the Minister paid London Transport £3,850,000 as compensation for postponing the increase" (Day, 1972: 163).

Overlooked in the British concept of the self-sustaining special public authority had been the American understanding that they could exercise both planning and operational functions and pay for them from the charges made for the use of their facilities. The public authority in the United Kingdom, as illustrated by these under the Transport Act of 1962, were assigned to functions both traditionally deficit and normally profit-making. When public transport was nationalized in 1947, for instance, the buses were making large profits in London, whereas the underground railways were showing a loss. The public authorities in the United States came mainly for those functions, generally those associated with the automobile, whose users were willing to pay the extra costs. The British had relied on the idea that its authorities could borrow through the minister, whereas the Americans had forced the public authorities into the market where they not only would have to compete with private bonding issues, but would have to do so in their own equity, as individual authorities, without resort to the underwriting of the national and state governments. (A few in the United States such as housing authorities, had such recourse, but not those in the pure sense of the special public authority in the states.) Both countries based their financial restrictions on these agencies on the basis that, as ad hoc units of government, outside the normal constitutional framework, they should be forced to "efficiency, economy and safety of operation," and that this "businesslike" attribute best could be assured by the profit-and-loss kind of bookkeeping. Insistence on this private-enterprise characteristic meant, in America, that the toll-producing functions spread freely under the flexible special public authority mechanism, while the deficit functions, especially the "software" ones of welfare and education, were left at the starting gate. Furthermore, these latter functions remained the concern of the general governments, threatening to bog them down with the unpopular, housekeeping duties of government, with the public authorities moving away under the spur of the more dynamic functions of modern metropolitan government. In the United Kingdom, under the socialized industries, the same pay-as-you-go principle for the ad hoc governments began to be retained simply as an ideal, but gave way to increasing demands for funds from the central government to meet annual deficits.

In both countries, the considerable planning carried on by the ad hoc governments—by the quasi-public special public authorities in the United States, and the boards, in Britain—exhibited a marked predilection for the functions of government that would not increase the deficits. Mass transit suffered in the United States; and road construction in the United Kingdom, as, in each case, through the peculiarly different developments of transportation facilities between the two, those functions would have required large capital outlays without corresponding returns.

Chapter 6

CONVERGENCE OF PUBLIC CORPORATION

AND SPECIAL PUBLIC AUTHORITY

The London Transport Board, which assumed its responsibilities on January 1, 1963, resembled in certain major aspects, the special public authorities that had been developing since the 1930s in the United States. Some of these similarities have been noted in the previous chapter, but, taken as a whole, these factors were:

1. the involvement of the Board in decision making, giving it genuine policy-making powers, but with a clear line of accountability to the minister (This latter sort of relationship to an executive official, however, had not been delineated in America)
2. the requirement that revenues were to cover costs of the board's functions
3. the board's right to borrow for capital expenditures either from the minister or from "any other person"

4. the small numbers on the board, 4-9 persons, with a chairman and vice-chairman, all appointed by the minister after consultation with the chairman
5. the composition of the board from among certain areas of experience, such as "transport, industrial, commercial or financial matters, administration, applied science, or the organization of workers," although these were more inclusive than were designated categories in the United States
6. the selection of board members who were familiar with the region of the board, as in the case of special districts in America
7. the stress on "efficiency, economy and safety" in connection with the operational activities of the board

All these points of emphasis were to be found in the American counterpart, the special authority. Lacking in the United States, however, were several principal assets enjoyed by the London Transport Board, including:

1. its multimodal coverage of transportation
2. its regional jurisdiction over a broad area
3. its interrelationships with the minister
4. its ability to resort to funds from the government, when it became obvious that tolls, in themselves, would not suffice, without a sacrifice of effectiveness in the carrying out of the transport functions
5. its independence from the bonding investment complex, even with its powers of borrowing for capital expenditures.

During the 1960s, just as the London Transport Board was becoming meaningful, with all these powers, a few large cities or metropolitan areas in the United States formed a new kind of special authority containing the very five characteristics of the London Transport Board that the American agency had lacked theretofore. With seven points of clear resemblance, and now the addition of the five major points of former divergence, the American special public authority and the British public corporation began to converge, for the first time in their mutual history of some 30 years. Although generally unnoticed, the similarities are marked.

AMERICAN METROPOLITAN
TRANSPORTATION AUTHORITIES

In the Boston region in 1964 these new special authorities began with the formation of the Massachusetts Bay Transportation Authority from an enlargement of the powers of the Metropolitan Transit Authority there that had reflected the earlier type special public authority. They gained impetus that same year with the creation of the Southeastern Pennsylvania Transportation Authority in the Philadelphia region. Detroit followed in 1967 with the Southeastern Michigan Transportation Authority, which, on paper, at least, was to be one of the most comprehensive in scope, encompassing six counties and Detroit, and having within its purview undertakings of passenger transport by means of, "but not limited to street railways, motor bus, tramlines, subways, monorails, rail rapid transit," and facilities also for tunnels, bridges and parking. The Metropolitan Transportation Authority of New York, which became legal on March 1, 1968, gave the big boost to this new kind of agency. In the meantime, the Metropolitan Atlanta Rapid Transit Authority has survived a rough "honeymoon" and seems to be more firmly grounded, and the Washington (D.C.) Metropolitan Area Transit Authority has its subway under construction and has taken over the buses. The Metropolitan Transportation Authority, therefore, has become a new category of special-purpose government in the United States. Indeed, the initials by which such agencies commonly are known are beginning to sound alike, with: MBTA, SEPTA, SEMTA, (NY)MTA, MARTA, WMTA, and CRTA (proposed) for the respective areas of Boston, Philadelphia, Detroit, New York, Atlanta, Washington, and Chicago.

Each of these MTAs is regional, extending beyond the central city, and each covers more than one mode of transportation. The MBTA includes Boston and 78 communities and is empowered by legislation to handle "any mass transportation facility." SEPTA includes Philadelphia and four counties, and has jurisdiction over the Philadelphia subways, bus undertakings, trolleys, and, by special arrangements, the railroads. The New York MTA includes within its scope all of New York City and the seven commuter counties wholly within the state of New York. Its modes include the New York City subways, buses, certain automobile bridges and tunnels, ferries, railroads and a few aviation functions. MARTA is busy constructing a subway for Atlanta and two counties, while assuming responsibilities for bus transit. The Washington, D.C., MTA also is building a subway within and outside the national capital, and has taken over major bus facilities. Chicago's RTA recommendations are for the inclusion of that city and six counties, for the coordination of the city subways, railroads, buses, and "special services" as the need may present itself. This was just a beginning, but the new type units did represent the largest city in the country, New York; proposals for one in the second largest city, Chicago; and MTAs in existence in the forth-, fifth-, ninth-, sixteenth-, and twenty-seventh-sized cities. Moreover, together, even though small in actual number, they constituted a sharp break with the several thousand special public authorities throughout America. As these half-dozen were stretching over both city and suburbs, the 1967 Census of Governments was showing that only 2,300 of the more than 20,000 special districts extended even beyond one county, and that a mere 453 of the total involved two or more functions. The regional, multimodal MTAs, therefore, were pioneers in a very real sense. The method of drawing their boundaries also was different: the demarcations of their jurisdictions were made to encompass whole units of local government, either county or municipality. This had not been so in all special public authorities of the older variety. The 25-mile radius around the Statue of Liberty that frames the activities of the Port Authority of New York and New Jersey, for instance, includes all of New York City, and all of Hudson County in New Jersey across the Hudson River, but it cuts through 11 other counties, although it does include entire communities. The significance of this newer concept of district, embracing whole units of local government, lies in the realization by the regional authorities that they no longer can depend entirely on the user charges, as their responsibilities now involve both profitable and deficit modes of transportation. Tolls, or user charges, can be collected anywhere along the path of the particular means of transportation. But other forms of taxation, such as the property tax, upon which these authorities now will have to depend to supplement the user charges, may require assessment and collection by the local governments, as is common in the United States. For this purpose, these governments' inclusion in the authorities as whole entities is essential.

The base of financial support predetermines the nature of the special-purpose governments in America, as that has been their most distinguishing feature. The better known and older kind of special authority had been tied to the revenue bond, for its capital funds, and to the user charge for its income. This fact, in itself, had meant that its delimitations were those of the one function it was to handle, and, in following that activity, the authority could ignore the boundaries of counties and municipalities in the area. For the authority these lines had little meaning. The user charge could be collected from those availing themselves of the authority facilities at their point of use, either by a meter, or toll-booth collectors, or through franchises. There was no need for assessments of real or personal property that had made obligatory the fixed boundary lines of the more conventional local governments. In fact, it had been that very rigidity that had given the special governments their greatest acceptance, as they could move with expanding functions and could do so without further overburdening the harassed property owner who bore almost all the costs of local government. Those attractions still were to be exploited by the new authorities, and the user charges would be made to bear the brunt of the costs of the transportation facilities wherever they could. When, however, it was clear that commuter railroads or city subways could not be made to depend solely on the tolls, by the sheer fact that if they were to be raised any higher they would be self-defeating in that riders would not continue to use the facilities, then the other forms of taxation were to come in to play as supplements. These latter might well require a form of fixed boundaries for assessment or collection.

The London Transport Board of 1963 inherited, almost intact, the very large physical region that had been drawn for the London Passenger Transport Board back in 1933. The communities of Gray and Tilbury, East of London, were added, but, otherwise this was the same territory. Within that region, 184 local governments were enclosed, but only the administrative County of London and the County of Middlesex were included in their entirety. Only parts of seven other counties were within the boundary lines. This failure to preserve the county as a whole within the jurisdiction of the London Transport Board did not begin to have the same significance, however, that it does for the newer American special authorities. The reason is that the British special corporation's fiscal nexus was with the minister and central government, rather than to local governing bodies, whereas the American authorities, in forming their districts must take into account the traditional financing of governments in the United States by the local residents, usually through property taxation. And, as will be seen in a fuller description of these new authorities, their source of supplementary funds in most instances is to come from the conventional local governing bodies. That difference between the British and American special agencies, may be a further extension of the centralized orientation of the special British corporations, under the minister, until the very recent changes, rather than the sense of pluralism, to bring such functions closer to the people in America. To be sure, the large transportation agencies are looking beyond their immediate source of income locally to help from the state and the federal government. But they must start at home with the kind of taxes that people are accustomed to paying for local services.

Shift from Bondholder Dependency

The greater signification of the decision even to permit the tapping of tax money by the special authorities in the United States is that that additional avenue of finance must mean a lesser dependency on the bonding interests. This is very important; it is coming to mean a totally new frame of reference for the American special governments, much more conformable to that within which the British public corporation functions, but without socialization of the transportation industry. The movement in the United States appears not to have been influenced primarily by the British examples, as even those closely associated with special governments know little about such agencies from one American city to another, let alone from one country to the other. There has not been in America an "authorities concept" under which these thousands of units have conceived of themselves as representing a new level of government, or a new device. One does not speak of *the* special public authority, as one does of *the* public corporation in Britain, although there is no general agreement among the British that public corporations should act in consort. The corporation, however, is recognized as something unique and permanent. One reason for the lack of similar recognition in America has been the continued thought that they are ephemeral, and are necessary only during periods of emergency, with the entire period of the 1930s through the 1970s seen as comprising a series of crises, depression, wars, a population explosion, and the like. Most special authorities contain provisions for their own dissolution when their task has been performed, and, of particular concern to this American institution, when their bonds all have been paid off with interest. The Port of New York Authority, in its agreement with the city of New York by which the Authority leased the city's airports at Idlewild, LaGuardia, and Floyd Bennett field, agreed not to "issue any bonds for Municipal Air Terminal purposes maturing later than May 31, 1997," for, in that year, 50 years after the beginning of the agreement, the Authority

> will give up, surrender and deliver to the City the demised premises including all the buildings, structures and improvements, together with, all furniture, equipment, and other personal property contained therein.

As this was a 50-year lease, and as most of the bonds for special public authorities mature in 40 years from date of sale, there has not been time for Americans to discover what will happen when the terminal dates do arrive. Most of the authorities were established during the Depression period of the 1930s, and the 40-year maturity periods of their bonds are soon to be reached. There is indication, however, that most of the special authorities will continue in effect despite their terms for discontinuance. What appears to be taking place is that the special agencies are issuing, regularly, new revenue bonds for various new facilities, or for improvements to existing buildings, and each such new issue postpones by that many years the date of dissolution of the authority (see Smith, 1969: 307-318). They give evidence, therefore, of being permanent fixtures in American government. If this fact becomes better understood, a far more realistic attempt could be made to find their role in federalism, rather than to go on pretending that they are expedients.

The transitory concept of special-purpose units has not been unknown in Britain. Professor Robson has pointed out that "(t)hese boards grew up in a typically British fashion. They were not based on any clearly defined principle: they evolved in a haphazard and empirical manner" (1937: 359). Professor Friedmann also stresses their expedient role of meeting political exigencies: "In the great majority of cases a blend of political and practical factors has been the determining motive for the constitution of the public corporation" (1954: 544). The acceptance of the public corporation as the vehicle for the nationalized industries, however, has lent a semblance of stability to the image of special government in Britain. Special agencies for transportation in Britain have been changed with considerable regularity since 1933, as with the transport acts of Parliament of 1947, 1962, 1968, and then, as applied to London, in 1969 and 1971. As a statutory action, however, the one special agency established in any act is considered to be in effect until superseded by the succeeding act of Parliament. The transfer of properties, responsibilities, and financial holdings are spelled out in the amending legislation. The overwhelming difference between this procedure and that in the United States is that the life of the British special authority does not depend upon the agency's amortization of its bonded indebtedness. This is but another illustration of the very unusual infiltration of the bond investment into all phases of the special authorities' operations in America.

The new multimodal, regional transportation authorities in the United States seem to derive their features from a combination of those of the early special districts joined with those of the post-1930 special authorities. Just what terminology is suitable to this synthesis has not yet been made clear, as the agencies simply use the words "Metropolitan Transportation Authority." The use of the identical title, "authority," by these and the older special authorities, serves to hide the very different characteristics of the MTAs. The author has suggested the use of the term, "Authority-District," and that has caught on here and there, as in the Chicago proposal. A better label than that could be found. It does have the benefit, however, of separating the new from the old type, and it does recognize the dependence of the new ones on both kinds of special-purpose governments America has known: namely, the special district and the special public authority. From the special district, the Metropolitan Transportation Authorities have adopted the potentialities of the relatively settled features of a fixed constituency, within recognized boundaries, agreeable to the payment for a desired service, such as mass transit, even by a special tax levy on their property, in return for which it has the assurance of a board, the majority of whose members must reside in the district. The new authorities encompass whole units of local government as media for political identification. From the special public authority, the new authorities inherit the primary focus on revenue-bond capabilities, with the correlary confidence that the user charges will defray most of the costs, at least, in so far as possible. With such reliance, the new authorities again are free to follow their transportation functions without regard to boundary lines of the individual elected conventional governments— lines which still serve for the everyday functions of the general governments, but which have lost their meaning for the expanding modes of travel. The amalgam of these attributes of the special district, on the one hand, and of the special public authority, on the other, has produced the so-called "authority district" of the 1960s in the United States. Britain's present public corporations have profited from that country's experience with mixed enterprise agencies; representative trusts, as for the ports; and the joint stock company, but the public corporation has come to supplant most of the other forms, and almost as a reaction against the other efforts. In the United States, to the contrary, special districts, special public authorities, and authority districts all continue to function side-by-side, and all are proliferating.

It is probably through a series of coincidences in Britain and the United States, independently, therefore, that the London Transport Board of 1963 and the metropolitan transportation authorities, beginning in 1964, have come to such striking resemblance. The public corporation has been considered in some detail. The MTAs need more attention than they are getting in America, where they still are thought of as parts of the special public authority movement that has been with the country since the Roosevelt era of the 1930s. The lack of understanding of the significant differences between the traditional special authorities and the MTAs has been caused by the reliance on the same terminology, of the "authority," but also by the fact that there is nothing in the United States to which they can be compared. It is only by seeking perspective by an examination of the counterparts in another country, particularly one that is English-speaking and draws on many of the same traditions of government, that one comes to appreciate such new techniques as the MTAs and the London Transport Board share in common. If any one illustration is needed of the difference between the more customary special public authority of the United States and the MTA, it can be found in an event that involved the two of them in late 1971 and early 1972. In December 1971, Austin J. Tobin, who had served as executive director of the Port of New York Authority since 1942, and had been with the Authority since 1927, announced that he would retire. The Port Authority represented the older-type special authority, and Tobin was the staunchest supporter of the need to uphold its bonded obligations and not venture into mass transit projects that might impair confidence among its bondholders. One of the persons considered for appointment to succeed Tobin, was Dr. William J. Ronan, chairman of the newer Metropolitan Transportation Authority of New York. In March of 1972, however, Ronan publicly withdrew his name from consideration for the post, a most prestigious one that carried one of the highest governmental salaries in the country, $75,000. In a letter to W. Paul Stillman, chairman of the Selection Committee of the Port of New York Authority, Ronan expressed his reasons for declining the chance to gain the office:

> As I indicated to the members of your committee, my principal interest lies in the earliest redirection of the Port Authority into a major role in mass transportation in this region. Frankly, I have concluded that I can do far more to achieve this purpose by continuing in my present M.T.A. post and my role as a member of the board of the Port of New York Authority for the next five years. [He already was one of the six commissioners from New York State on the Port Authority's Board] . . . I reluctantly concluded that, with notable exceptions, Port Authority commissioners appear to assign a higher priority to the bond market than to mass transportation. . . . The Metropolitan Transportation Authority's progress in mass transportation in but four years of existence, despite all its financial, physical, labor, managerial and

political problems, frankly offers more real opportunity than the Port Authority with all its resources unless there is a clear cut change in its policies and direction (*New York Times,* 1972b).

Despite this severe criticism, however—or perhaps because of it—Dr. Ronan was elected by the commissioners of the Port Authority to serve as vice chairman, in June of 1972, while continuing as the chairman of the Metropolitan Transportation Authority.

A bond analyst had warned his colleagues in the investment world of the "threat" from the new special-purpose agencies some three years earlier (Rosenberg, 1969):

> Once considered to be virtually impregnable, the revenue bond indenture over the past two years has become the target of a series of explicit and implicit challenges to its sanctity, which would remove completely, siphon away or substitute for the basic security behind such an obligation to the detriment of the bondholder. The threat is contained in a unilateral alteration of the revenue bond contract through the enactment of a new law whereby the bond security may be supplanted on terms that violate the bond contract. . . . The handwriting is on the wall, and investors in toll-supported revenue bonds can do little but wonder about the true risks involved in committing their capital to enterprises in which the bondholders' prior lein has become subordinate to the lien of the "public interest."

The British understanding of the obligations of the special governments would read exactly the opposite from his conclusion, that a cause of alarm should be that "the bondholders' prior lien has become subordinate to the lien of the 'public interest'." The British attitude is that the "public interest" of the special agencies in the United Kingdom is superior to, or prior to, that of the "bondholders . . . lien."

The reference by the bond specialist to the "sanctity" of "the revenue bond indenture" emphasizes the extent to which this means of financing had become exaggerated. The inviolability of the special authority's bonds is one of the strangest developments in modern government, and can be appreciated fully only when compared to the opposite viewpoint of the public lien, as practiced in the United Kingdom. Dr. Ronan stated the shift to the public focus this way: "The pristine purity of revenue bonding simply can't be sustained" (*New York Times,* 1971d). The problem faced by the Metropolitan Transportation Authorities was that they would inherit the bonded indebtedness of any of the older kinds of special public authorities that they would take over; would continue, themselves, to use revenue-bond-user-charge financing wherever practicable; and would have to seek other funding from other sources. The ways that each of the MTAs attempted to resolve these diverse interests should reveal much about the general nature of this latest version of special governments in America, as each one adapted measures and organizational structures to the peculiar conditions of the tradition and environment in which it was starting its operations.

Massachusetts Bay Transportation Authority

The Massachusetts Bay Transportation Authority, the first of the MTAs, was based on the New England tradition of the small town. Metropolitan structures had been forced to adjust to that orientation over the years, as it represented the dominant political force there. Whereas the definition of a Standard Metropolitan Statistical Area, used by the federal Bureau of the Census for the collection of statistics, had been predicated on the core city and surrounding dependent counties, for example, in New England an exception had been made, as the bureau explained, so that "towns and cities are the units used," as they "are administratively more important than the county. . . ." When the Office of Management and Budget recommended changes in the definition of the SMSAs, in 1973 an exception still was maintained for the New England area (Executive Office of the President, 1973).

Regionalism had roots in the Boston area but always in the context of the joining of towns and cities for specific functions. As early as 1920, for instance, 50 Boston-area communities had united for jurisdiction over parks, water, and sewerage, to form the well-known Boston Metropolitan District. Since 1949 there had been metropolitan concerns for transportation in and around Boston, first with the so-called Metropolitan Transit District, comprised of fourteen cities and towns, including Boston, that had operated elevated and subway lines. When this district setup had not worked, the same fourteen cities and towns had been made members of the Metropolitan Transit Authority, the immediate forebear of the Massachusetts Bay Transportation Authority. The MBTA started with these same fourteen units of local government, but in its enabling legislation, immediately added to them 64 more communities within the Boston commuting area. The MBTA, then, represented 78 cities and towns in all, each very conscious of its place of importance in Massachusetts government and politics. (A 79th was attached to the MBTA in 1967). The total organization of the MBTA, even though regional and multimodal, had been framed to accommodate these component parts.

The strength of the member groups was given play, first of all, in the board of directors of the MBTA. The governor had the responsibility for naming all five members of the board, and of designating one of them as its chairman, but he must make his selections for the board after consultations, as follows: two with the approval of the governor's own council, but then one with the approval of the Advisory Board of the MBTA, described below as controlled by the 79 cities and towns, one with the approval of the original fourteen cities and towns that had been the members of the former Metropolitan Transit Authority, and one with the newly added 65 cities and towns. Of the five choices to be made by the governor, therefore, three of them were to have the approval of the local governments. The method for expressing this consent to his appointments even was spelled out in the legislation (sec. 6), indicating that it was not to be a mere perfunctory expression of satisfaction:

The approval of the fourteen cities and towns and of the sixty-four [later sixty-five] cities and towns, respectively, shall be determined by a majority vote of their mayors (or city managers in the case of Plans D and E cities) and chairmen of selectmen with the vote of each city and town counted as on the advisory board [below] . . . ; provided that the vote of at least four municipalities shall be required to constitute the majority of the fourteen cities and towns.

The governor further was directed to select one of these members as "experienced in transportation, one a member of organized labor who shall be a member of a national or international labor organization [shades of the London Passenger Transport Board of 1933], and one experienced in administration and finance." No more than three of the five could be from the same political party.

The real power of the local communities in the MBTA was to be exercised, however, through an additional body, known as the Advisory Board. This was their province. It consisted of "the city manager in the case of a Plan D or E city or the mayor of each other city, and the chairman of the board of selectmen of each town, constituting the authority." The very large board was made the more unwieldy by the use by it of an unbelievably complicated system of weighted voting, in which, initially, 195 votes were to be cast on it. The weighting was dependent on the amount of money paid to the MBTA each year by the city or town as its share of the costs of mass transit. It was described in the statute (sec. 7) as follows:

Each city and town shall have one vote on the advisory board plus additional votes and fractions thereof determined by multiplying one and one half times the total number of cities and towns in the authority by a fraction of which the numerator shall be the total amount of all assessments made by the state treasurer to such city or town . . . and the denominator shall be the total amount of all assessments made by the state treasurer to all such cities and towns.

The assessments, referred to above, are supplements to the user charges that are inadequate to support the deficit operations of the MBTA in the mass transit field. The state now comes into the picture, as the minister and government do with the British public corporation but in far different ways. Massachusetts is required to pay to the MBTA at the end of any year an amount to compensate for the Authority's net loss for the cost of its services. The Commonwealth, however, before calculating the amount that it owes the MBTA under this provision, will assess each of the component cities and towns in the MBTA for the relative proportion of services each has received from the MBTA. This assessment is of two kinds:

(1) For express commuter services: 75 percent of this express cost is to be paid by the cities and towns enjoying it, according to the proportion that the number of commuters in each community bears to the total number of commuters in the whole area of the MBTA; (2) Twenty-five percent of the cost of express services is to be paid by those cities and towns that actually have express stations, according to the proportional numbers of riders using those stations. For commuting services other than those for express travel, other proportions are assessed.

The determining of the weighted votes on the Advisory Board on the basis of these proportional assessments for the services of the MBTA resulted, from the very outset, in Bostons' being outvoted by the surrounding towns. In the first computations of the votes on the Advisory Board, Boston came out with only 73.29, out of the total of 195.00, and even if she joined with Cambridge, adjacent to her at the core of the metropolis, they would have only 83.85 votes, or 13.65 votes less than half.

The Advisory Board, moreover, was far more than "advisory." It had control over the finances of the MBTA. The statute (sec. 5[i]) was quite clear at this point:

All current expenses of the authority shall be in accordance with an itemized budget prepared and submitted by the authority to the advisory board not later than November first of each year for the ensuing calendar year. Within thirty days after such submission, the advisory board shall approve said budget as submitted or subject to such itemized reductions therein as the advisory board shall deem appropriate. The budget shall govern the current expenses of the authority during such calendar year. No such expenses may be incurred in excess of those shown in the budget.

In other words, the Advisory Board had an itemized veto over the budget of the MBTA.

The state was authorized to make certain payments for services to the MBTA itself, without assessment on the cities and towns in the MBTA, for capital construction such as for express facilities. The MBTA, also, in its own name could borrow by the traditional special public authority method of the issuance of revenue bonds. These were floated in the name of the MBTA, but their assurance came from the fact that, even though the entire operation of the MBTA might well prove to be a deficit one for any year, the Commonwealth of Massachusetts would shore up the bonds, and guarantee their periodic repayment, through its responsibility to make up the difference between the income of the MBTA and its costs each year after local assessments have proved inadequate. Technically, the obligation of the commonwealth protects the bondholders because, included in the net debt to be met either by assessment or direct payment by the state is that of the debt service, or periodic payments of bond principal and interest.

The MBTA legislation met, head on, the intricate constitutional question as to the rights of the bondholders of the former Metropolitan Transit Authority that had been taken into the Massachusetts Bay Transportation Authority. It simply declared that "all mass transportation facilities . . . and all other property, real and personal, owned, controlled by or in the custody of the Metropolitan Transit Authority is hereby transferred to the ownership, control and custody of the Massachusetts Bay Transportation Authority." The MBTA would assume "all debts, liabilities and obligations of the Metropolitan Transit Authority" (sec. 20). Assessments for the purposes of defraying the former debts of the Metropolitan Transit Authority, however, were not to be saddled on the new members of the MBTA, but were to be chargeable against the fourteen cities and towns that had comprised the MTA and now were members of the MBTA.

The state, or commonwealth, thus had undertaken major obligations for mass transportation through the MBTA. It was to guarantee help to the Authority over and beyond the user charges that no longer would be anywhere nearly adequate to meet the costs of railroads, buses, subways, and the like. To help meet these new financial burdens, Massachusetts imposed on the citizens of the entire state—not just those in the MBTA district of the 79 cities and towns—a $0.02 tax on each pack of cigarettes. The Supreme Judicial Court of Massachusetts (I, II, sec. 1IIB) upheld this right of the state to tax the entire state for help to the MBTA, even though it might seem to favor one geographic part of the state at the expense of the others:

> Transportation concerns every inhabitant of the Commonwealth and every aspect of our society. . . . The Authority is that kind of agency of the sovereign for which broad general powers and standards are appropriate. . . . To meet the public need the Legislature has created a "political subdivision of the Commonwealth." The Authority has some resemblance to a county, a regional school district, or a fire, improvement, or incinerator district. . . . The Authority is suitably placed within the existing political framework of the Commonwealth. . . . Doubtless in exercising that discretion the Executive Office will take into account . . . the extent to which the project will be of benefit to an area larger than the seventy-eight cities and towns in relieving highway congestion, and providing facilities of value to the entire Commonwealth. [Massachusetts Bay Transportation Authority vs. Boston Safe Deposit and Trust Company et al. (1965).]

This total involvement of the cities and towns in so all-embracing a transportation agency as that of the Massachusetts Bay Transportation Authority—through their advice to the governor on appointments to the board of directors, through direct participation by their leaders on the Advisory Board, by their itemized veto powers, on the board, over the budget, and by their use of state monies over and beyond the user charges and assessments—all became so complex that it interfered with the functioning of the Authority, as very awkward interrelationships developed between the Advisory Board and the board of directors, particularly over budgetary matters.

Southeastern Pennsylvania Transportation Authority

The Southeastern Pennsylvania Transportation Authority placed its emphasis in exactly the opposite direction from that of the Massachusetts Bay Transportation Authority. Whereas the latter had given priorities to the communities surrounding Boston, rather than to the central city, for transportation coordination, the Philadelphia-based SEPTA stressed the essential role of the city. The city was central to its formation, as SEPTA grew out of existing special-purpose units, as have so many of these new MTAs. (The Massachusetts Bay Transportation Authority, as has been described, evolved from the former Metropolitan Transit Authority.) The two units that were taken over by SEPTA centered on Philadelphia: one, the Passenger Service Improvement Corporation (PSIC) included a commuter railroad program within the city itself, and the other, the Southeastern Pennsylvania Transportation Compact (SEPACT), also had to do with commuter railroads, but in this case the railroads serving commuters to Philadelphia from three suburban counties. The newly formed SEPTA assumed management services for both PSIC and SEPACT. That, per se, helped make the city of Philadelphia the focus of the new MTA. The composition of the board for SEPTA also pointed in the direction of city influence. The Southeastern Pennsylvania Transportation Authority, approved in 1963 for operation beginning in 1964, consisted of the city of Philadelphia and four commuter counties, Bucks, Chester, Montgomery, and Delaware, all in Pennsylvania. Delaware had been a reluctant addition to the compact at the last minute, as it had expressed fears of the dominance of Philadelphia's interests. One of the commissioners of that Delaware County had been quoted as having declared that his county "will never give one subsidy dollar to the railroads or Philadelphia. What Philadelphia has it can keep. We don't need it" (Philadelphia *Evening Bulletin,* 1961). The voting on the board was apportioned as shown in Table 1.

TABLE 1
VOTES ON THE BOARD OF THE SEPTA

City of Philadelphia	2 votes
Bucks County	2
Montgomery County	2
Delaware County	2
Chester County	2
Appointee of the governor	1
TOTAL	11

All units, the four counties, and the city of Philadelphia, have the right to veto regional actions of the board. To override a veto, nine of the eleven votes are required. That means, in practice, that if Philadelphia vetoes an action of the board it could not be overriden, except by the unanimous vote of all the other members, including the two votes from each of the four counties and the veto by the governor's appointee. Conversely, of course, each of the other units has a veto that can be used against Philadelphia, or any of the other units' desires. Those interests of the city, however, would seem to stand in distinction to those of the suburban counties in general, or as related to certain of the suburban counties for commuter transportation. The chance of united action against Philadelphia's wishes to the extent of unanimous voting would seem to be lessened by the requirement of at least nine votes to override the veto. Indeed, the first year of the operation of the Southeastern Pennsylvania Transportation Authority, the board was plagued by vetoes, tying up any productive action. Delaware County, including both of its representatives, led in the employment of this device, but was joined by one of the members of the board, oddly, from Philadelphia. These three stood together not only in the veto process, but more significantly, in any attempts to overcome the veto, thereby making the nine votes required impossible. Vetoes by the group included one to prevent the board from meeting in executive session to block the leasing of office space, and two to block the appointment of a deputy general manager as acting administrator. Finally, in October 1964, Mayor James H. J. Tate, of Philadelphia, dismissed the Philadelphia member who had been supporting the vetoes from the board and appointed a new one. The mayor accused the recalcitrant member of trying "to force the adoption of personal views by blocking action of a majority of the board."

The *Evening Bulletin* of Philadelphia (1964) editorialized:

> Placing SEPTA into effective operation is a very delicate matter because of the inevitable regional animosities and superficial conflicts of interest. The political realities require that it move forward slowly and at times inefficiently; but the economic realities require that it at least move forward. The veto and the stirring of sectional rivalries within the SEPTA board have thus far checked such forward movement.

The *Philadelphia Daily News* (1964), on the other hand, recognized the tenuous nature of SEPTA's beginnings:

> With more than 3.5 million taxpayers in five counties having a stake in SEPTA's decisions, it would seem that the authority must bend over backward to satisfy the diverse demands of its members and to insure public confidence in its operations. With this in mind, the veto may be well taken.

The veto involving the appointment of an acting administrator for SEPTA, which finally was resolved when the Philadelphia member who had voted for the veto changed her vote just before she was removed from the board, again illustrated the centrality of Philadelphia in SEPTA. The person being considered for the position was John A. Bailey. He was, at the time, the executive director of PSIC, for railroads within the city, and the executive secretary of SEPACT for the commuter railroad project connecting Philadelphia and the suburbs. His appointment was considered favorable to Philadelphia. Indeed, the Philadelphia member had vetoed his appointment to the administrator's post of SEPTA because of alleged conflict of interests and the Delaware County members had vetoed the choice on the basis of his possible predilection to railroads, when that county's means of transportation was the bus. Bailey was appointed, however.

The city's role in SEPTA was marked in another way in that during the first year, Philadelphia contributed $80,000 and each of the four counties only $20,000 to get the new authority's projects underway, in addition to the PSIC and SEPACT railroad experiments that were receiving federal funds. SEPTA has been required, from its inception, to perform its tasks by resort to fares, without help from tax sources, and has had to rely on matching grants from its component members, state appropriations, and federal grants. In 1973, nine years after its inauguration, SEPTA still was seeking additional fiscal sources, and was asking for $75,000 just for operating expenses. (In fact, the special authorities in America were insistent by the 1970s that they receive help for their daily operations, in view of the fact that most all grants were for capital costs. Operational obligations had kept rising, as labor costs continued to jump, and are chargeable to the operations budget.) By then, SEPTA was being aided by bookkeeping techniques in which, for example, the city leased the transit property from SEPTA to support the Authority's revenue bonds, and then leased this property back to SEPTA for its operation of it. This leaseback type of special authority is used rather extensively in a

few states, such as Pennsylvania, for instance, for the construction of school buildings, each by a separate special
authority, and then the leasing of that school building to the
township, or other municipality, over a period of years until
the cost of construction is paid. SEPTA subsidizes railroad
lines, and, in the spring of 1973, received permission from
the United States District Court to take over the Reading
Railroad's commuter operations in its five-county area. It has
under its jurisdiction also trolleys, trackless trolleys, and
buses. Its 6,200 transit employees, and 1,800 railroad commuter employees make possible a network of transportation
modes:

> a million person trips per weekday using 1600 diesel buses, 491
> subway-elevated cars, 440 electric railroad cars, 450 high and low
> speed cars generally of the trolley type, and 128 trackless
> trolleys. The annual budget is running $140 million per year for
> operating and other annual expenses. Capital improvements aver-
> age about $30 million per year [Tennyson, 1972: 18].

As in Boston, however, the new Authority had been unable
to tap the surpluses being accumulated by the special public
authorities from automobile tolls. In Boston, the user charges
from the Massachusetts Turnpike Authority that runs directly across the state of Massachusetts into the very center
of Boston were not to be employed to help to defray the
rising costs of mass transit under the separate Massachusetts
Bay Transportation Authority. Similarly, in Philadelphia, the
lucrative tolls from the Pennsylvania Turnpike Commission's
highway that physically crossed some half-dozen of the lines
of the deficit-plagued commuter railroads were denied
SEPTA to help balance its debts. The new MTAs, with the
partial exception of that for New York, were being established for the coordination of mass transit, but there still
remained, independent of them, the former special public
authorities that had grown up around the automobile and
still benefitted from its tolls. In 1970, the chairman of
SEPTA proposed that a portion of the tolls from the automo-

bile bridges connecting Philadelphia with New Jersey, across the Delaware River be given to SEPTA. The bridges, however, are under the jurisdiction of still another special public authority in the area, the Delaware River Port Authority. The SEPTA chairman argued: "Surely, if it is valid to spend $94 million on bridge tolls to furnish modern transportation to 30,000 passengers a day in New Jersey, it is valid to provide an equal amount from the same bridge tolls for the 1,000,000 daily riders of Southeastern Pennsylvania" (Philadelphia *Evening Bulletin*, 1970). He had reference to the Port Authority Transit Corporation, a subsidiary of the Port Authority, consisting of a 14.4 mile highspeed, entirely automated, rapid transit line system, known as the Lindenwold Line, extending from Philadelphia eastward into the New Jersey commuter communities.

Southeastern Michigan Transportation Authority

The Michigan Transportation Authorities Act of 1967 sought to encourage the development of MTAs in that midwestern state and to have them reflect regional associations of elected officials of local governments in the area. The basic problem in this effort, however, lay in the fact that no such general-purpose regional governments were in existence in the state. Board membership, therefore, had to be stated in conditional terms:

After the initial appointments are made by the governor to the southeastern Michigan transportation authority, and if a southeastern Michigan council of governments is created by the legislature, those members of the council of governments who represent governmental units within the authority shall have the power by a majority vote to appoint 6 of the 7 members of the authority. . . . The power of appointment of a seventh member shall remain with the governor [No. 204, Public and Local Acts of the Legislature of the State of Michigan, 1967, 124.410, see 10 (5)].

In 1971, the board was increased to nine members, six of whom were to be appointed by the Council of Governments.

That pattern of the special government's desire to forge ahead and form new geographic conformations for expanded functions, and of the general government's hesitancy to do so, has prevailed throughout American history. Any idea of fluid boundaries flexible enough to accommodate to changing circumstances has been alienable to the conventional governments, tied as they have been to fixed boundaries within which they could continue to assess property and collect the taxes thereon. Accordingly, the Southeastern Michigan Transportation Authority began operations before there was an organization of the general-purpose governments to name members to its board. England, until recently, has experienced the same sort of pioneering by the ad hoc units without corresponding enlargements of the scope of action by the conventional governments. A Royal Commission of 1853 looking into the possible expansion of the municipal government of London to an area of the metropolis, recommended that one way to do so would be simply to incorporate the city with the Metropolitan Police who had been established as a special-purpose agency on a metropolitan scale as early as 1839. Another suggestion by the Royal Commission was that the Thames Conservancy, an ad hoc organization, be transferred to the city. There, as in America, the special units have had the freedom, denied generally to regular governments, to draw new boundaries in the interest of economy of scale. In the case of the United Kingdom, however, the modern reorganization of governments demonstrates a willingness to change as yet unknown in the United States. And, indeed, as far back in history as 1855 London had a Metropolis Management Act, under which, for one thing, the Metropolitan Board of Works members were elected (Robson, 1948: 56-58). The boundary lines of the Greater London Council today, however, resemble, to a large extent, those of Metropolitan Police District and those of the Metropolitan Water Board, of 1902, both special-purpose agencies. One result, in both countries, has been that regional, and especially metropolitan, planning, such as there has been, had been done by the ad hoc governments. Carrying out projects for their particular functions, these units have had to make decisions as to their location and use. Within their limited functional orbits, thus, they have developed metropolitanwide plans, long before consideration of the more comprehensive regional plans by conventional government. Transportation special authorities, as discussed in this book, have carried on extensive regional planning, in default of any overall plans. A moment's thought will indicate the weaknesses inherent in this kind of piece-meal allocation of priorities and goals. The very meaning of the planning process is that it be comprehensive, and take into account the total picture. The least qualified agency to plan is the special government, for, by its very nature, it has an obsession for the one function, or the closely related functions entrusted to it.

By January of 1968, however, the Southeastern Michigan Council of Governments was organized in the Detroit area, covering the same units of government that were encompassed in the Southeastern Michigan Transportation Authority of 1967. Councils of Government were appearing throughout the United States at that time, under the spur of federal financial support. They were not, in most instances, units with governing powers, but merely voluntary associations of local government officials. A few, such as the Metropolitan Washington (D.C.) Council of Governments were entrusted with coercive powers and a real role in the metropolitan area, but they stood out as the exception. A National Association of Regional Councils represents them in Washington, D.C. The point of interest in the Detroit area interrelationship of the Authority and the council is that here was an attempt to establish a regional special authority under the guidance of a regional representation of elected officials. In addition to the power of appointment of board members, the Council of Governments was to review the budget of the Transportation Authority each year:

The authority shall submit its annual operating and capital budget, financial audits and construction plans to a regional government . . . for review and comment a reasonable time prior to final approval by the authority board of directors [124.415, sec. 3].

As has been mentioned, its responsibilities, by statute at least, were to be as comprehensive as that of any MTA in the country:

An authority is a public benefit agency and instrumentality of the state with all the powers of a public corporation, for the purpose of planning [note this specific provision for planning], acquiring, constructing, operating, maintaining, improving and extending public transportation facilities, and for controlling, operating, administering and exercising the franchise of such transportation facilities, if any, including charter operations as acquired [sec. 3].

For the first 18 months, the Southeastern Michigan Transportation was limited by this act to two projects: (1) "the acquisition, improvement and operation of existing bus systems"; and (2) "attention to existing rail commuter facilities serving the Woodward avenue corridor" northward to the city of Pontiac, working with the management of the affected railroad companies and the public.

The Authority was given the traditional right of special authorities to issue revenue bonds, which were to be self-liquidating and were to be "payable solely from the revenues of such property" (sec. 16). It was to rely on "fares, rates, tolls and rents," wherever possible, but, in addition, was to finance its facilities by:

other income or revenues from whatever source available, including appropriations or contributions of whatever nature of other revenues of the participating counties and political subdivisions within the geographical boundaries of the authority.

grants, loans or contributions from federal, state or other governmental units and any other grants, contributions, gifts, devises or bequests from public or private sources [124.414, sec. 14].

In the fall of 1970, SEMTA announced a $9.2 million budget for the year, much larger than previous ones. A total of $637,000 of this amount was to be required from the six participating counties, based on a population formula of 11.9¢ per capita. The contributions from the counties were to be "matched three for one with state funds, and the total of local and state funds matched two for one with federal monies" (*Passenger Transport*, 1970). Effective on February 1, 1973, an increase of $0.02 a gallon on gasoline was to permit $0.05, or $21 million a year, for public transit, as an advance, or loan. The proposal was that "any transit construction project costing more than $10 million would have to be approved in advance by a two-thirds vote of the legislature and a three fourths vote of a local or regional transportation authority" (B. Jones, 1973).

The new concerns for representation of constituent units by the MTAs were influenced, in no small amount, by the fact, as illustrated by SEMTA, that these components now would be helping to defray the costs of the actions by the Authority.

New York Metropolitan Transportation Authority

There is the attitude among urban experts in the United States that if anything can work in the New York metropolitan area, with its intricate maze of complexities, it can be made to succeed in any other metropolitan center in the country. Experience in New York is rated highly, and specialists feed in and out of New York City positions to serve other cities and regions. The attempts, beginning with those of Mayor John V. Lindsay, from his very assumption of the office, January 1, 1966, to coordinate the web of transportation modes in New York, attracted nationwide attention, despite the fact that there had been relatively little awareness of the pioneering MTA efforts of Boston, Philadelphia, and, in legislation, at least, of Detroit. The *New York Times* (1967) stressed New York's prototype role here:

The experiment will be watched closely by urban communities all over the nation, such as San Francisco and Chicago, which have congestion problems almost as severe as New York's. If New York's plan succeeds, it could prove a model for these other equally strangled cities.

The strangulation, for the New York region, had been outlined by Lindsay, in his campaign for mayor in the fall of 1965. A "white paper," entitled "A Modern Transportation System for New York City" at that time had made the point that, not only had no new subway lines been constructed for the past 25 years, but that the city actually had fewer lines than it had had in 1940. The elevated lines on Second and Third Avenues had been torn down but not replaced in any way. "Loads carried by many subway cars," the report stated, "during the rush hours exceed seating capacity by as much as 400 percent and standing capacity by 50 percent." The subways were "inconvenient, ill-equipped and ill-maintained," with long-distance rides too slow, delays on all lines, no significant progress toward air-conditioning, no modernization of the ventilating systems, platforms and entrances filthy, lighting poor, and "fear of criminal attack" by subway riders.

The conclusion of the report was that "mass transit must survive—and to survive, must be vastly improved." This was to be done through the allocation of the resources necessary, "planning each new link in the overall transportation structure to promote, rather than detract from, mass transit," and "neither paving our City over with asphalt nor making its heart into a vast parking garage."

To carry this into effect, there was to be "no equivocation on the basic need for an integrated approach," to overcome the "fragmented monstrosity of the City's transportation structure" (Lindsay, 1965: 1-4). As mayor, one of Lindsay's early proposals was legislation to effectuate these recommendations. When this proposal failed to win the approval of the state legislature, Governor Nelson Rockefeller submitted a plan, which became the basis for the creation of the Metropolitan Transportation Authority (Smith, 1969). The M.T.A. began operation on March 1, 1968. It was designed to serve as an "umbrella" or "holding company" agency, including within its jurisdiction the Metropolitan Commuter Transportation Authority (the Long Island Rail Road), the New York City Transit Authority (with its subsidiary for the Fifth Avenue buses, the Manhattan and Bronx Surface Transit Operating Authority [MABSTOA]), and the Triborough Bridge and Tunnel Authority. One and the same board of nine members (later expanded to ten and the chairman) was to serve to govern the M.T.A., and, in an ex officio capacity, as the board for the New York City Transit Authority, the Long Island Rail Road, and the Triborough Bridge and Tunnel Authority. All members are appointed by the governor, with the consent of the Senate. Three of the members of the board are to be appointed "only on the written recommendation of the mayor of the city of New York." "No more than two of the members may be nonresidents of the district" (New York State Laws, Art. 5 Title 11, sec. 1263, par. 1).

A balanced approach to transportation in the New York metropolitan region was anticipated. In regard to the New York City subways, they now came under the jurisdiction of the overall board of the M.T.A., but they no longer would have to support their daily operations by the fares collected for their use. This had become unfeasible, especially when labor costs are chargeable against the operating budget. The M.T.A. was to attempt to balance out the surpluses being accumulated by the Triborough Bridge and Tunnel Authority against the deficits of the New York City Transit Authority, both of which Authorities now are under the same aegis of the M.T.A. The M.T.A. was to establish tolls and other charges "to maintain *the combined operations* of the authority . . . on a self-sustaining basis," rather than just the operations of the subways. This provision would enable the M.T.A. to undertake nonprofitable ventures without making their use prohibitive through excessive tolls, or restricted to those who could afford to pay high charges. The New York City Transit Authority, within the "holding company" of the M.T.A., finally could be relieved of the necessity, imposed by the state back in 1953, to finance its operations exclusively from subway fares. The Transit Authority still has the responsibility "at all times to fix or adjust the rate or rates of fare to be charged . . . as may be necessary to maintain the operations of the authority on a self-sustaining basis," but the term, "self-sustaining," has been liberalized to include revenues, not only from fares, but "from any funds granted or transferred to the authority pursuant to any provision of law" (New York State Laws, sec. 1266, par. 3; Title 9 1205, par. 1).

The law referred to was the amendment to the legislation of the Triborough Bridge and Tunnel Authority that had been worded to read, that, after certain conditions to protect the bondholders had been met, the Triborough Authority could "from time to time transfer and pay over to Metropolitan Transportation Authority or New York City transit authority all or any part of its surplus funds" (Art. 3, Title 3, sec. 569-c, par. 1). For the first time, therefore, surpluses from automobile traffic could be transferred to help defray the deficits of the mass transit operations. Practically, this meant that the state legislature in 1969 gave the M.T.A. the right to pay the holders of the outstanding bonds of the Triborough Bridge and Tunnel Authority from one-quarter to one percent more interest, in return for which the bondholders would agree to the transfer of the Triborough surplus of $26,064,296 to the New York City Transit Authority.

The M.T.A. represented, therefore, a new kind of co-ordinating special-purpose government, with its stated purpose as that of "the continuance, further development and improvement of commuter transportation and other services related thereto within the metropolitan commuter transportation district, including but not limited to such transportation by railroad, omnibus, marine and air." Its boundaries include all of New York City, and the seven commuter counties within the state of New York, of Dutchess, Putnam, Orange, Westchester, Rockland, Suffolk, and Nassau.

As a coordinating comprehensive unit of government, the M.T.A. was assured the financial support for deficit operations that the former public authorities had lacked—namely, the guarantee that its bondholders would be protected even if the deficit functions were to prove greater than the productive sources. A practical and direct recourse was provided by the M.T.A. legislation: "The chairman of the authority shall annually, on or before December first, make and deliver to the governor and the director of the budget his certificates stating the amount, if any, required to restore each debt service reserve fund to the amount aforesaid and the amount or amounts so certified, if any, shall be apportioned and paid to the authority during the then current state fiscal year" (Art. 5, Title II, sec. 1270, par. 3).

Metropolitan Atlanta Rapid Transit Authority

The Metropolitan Atlanta Rapid Transit Authority went just about all the way in relieving itself of dependence on revenue bonding. It set out to develop bus and rail facilities in the city of Atlanta, Fulton County (in which Atlanta is located), and adjacent DeKalb County, on a "pay-as-you-go" basis. This drastic approach had been forced on the Authority by the fact that its first referendum for a rapid transit program, which had called for $992.8 million in bonds, had been soundly defeated in 1968 by the voters in all three units, the city, Fulton, and DeKalb counties. Many attributed the negative response to the fact that the bonds would have to be paid for from taxes, as they would be for nonprofitable mass transit, requiring increases in the property tax. The voters felt, as they had begun to throughout the United States, that the saturation point had been reached. The Authority had been established in 1966, but, without approval for the bond issue, it could not begin operations. Its board instituted a whole fresh attack on the problem. Its plan presented to the voters on November 9, 1971, contained the safeguards against further heavy bond indebtedness. The program called for large expenditures, a $1.4 billion capital outlay, for the buying and improving of a private bus company, and for the construction of a rapid rail system. One of the promises of the Authority to the voter this time was that just as soon as possible after the successful vote on the referendum, the Authority would buy the private bus company and would reduce the bus fares from $0.40 to $0.15. The reduction would be in effect for the next seven years, and the fare would be increased only to $0.20 at that time, to $0.25 in the ninth year, and, finally, $0.30 in the tenth year. There were to be no additional charges for transfers. It was estimated that the first reduction "will mean an immediate, direct saving of about $2.50-$3.00 per week for the person using transit to get to and from work five days a week" (*Passenger Transport,* 1972b). All this unheard of largess was to be made possible by several factors:

1. Action by the state legislature, which for the first time since Atlanta's charter in 1873, had voted a new source of revenue to the city, namely, the increase of 1 percent on the sales tax for Atlanta, Fulton, and DeKalb counties. Noteworthy is the fact that this was not an increase in the property taxes of any kind. The legislature had done so in March of 1971, in anticipation of the possibly favorable vote by the residents in the November referendum. So excited had been the mayor of Atlanta, Sam Massell, at this legislative action that he had had a large billboard erected across the street from the Capitol, reading "Thank You, Georgia Lawmakers."
2. Approval by the federal government, under the Urban Mass Transportation Act of 1970, of funds to cover two-thirds of the total cost of the undertakings.
3. Agreement by local banks to advance to MARTA the one-third local share and part of the operating costs.

The chairman of the Authority declared that by not relying on bonding to borrow the money, there would be a saving of

$150 million in long-term interest on the bonds. Revenue bonds generally require interest payments of about ½-1 percent higher than for the bonds usually floated by general-purpose governments, called general obligations. The reason is, of course, that the latter have as their equity the entire property of the local government that issues them, whereas the revenue bond has to depend on the income that it is anticipated the facility to be built with the money will draw. Revenue-bond financing, then, even though touted as relieving the property owner of additional taxation, introduces considerable extra costs into the financing of governments.

The Metropolitan Atlanta Rapid Transit Authority more than made good on its promises. Sooner than expected, it purchased the private bus company, and, on March 1, 1972, just four months after the voters' approval, the reduced fare of 15¢ was instituted. The Authority now is proceeding with the construction of the new rail transit. The "pay-as-you-go" features are to be applied through advancing the program step-by-step, as follows:

Early 1972: Acquire the Atlanta Transit System (Feb. 17, 1972); reduce fare to 15¢ (March 1, 1972); sales tax becomes effective (April 1, 1972); award contract for 125 new air-conditioned buses (June 20, 1972).

Mid 1972: Begin final design criteria and standards procedures and prepare Environmental Analysis Statement.

Early 1973: Complete major improvements to the surface bus operations; receive first shipment of new, air-conditioned buses.

Mid 1973: Begin acquisition of rapid rights-of-way and begin implementing park-and-ride facilities.

Early 1974: Begin system construction.

Early 1977: Open the East-West Line . . . for revenue service; open the South Line . . . for revenue service; open the Tucker-North DeKalb and East Atlanta busways.

Mid 1977: Open the entire Central Line and the Northeast Line to the Lenox Station and the North Atlanta busway for revenue service.

Early 1978: Extend the East Line . . . ; the West Line . . . ; the
South Line to the Airport station; and the Northeast Line to the
Brookhaven Station for revenue service.

Early 1979: Complete construction of the system by extending
the Northeast Line to the Doraville Station; the Northwest Line
to the Northside Drive Station and the Southwest Branch to the
College Park Station [*Passenger Transport,* 1973b: 4].

Washington Metropolitan Area Transit Authority

The Washington (D.C.) Metropolitan Area Transit Authority, approved in the fall of 1966 but delayed in its
financial planning until a favorable vote on its referenda two
years later is the first of the MTAs to involve more than one
state. It is multimodal, and interstate. Philadelphia is situated
along a river, the Delaware, that divides two states, Pennsylvania and New Jersey, but its activities are confined within
Pennsylvania. Interstate transportation is cared for by
another special public authority, the Delaware River Port
Authority. The New York metropolitan area extends into
three States, New York, New Jersey, and Connecticut, but
the New York MTA is chartered only in New York State as
its components are New York City and the seven commuter
counties of New York State. In the cases of both Philadelphia
and New York, the isolation of the "regional" MTA to one
state is illogical, but interstate compacts that would be
needed, provoke all kinds of legal intricacies. In fact, Mayor
Lindsay had confined his ill-fated proposal for transportation
coordination simply to New York *City,* without even the
inclusion of the New York State commuter counties, for fear
of the legal implications that even that would entail. His
thought was that the city might first put its house in order,
and, only then, think of extending its control outward.

Washington, D.C., was in a somewhat more favorable position when it sought to frame a regional M.T.A. For some
reason, regional activity is accepted in the counties surrounding the nation's capital. One reason may be that there is

a more homogeneous ambience in those suburban units through the fact that so many of the residents have the same employer—the federal government. Still another reason may be found in an unrecognized recoiling from the influence of the same federal Government, in which the local governments join together to compensate. At any rate, in both of the states on either side of Washington, there had been, and still were in 1966, transit commissions. The Washington Suburban Transit Commission embraced two key commuter counties in Maryland, Montgomery and Prince Georges; and in Virginia, on the other side, the Northern Virginia Transportation Commission, Fairfax and Arlington counties as well as the cities of Alexandria, Fairfax, and Falls Church. There was prior recognition, therefore, of regional action and for transportation. For whatever reason, the referenda on bond issues for the WMATS, commonly referred to as "Metro," were approved on their first try in November 1968. The formula on the basis of which payments would be expected, had been worked out with the two regional agencies and the city. It was based on the following factors: the largest percentage for the amount of construction; the next largest for the quality of service; and equal percentages for the source of the rides and the projected population of each area by the year 1990. Amounts owed by each unit would be predicated on the degree that each of these elements affected it. The money is being raised by additional taxation by the units, which means, again, a further burden on property owners. There was a difference in regard to the proportions for each factor between the two regions, but the principle was accepted by both.

These assessments alone could not have served to make feasible the construction of the subway. Help was needed from the beginning from the Congress. This was to be in two forms: first a direct grant of money from Congress; and, then, the guarantee of much of the bond issue by the United States government to help support its sale in the open market. There was very real doubt that fares and other charges could provide enough money to repay the obligations. Aid of both kinds was forthcoming from Congress, but only after a delay of some months. Congress withheld legislative approval until the City Council of the District of Columbia agreed to the construction of an automobile bridge across the Potomac into Virginia, and of a new freeway from the Maryland side. Opponents of the congressional stalling charged that Congress was "holding the Washington Metro hostage for the highway lobbies." Leaders for the black residents in the District argued against the freeway on the fear that it would cut through black residential sections of the city. Certain businessmen supported the plan for the bridge and freeway. The stalemate was made the more difficult to resolve because it was accepted by many as a test of strength between the Congress, on the one hand, and the City Council, on the other, as the District of Columbia had just been granted the right to have its own Council after Congress had run its local affairs throughout its history. The City Council finally agreed to the construction of the two projects but with the understanding that it could seek an alternate route for the freeway so that it would do the least damage to residential areas. Other opposition from within the Congress focused on the charge that Congress' action would constitute unfair treatment vis-à-vis other metropolitan centers not so favored. The District of Columbia's own share of the costs had been held up by congressional inaction, as that body had to grant the District the right to assume the obligation and make payments.

The 98-mile subway was one of the longest ever to be constructed at one time in the world. Other systems, of course, are longer but have been built in sections. The London subway, for instance, extends for 257 route miles.

Beginning at 2 o'clock in the morning, January 14, 1973, the Metro started its take-over of the four major bus companies in the area: in all, some "1,700 buses carrying some 128.3 million passengers over 47.1 million route miles" and, underscored, "at a net loss of $628,700 yearly" (*Passenger Transport*, 1973a). The federal government agreed to pay $70.3 million, and the eight political participants of the

WMATA $35.2 million of the costs of purchase and improvements. Riders were handed cards right after the takeover by the Authority, which read, in part:

> Welcome aboard. This is YOUR bus. You and all the people of the region own it because of action by citizens, the Congress and President Nixon. . . . As the weeks go by, the buses will get cleaner, maintenance will improve, and telephone information service will get better. . . . Hang in there. Improvements are in sight (2/5/73).

The United States Department of Transportation signed a contract with London Transport for consultancy service, particularly by the latter's retired and serving personnel, with the Washington, D.C. Metropolitan Area, with the aim to prepare "an action plan for improving transport systems" there. Subsequently, this service has been extended to other American cities, as well as to already existing, or new, assignments for London Transport consultants in Melbourne, Toronto, Montreal, Johannesburg, Helsinki, and cities in France (London Transport Executive, 1972: 25). The same year, the London Transport Executive Association, with Barton-Ashman Incorporated, published a book, *Action Plan for Improvement in Transportation Systems in Large U.S. Metropolitan areas* (National Technical Information Service, 1972).

(PROPOSED) CHICAGO REGIONAL TRANSPORTATION AGENCY

The most novel proposal for an MTA is found in recommendations not as yet implemented that came in the report of the Governor's Transportation Task Force for Northeastern Illinois in 1973. The agency would be known, appropriately, as the Chicago Regional Transportation Agency, and would coordinate various modes of travel in the city of Chicago and its six commuter counties. Referred to as an "authority district," the CRTA was thought to be the best type of organization to incorporate the following features:

> Be a single agency in order to provide the best mechanism for regional coordination of modes, fares, routes, and scheduling, and for achieving maximum efficiency through elimination of duplicative or uneconomic services and facilities.
>
> Have responsibility for performing those functions which are crucial for achieving regionalization and which can best be performed in a centralized manner: e.g., marketing; fare schedule and route coordination; research and planning; and determination of capital investment priorities.
>
> Provide suburban interest with sufficient local control over suburban service and the city of Chicago sufficient control over city service.
>
> Provide a means of stabilizing the present labor situation between city and suburban transit services so as not to make the suburban services completely uneconomic. Provide for contracting for services through 'purchase of service' agreements. It should *not* mandate the purchase of private systems since each purchase may not be in the best interest of the Regional Transportation Agency, hence the public [Governor's Transportation Task Force, 1973: 83].

The uniqueness of these purposes lies in the extent of the use of the "purchase of service" technique. Such a device has been used by other MTAs, such as SEPTA, for the shoring up of commuter railroads. The Chicago Regional Transportation Agency, however, would rely much more extensively on it for various modes of transportation in the six-County region. Other than for the operating of the buses, which would be purchased from private companies, the CRTA would contract out for services from the Chicago Transit Authority, which would be left intact as a separate special Authority; from the commuter railroads; and from any other modes, or the same ones, for special services, such as those for the aged or infirm. The contracts would include not only capital investments, which had been the backbone of the more common special authorities, but, as well, operating costs:

> To make these capital programs more effective, the RTA should be given sole responsibility in the region for applying for mass transportation grants. Assuming that some source of operating funding must also be provided in order to preserve and improve transit services in the region, the RTA should be given responsibility for distributing such funds through operating subsidies tied to "purchase of services" agreements (which could include incentive features for improving transit service) [Governor's Transportation Task Force, 1973: 84].

The overall policy for the region would be determined by a governing board of eight members and a chairman. Representation would be predicated on "the area's political jurisdictions based on population in a form of constituent representation roughly in accord with the one-man-one-vote principle" (Governor's Transportation Task Force, 1973: 91). This would work out as shown in Table 2.

Nominations would be made by the constituent political jurisdictions, and appointments by the governor. "(T)he preferred method is to give the governor final responsibility for

TABLE 2
PROPOSED REPRESENTATION FOR THE CHICAGO RTA

	Number of Appointments	Regional Representation (in percent)
City of Chicago	3	50
Suburban Cook County, DuPage County	2	33.3
Kane, Lake, McHenry, Will Counties	1	16.7
At Large (including Chairman)	3	100.0
Total	9	100.0

appointing all board members. This fixes accountability. The governor is the only general government official elected by all citizens within the region, and these citizens represent fully seventy percent of the state-wide constituency" (Governor's Transportation Task Force, 1973: 93-94). The generalist was to prevail: "The Board members should not be specifically required to possess special skills or qualifications other than the capacity to represent their constituency."

The suggestion was that the board of directors should maintain an "arms length" relationship with the organizations of transportation with which it would be dealing, even to the extent of "a healthy adversary relationship." To make this attitude possible, the recommendation was for a regional management group to be interposed between the board of directors and the operating units. This would be a "staff" of "competent professionals, performing fiscal, technical, managerial, program and other analytical assignments for the Board" (Governor's Transportation Task Force, 1973: 91).

There is something reminiscent here in the structure of governor, board of directors, regional management group, and four operating units (Chicago Transit Authority, Commuter Railroads, Surburban and Satellite City (Bus) Systems, and Special Services), of the organization under the British Transport Act of 1947, which had had minister, National Transport Commission, and six Executives (railways, road haulage, road passenger transport, hotels and catering, docks and inland waterways, and London passenger transport [which soon had been reduced to four]). The interposition of the regional management group, unless its relationships to the board on the one side, and to the operating units, on the other, were carefully spelled out, could lead to the same sort of unnecessary overlapping of responsibilities as it did with the British interposition of the National Transport Commission.

The funds necessary for the purchase of services would come from additional taxation from people in the six-county region of CRTA, probably through a combination of special taxes. "An additional motor fuel tax and a regional income tax might provide the most advantageous approach":

Administration of an income tax should present few problems. Collection could be facilitated through use of a piggy-back surcharge mechanism which is processed at the same time that state returns are processed. . . . Other features of this tax, which add to its attractiveness, are a strong growth rate and limited regressivity when compared with a sales tax or motor fuel tax. The vigorous growth rate of this tax indicates that it would remain a viable revenue source to meet changing conditions in the future. The feature of limited regressivity presents an opportunity to shift some burden of financing from lower income classes to those more able to bear the burden [Governor's Transportation Task Force, 1973: 58-59].

M.T.A. Characteristics

The metropolitan, or regional, transportation authorities were coming by the early 1970s in varied shapes and forms. In view of the fact that they were differentiated from the thousands of special authorities that had developed since the 1930s by their method of finance, it was that factor that produced the greatest variety among their provisions. As these new MTAs broke away from subservience to the revenue bond, and sought other financial sources, as they now have to do to coordinate revenue-producing modes with deficit activities, they were experimenting with widely diversified forms of income. The MBTA, of the Boston region, drew on a statewide cigarette tax, with considerable support from assessments against its 79 cities and towns based on their use of the services; SEPTA, in the Philadelphia area, had no additional tax sources allowed it, and therefore had to depend on contributions from its constituent units of local government, as well as on grants from the state and federal governments. SEMTA, with its center in Detroit, was to continue with the former method of special authorities of the revenue bond insofar as possible, but then each of its constituent local governments (the six counties) was to be assessed on the basis of a per-capita amount. Again, as more money was needed, an increase in the gasoline tax also was added.

MARTA, of the city of Atlanta and two Georgia counties, was granted the right to a special sales tax within the region, as well as a large federal grant. The New York MTA was expected from the beginning to count heavily on state help, and began its operations by dint of $1 billion received from a $2.5 billion bond issue by the state after a statewide referendum. Two succeeding bond issue referenda were voted down decisively by the state's citizens, however, indicating that this resource was not unlimited. The WMATA of the nation's capital and surrounding counties and cities was financed by constituent appropriations, determined by a formula of population and use of services, as well as by a very large federal grant. And the proposed CRTA, of Chicago and its six counties, was to put together a package of regional taxation, probably centering on income and motor fuel taxes. When one examines this overall picture of the MTA's groping for funds—from cigarette taxes, constituent assessments with various formulae, gasoline taxes, sales tax, state bond referenda, federal grants, and possibly now income and motor-fuel taxes—one better can understand the sheer simplicity of the revenue-bond-user-charge device that had given rise to some 9,000 special authorities throughout the United States. He can appreciate, also, however, how that method, dependent as it was on profitable ventures as epitomized by the automobile, had set back the parallel development of mass transit, until now these billion dollar expenditures had become a matter of urgent necessity.

M.T.A. and London Transport Board Similarities

Although their flexibility, in all aspects, except for their basic intermodal, regional, characteristics, makes generalization dangerous, it is of interest to attempt to compare the features of the group of MTAs to those of the London Transport Board of 1963, as they were operating during the decade of the 1960s as unwitting counterparts. The numbered categories below were suggested at the beginning of this chapter, as those descriptive of the London Board. In lettered notes under each are suggestions as to the comparisons with the American MTAs:

1. The involvement of the board in the planning process, giving it genuine policy-making powers, but with a clear line of accountability to the minister.

    (a) The MTAs clearly were expected to be policy makers in regard to transportation in their areas. The word, itself, was used in legislation establishing the MTA. In the statute for the New York MTA, for example, the purposes of the Authority are described, in part, as "to develop and implement a unified mass transportation policy for such district" (sec. 1264 2.).

    (b) The line between the chief executive officer, the governor of the state, and the MTA was not nearly so clearly drawn as was that between the minister and the London Transport Board, but it was beginning to become visible. For one thing, the state had come very much into the picture of the MTA financing now that sources other than revenue-bond-user-charge avenues were needed. The power of the purse string was beginning to assert itself. For another, President Nixon was insisting on a new role for the states in the "New Federalism" that he had adopted as a motto, and federal funds were starting to funnel through the office of the governor rather than, as in the past, directly from federal departments to special-purpose authorities within the states. As a concomitant of the formation of the MBTA, in Massachusetts, for example, there was provided for, in the same legislation that made the MBTA possible, the Bureau of Transportation and Development, and a Director of Transportation Planning and Development, as "the principal source of transportation planning in the commonwealth" (sec. 3A). Departments of Transportation, on the state level, were organized in many states. A number of experts on special-purpose authorities in the United States had come to the conclusion that the most effective means of accountability for them was through the office of the chief executive, meaning, in most states, the office of the governor.

2. The requirement that revenues were to cover costs of the board's functions.

    (a) Statutory requirements for the MTAs continued to insist, in most instances, that operational costs be covered by the fares charged, in the interest of efficiency and economy. A United States senator from Colorado, for example, feared that national assistance for operations would be tantamount to subsidizing "the worst systems, the worst management, the worst operation, the worst overloading of personnel—everything that is bad about the operation of any system" (*Passenger Transport*, 1972a: 8). The British and American attitudes seemed similar at this point. In both countries, operating costs were expected to be borne by the special-purpose unit, but with a growing suspicion in both that this practice was rapidly becoming unfeasible. The British continued to insist on total costs of special authorities being covered by tolls and charges in general, while actually winking at subsidies where it was becoming crystal clear that such increased fares would be self-defeating. The Americans had come to expect with the MTAs, that operating expenditures were to be covered by the user charges but generally not the capital obligations.

3. The board's right to borrow for capital expenditures either from the minister or from "any other person."

    (a) There was growing concern in America over the competitive nature of special-authority borrowing, geared as it was to the open market, in a contest with other tax-exempt bonds from general-purpose governments, and with the bonds of private corporations. Talk was heard of a possible state fund where the state would do the bonding for all of its subdivisions, including special authorities; and also of a federal bonding fund where that level would assume the responsibility.

        The United Kingdom's use of pooled borrowing for its smaller units of government, and for its public corporations, was slow to catch the eye of the American public, as it was fought by the bonding investment interests. The MTAs continued to exercise the right to borrow through revenue bonds, wherever possible, and only then resort to help from other sources. In the case of holding company organizations of the MTAs, such as that of the New York MTA, where former units with bonding powers had been taken under its umbrella, the individual units continued to have the right to bond. In fact, one of the principal reasons for their inclusion as intact entities within the holding-company type of special authorities was that they still had highly favorable ratings in the bond market, and/or still had bond issues outstanding. In the case of the New York MTA, the MTA, itself, as a holding company special authority could issue bonds in its own name, or its subordinate units, such as the New York City Transit Authority and the Triborough Bridge and Tunnel Authority could issue bonds. The TBTA continued to be relied on by the MTA, after its formation, because of the high ratings it had, and the correlative low interest on its bonds in the market.

4. The small numbers on the board, four-nine persons, with a chairman and vice-chairman, all appointed by the minister, and after consultation with the chairman.

As part of the new influence of the state in regard to the special MTAs, the governor was given far more of a hand in the appointment of the members, rather than have this done by the local units of government, although there is anything but unanimity in practice. For example:

(a) In the Boston area MBTA, the governor named all five members of the board after consultation with the groups represented. He did not have this control over the Advisory Board, however, which had strong power.

(b) In Philadelphia region's SEPTA, the governor had only one of the eleven appointments to make.

(c) In Detroit, the governor appointed only three of the nine members of SEMTA as the other six were chosen by the Council of Governments.

(d) In New York's MTA, all eleven members were appointed by the governor, although three were nominated by the mayor of New York City.

(e) In both Atlanta's MARTA and the District of Columbia's WMATA, constituent representation resulted in the naming of representatives by the local governing bodies concerned.

(f) In the proposed Chicago Regional Transportation Authority, all nine appointments would fall to the governor, with nominations by the constituent groups.

5. The composition of the board from among certain areas of experience, such as "transport, industrial, commercial or financial matters, administration, applied science, or the organization of workers."

(a) Persons were selected for the MTAs usually to represent collectively the area, as a whole, or its constitutent units. Recommended backgrounds generally were related to the fields of transportation, including its financing, but they varied all the way from the MBTA suggestion for "one experienced in transportation, one a member of organized labor who shall be a member of a national or international labor organization, and one experienced in administration and finance," to the stipulation by the recommended Chicago RTA, that:

> Persons holding other government positions should not be barred from Board membership. Appointments to the board should be based solely on the merits of each nominee. The Board members should not be specifically required to possess special skills or qualifications other than the capacity to represent their constituency [Governor's Transportation Task Force, 1973: 94].

6. The selection of board members who are familiar with the region of the board,

(a) Requirements that members live in the region are almost universal in the MTAs. Occasionally ex officio members from state offices are included in the board, and they, of course, may not live in the region.

7. The stress on "efficiency, economy and safety" in connection with the operational activities of the board.

(a) The similar insistence of the MTAs on this prime characteristic of the special government has been discussed above, under number (2).

8. Multimodal coverage of transportation

(a) This was one of the required characteristics for inclusion here as an MTA. None of the listed MTAs controlled fewer than two modes, and the usual combination was that of rail mass transit and buses, commonly in a main line-feeder type of coordination.

9. Regional jurisdiction over a broad area
   (a) The clear pattern that has emerged with the MTAs is that of the inclusion within it of the entire core city and its commuter counties. SEPTA involved Philadelphia and four Counties; SEMTA, Detroit and six counties; New York MTA, New York City and seven counties; MARTA, Atlanta and two counties; WMATA, Washington, D.C. two counties in Maryland, two counties in Virginia, with three cities in Virginia. The recommendation for the CRTA is for the inclusion of Chicago with six counties. The one major exception of course is that of the MBTA, which includes Boston and 78 cities and towns, but this is attributable to the tradition of the small-town, and the correlative weakness of county government in Massachusetts. The pattern for the MTA is that of city and surrounding commuter counties, with the city and counties being enveloped in their entirety rather than sections of them.

10. Interrelationships with the minister
    (a) As has been noted above under (1)(b), the nexus between the American MTA and the governor seems to be strengthening, but is by no means a universal characteristic.

11. Its ability to resort to funds from the government, when it became obvious that tolls, in themselves, would not suffice, without a sacrifice of effectiveness in the carrying out of the transport functions.
    (a) As has been considered above, under (2) and (3), the MTAs, having broken with the dependence on the bond-holders now are expected to find other means of support, and among the recognized channels are those of the state government and, increasingly, the federal government. This is true today for capital funds, and there is a trend toward recognition of the need for help, particularly from the federal government, for operating costs.

12. Its independence from the bonding investment complex, even with its powers of borrowing for capital expenditures.

(a) This freedom has come, of course, to be the trademark of the MTA as contrasted to the former special public authorities. The distinctive change has been noted by the *Weekly Bond Buyer* (Heffernan, 1972):

> The retirement of Austin J. Tobin [in March, 1972] as executive director of the Port of New York Authority after 45 years of service with the bi-State agency may well signalize the end of an era—the "era of the authorities." There is, of course, no shortage of public authorities set up as subdivisions of local government to fulfill certain special functions. But the "era of the authorities" represented by the New York Port Authority's multi-billion-dollar complex of public investments is something else—incomparably so. For such a tremendous public investment in airports, tunnels, bridges and bus, marine, truck and grain terminals to have been administered efficiently and innovatively for nearly half a century on a basis independent of both politics and public taxation is something for which there is no precedent in modern history. It is not likely to happen soon again. Coincident with the Tobin retirement, heavy clouds engendered by mounting political pressures, are finally gathering around the Port Authority.

These political pressures had been expressed by a New York State Assemblyman, G. Oliver Koppell, in 1971: "The time has come to recognize what distinguishes an authority from a private corporation. The Port Authority must see its role first and foremost as a 'public' authority, and only secondarily as a 'revenue bond' authority" (*The New York Times,* 1971c). Similar sentiments were being expressed here and there. In a judicial decision upholding the creation by the state of New Jersey of the New Jersey Sports and Exposition Authority, also in 1971, Chief Justice Weintraub, while declaring its formation constitutional, had issued this warning about extreme powers granted the new Authority:

> It is axiomatic that the police power of the State cannot be bargained away. The term, police power, in its largest usage, embraces all the powers of government other than eminent domain and the power to tax. It probably is true that some part of the police power, as thus broadly defined, may be bargained away as an unavoidable incident of a contract required in the public interest.... [A] legislature [however] cannot contract away the power to protect the public safety, health and morals, and the power thus inalienable embraces the subject of racing and gambling.... Hence chapter 137 cannot obligate the State not to abolish racing or related gambling. The purchaser of bonds or notes are chargeable with that understanding and may not maintain either that the State is thus restrained [by the provisions protecting bondholders of the new Authority].... [New Jersey Sports & Exposition Authority v. Joseph M. McCrane, et al.].

From investors, politicians, and judges, there was emerging a new interpretation of the quasi-public, quasi-private concepts of the special public authority, with a growing consensus that its public side must gain precedence over its private inclinations, which had been overexaggerated through the forced dependence of the special authority on the revenue bonds as its sole means of support. The MTAs were leading the way into this new focus on the special public authority for transportation. They were converging, without realizing it, on the role of the public corporation in the United Kingdom, which, from the date of the legislation for the Port of London Authority in 1908, and the modern London Passenger Transport Board in 1933, had favored the public "lien" emphasis.

Chapter 7

FRAGMENTATION OF THE PLANNING PROCESS

One negative comparison between the metropolitan transportation authorities of America and the London Transport Board of the 1960s is that neither of them had been able to carry out the planning functions expected of them. Provisions in the state statutes setting up the MTAs had anticipated a planning role. The word "plan" commonly appears among the powers and duties of the MTAs in general. The New York Metropolitan Transportation Authority, to cite one, is required to "make plans, surveys and studies necessary, convenient or desirable to the effectuation of the purposes and powers of the authority and to prepare recommendations in regard thereto" (sec. 1265, par. 10). SEMTA duties in the Detroit area were stated as follows: "An authority is a public benefit agency and instrumentality of the state . . . for the purpose of planning . . . transportation facilities." Other functions, of course, were added. And for the suggested Chicago RTA, the Task Force has urged that it have "responsibility for performing those functions which are crucial for achieving regionalization and which can best be performed in a centralized manner: e.g. ... research and planning..." as among other responsibilities. Indeed, specialized planning, as that for transportation, had become recognized, and lent itself to this function of the special governments.

Expectations of planning by the London Transport Board also had been explicit in its statutory requirements:

> It shall be the duty of the London Board in the exercise of their powers under this Act to provide or secure the provision of an adequate and properly coordinated system of passenger transport for the London Passenger Transport Area, and to have due regard to efficiency, economy and safety of operation as respects the services and facilities provided by them [sec. 7 (1)]. The London Board shall cooperate with the Railways Board for the purpose of ensuring that the services provided by the London Board are properly co-ordinated with the railway services [sec. 7 (2)]. Subject to this section, each Board shall have power to develop their land in such manner as they think fit [sec. 11 (1)]. Each of the Boards shall from time to time submit to the Minister proposals as to the manner in which their powers of construction, manufacture and production ... are to be exercised [sec. 13 (4)].

As has been referred to earlier, special-purpose governments, in both the United States and the United Kingdom had been the only governments capable of regional planning, as they could expand outward with changing needs. They had become regional or metropolitan planning units, at least for their particular functions, long before general governments realized the problem this was to pose for them. In the United States, the emphasis on planning by the special authorities had become more entrenched through their role as the borrowers for capital construction in the region. As they proposed giant bridges, tunnels, turnpikes, sewerage layouts, and the like, they, of necessity, had to plan for their construction, determine the feasible sites from an engineering standpoint, and plan for their use in order to recapture their borrowed funds through the fees that users would pay for the facilities. As the areawide providers of capital funding, therefore, they had quite naturally assumed the role of areawide planners.

The disadvantages of special-purpose governments in the planning process are apparent. First of all, the requirements imposed on them in Britain and America that their revenues must cover their costs, at least of operations, has influenced their thinking inevitably toward plans that would best assure income. An analysis in 1972 of the problem by the Greater London Group of the London School of Economics and Political Science explained the British board's concerns this way:

> The railways, in particular, with their heavy annual deficits, were increasingly constrained by the need, as they saw it, to develop the most profitable activities for the future, such as high speed inter-city passenger trains and fast, regular, long-distance freight services. Improvement of London suburban services did not have the same priority. In any case, under the fragmented regional structure of administration which they had adopted, it was difficult for British Railways to concert a policy for such improvement. For London Transport it became increasingly obvious during the 1960s that their obligation to provide an adequate system of passenger transport was in conflict with their financial obligations, and this inherent conflict of obligations acted to inhibit their forward planning [Rhodes, 1972: 276-277].

For the American special authorities, such considerations were even more pressing, as they were foraging about to uncover new sources of income now that they could not depend so much on the user charges that had supported their predecessor special authorities.

In both countries, the fact that the special authorities had control only of certain mass transit modes and their facilities made the very concept of planning a misnomer. It was specialized planning in its most narrow sense, as not even all of the transportation functions were subject to their plans. The complaints in this regard almost echo each other across the Atlantic. The Royal Commission on Local Government in Greater London 1957-60 had found "the present machinery [for traffic management] chaotic, inefficient and totally out of date" (sec. 405). "The present machinery is so confused that it is difficult even to put down on paper a description of what it is, let alone how it works" (sec. 407). "These powers may be fairly termed a jumble of ad hoc provisions, each of them designed from time to time to help paper over the cracks in the administrative structure of traffic management which we have been trying to describe" (sec. 427).

From across the ocean, came almost the same expressions of despair, from mayoral candidate John Lindsay (1965: 3), in 1965:

> In spite of these self-evident facts, there is in our great City no coordination of transportation policy. Not only is coordination of planning and action wholly lacking; there is not even mean-ingful cooperation. And what is even more inexcusable, there is not even an established medium for coordination and coopera-tion. . . . On policy and operations we can no longer afford the ineffectiveness, the quarrels and the waste which characterize the hydra-headed and fragmented monstrosity of the City's trans-portation structure today.

The Greater London Group explained the fragmentation this way:

> Provision of off-street car parks, for example, was largely a borough function; it is true that the GLC [Greater London Council] was given a concurrent power to provide car parks but this was exercisable with the borough's consent or, failing that, with the consent of the Minister. The regulation of parking on the streets, e.g. by means of meters was, before the 1963 Act came into force, a Ministerial responsibility in the London Traffic Area. The Minister could make orders designating parking places both as a result of an application made by a local authority and on his own initiative. The 1963 Act gave the GLC these powers concur-rently with the Minister; applications by a London borough for an order were, however, to be made to the GLC except where they affected a trunk road [Rhodes, 1972: 269].

The Task Force on Transportation Organization in New York City in 1966 reported the same sort of overlapping duties there:

> The Department of Highways designed, constructed, and repaired public roads, streets, and highways, except marginal roads, parkways, and arterial highways, in certain respects; the Department of Marine and Aviation had the lot of constructing, closing, widening and regulating the use of the marginal streets, which, however, were to be maintained by the Department of Highways. The Park Department had the responsibility of regulating the use and construction of all streets within any park or within a distance of 350 feet [Smith, 1969: 129].

Any thought of comprehensive planning in either London or New York under this kind of disintegration was folly. Moreover, in each city, the agency charged with the responsibility for transportation coordination and planning, the London Transport Board, and the Metropolitan Transportation Authority, had no control over the fragmented traffic management and road construction and maintenance described above. Both special Authorities were limited in their coordinative efforts to modes of mass transit, principally rapid rail and bus travel. Each were expected to work out arrangements with the railways, but in both London and New York, railroad administration was itself disorganized and the special Authorities were having extreme difficulties in separating out the functions of the commuter segments of the railways from their intercity and countrywide operations. By coordinated transport activities, therefore, assigned to the London Transport Board, or to the MTAs, were meant a segment of mass transit, in conjunction with a hoped-for working arrangement with commuter railroads, but with no control over the facilities for the automobile. In Great Britain, concerns for automotive travel rested with the minister of transport, local governments, and, for a very large area beyond the boundaries of what was to become the Greater London Council region, the London and Home Counties Traffic Advisory Committee, created in 1924, as an ad hoc agency. In the

United States, highways, tunnels, and bridges for the car had
been supplied by federal, state, and local governments, and,
for the cities, largely by the special public authorities
emanating from the 1930s. In Great Britain, where there was
need for greater emphasis on roads, the traditional focus of
the special authorities on mass transit had come to narrow
their range of vision to the extent that they seemed out of
step with the needs of the times for travel. And in the United
States, where the overwhelming core of the special authorities' movement had been the automobile, the growth of the
MTAs, with their attention to mass transit for the first time,
seemed even the more to segment planning, as these new
giant special authorities found themselves unable to relate to
automotive planning and unable to benefit from the surpluses
from automobile tolls accumulated by the traditional special
units. The London Transport Board and the MTAs both
undertook planning functions under these almost insuperable
handicaps.

By their very nature, special authorities are the least suited
of all units of government to the planning responsibilities.
They are directed by statute to the sole function, or the
closely related functions, for which they were established,
and they are expected to concentrate their expertise on that
one concern. In fact, they are denied the right to apply their
skills to other functions. In this respect they differ most from
the general-purpose governments, which are required to
direct their attention to all the normal expectations of the
citizens, and even to anticipate new ones. In the performance
of their assignments, however, the special governments,
limited to one function, are almost entirely free as to how to
handle that activity. The general-purpose governments are
circumscribed, by laws, as to the methods they may employ
in the handling of their myriad duties. Planning, which en-
visages the interrelated panorama of governmental activities,
requires the purview of the general government in order that
it may fix priorities of needs and interests for any one year.
The assignment of planning to an agency prevented from
taking that overview is totally inconsistent.

Regional planning has come by default. It has been done by the special governments because conventional governments have been unable, or unwilling, to plan. Planning in transportation has been split off even from general land-use planning, because its scope has exceeded that of the local general governments responsible for land use. In the United Kingdom, this transportation planning had made use of greatly extended boundaries about London, including, from 1933 to 1969, the London Transport Area, some 60 miles in length, north and south, and about 36 miles wide east to west. Even the present boundaries of the Greater London Council seem restrictive in comparison. And, in an advisory capacity for traffic management, the bounds of the Homes County Traffic Advisory Committee, almost as expansive as those for the London Transport Area, gave the broader perspective for the same period of time.

The establishment of the Greater London Council area in 1963, however, even though not of the size of the London Transport Area or the region of the Homes County Traffic Advisory Committee, represented a considerable improvement over the delimitations under which the general-purpose governments had had to work, and made possible, for the first time, the kind of comprehensive planning unthinkable for the smaller illogical units of local government that had prevailed in the London area. The 1963 act, which had allocated the functions of government to either the metropolitan, regional, tier, or to the newly drawn boroughs, left a number of ad hoc governments out of either compartment and free to operate as they had. One such unit not enveloped in the tier structure was the London Transport Board of 1962, although the Homes County Traffic Advisory Committee was dissolved. The minister, in 1966, set up the Transport Coordinating Council for London, comprised of representatives of the Greater London Council, British Rail, London Transport, the London boroughs, and the trade unions. The interrelationships among these groups, however, remained awkward. The Greater London Council, heir to some 7,000 miles of roads within Greater London, most of which had been neglected over the years, leaned in its transportation interests to traffic matters for the automobile, even though the Greater London Development Plan of 1969, prepared by the Greater London Council, urged the need for a balanced system of modes of travel. After all, the handling of mass transit still rested largely in the hands of the London Transport Board and the railways boards. The London Traffic Survey, completed in 1964 and 1966, revealed that on "the average working day there are about seven million journeys to or from work in London. About two-and-a-half million are to or from the Central Area (roughly the area within a line joining the main line railway termini). Well over half of the work journeys to the Central Area are by train—many over long distances—and about a quarter by bus. Only about ten percent are by car" (Ministry of Transportation, 1968: 3). Nevertheless, the Greater London Council's preoccupation in transportation continued to shade to road traffic, and the awkward division of labor among the GLC, London Transport Board, Railways Boards, and the minister and the boroughs continued for the first five years after the GLC had become legal on April 1, 1965.

TRANSPORT ACTS
1968, 1969, 1971

Finally, on January 1, 1970, the responsibilities for London Transport were assumed by the Greater London Council. The government explained this 1970 action as a logical step following on the formation of the Greater London Council five years earlier:

London has already gone a long way towards the degree of unification which is now so necessary in urban passenger transport. And it has a local government structure which makes possible the logical further step—to the fullest possible integration of all forms of public transport, traffic measures, and development of the most important roads; and their close association with land use planning. In the Government's views, these are matters where the primary responsibility should be local [Ministry of Transport, 1968: 1].

Three weaknesses in the planning process were discerned (Ministry of Transport, 1968: 6-7). The fact that

1. there was no single body responsible for planning in London that could "broaden the range of interests considered and to seek out new—and perhaps unorthodox—alternative methods of meeting their needs." Its illustration was the plight of the pedestrian, who might benefit by his separation from moving vehicles, through "walkways, moving pavements or some other form of 'passenger transport.' "
2. Inadequate "co-ordination between those who provide public transport and those who determine . . . the traffic and pricing environment in which public transport operates."
3. The "arm's length" distance between transport planning and land use planning.

To decentralize the planning process for transportation, to the control of the Greater London Council, Passenger Transport Acts of 1968, 1969, and 1971 provided for a new relationship between special-purpose and general-purpose governments. The emphases were on giving comprehensive planning functions to the general-purpose government, the Greater London Council, which could relate transport and land use planning, and on the regional basis of the Greater London Council area. To implement those plans, the Executive form of special government, first used for transportation with the Executives under the Transport Act of 1947, was reinstituted. One principal difference between the Executive of the 1968 act as against those earlier agencies by the same name of 1947 lay in the fact that the former Executive was totally dependent on the national British Transport Commission, where the new Executive was to serve under the Greater London Council. The difference should be noted carefully. The Executive was to take over the duties for bus and Underground services that had been the province of the

London Transport Board. "The Executive," the government explained, "will in fact be very broadly in the same relation to the Council as the London Transport Board are to the Minister of Transport." In other words, the whole process has been moved down one step toward the local area. The minister, representing general-purpose government, had worked through the special unit, the London Transport Board. All this now moves down. The Greater London Council, representing general-purpose government, now will work through the London Transport Executive. To see it still another way, comprehensive planning, under the new organizational structure, now becomes the function of the general-purpose government, the GLC, and the day-by-day operations are to be managed by the Executive. Both planning and operations are so closely interrelated in practice that they can be stated accurately only as emphases, rather than separate roles, and that intimacy is to be recognized by placing them both down in the area of the Greater London Council. The much more extensive area of the London Transport Board that had been used since 1933 no longer would be in effect. Transportation planning would extend only over the area of the Greater London Council. Operations, under the Executive, "should in principle be Greater London" also, although the Executive was to follow its functions where they might lead and there would be "no formal mileage or geographical limits to their powers to operate transport services" (Ministry of Transport, 1968: 11, 10).

This arrangement reflects the "fluid-boundary" capabilities of the special units that can provide flexibility in the more rigid-boundary tradition of regular governments. For the first time, the planning and development of public transport, major highways, location of industry and housing are brought together under a single metropolitan government. The unremunerative public transport services within Greater London also would be subsidized by the Greater London Council as well as by individual London boroughs. The central government still will provide most of the money for approved capital construction projects, while the Greater London

Council will provide the rest, with London Transport having only to cover its operating costs, if it can do so.

The relative responsibilities of the Greater London Council and its Transport Executive were defined clearly in the Transport (London) Act 1969:

(I)t shall be the general duty of the Greater London Council . . . to develop policies, and to encourage, organise and, where appropriate, carry out measures, which will promote the provision of integrated, efficient and economic transport facilities and services for Greater London [Part I, sec. 1].

(I)t shall be the general duty of the Executive to exercise and perform their functions, in accordance with principles from time to time laid down or approved by the [Greater London] Council, in such manner as, in conjunction with the Railways Board and the Bus Company (National), and with due regard to efficiency, economy and safety of operation, to provide and secure the provision of such public passenger transport services as best meet the needs for the time being of Greater London [Part II, sec. 5(1)].

The Executive was to be the creature of the Greater London Council, the general-purpose government. Its chairman and all its members were to be appointed by the council "from among persons who appear to the Council to have had wide experience of, and shown capacity in, transport, industrial, commercial or financial matters, administration, applied science, or the organisation of workers" (Part II, sec. 4[2]).

The London region was the only conurbation in the United Kingdom to have organized a metropolitanwide form of government. The Transport Act of 1968, however, anticipated other such developments. It provided for the creation of Passenger Transport Authorities elsewhere in Great Britain, until areawide general-purpose governments should be established, and, under the Authorities, there would be Passenger Transport Executives. The same structure, then, that had been devised for Greater London—overall policy making and planning decentralized from the minister down to the metropolitan area, and professional operations in the hands of a Transport Executive was made available for England, Scotland, and Wales, at the discretion of the minister. Lacking general-purpose governments on the scale this would necessitate, however, a two-tier system of special government would be instituted until such areawide governments should be formed. It is of interest in this regard to note the traditional role of special agencies acting in default of regional efforts by local general-purpose governments. The act (sec. 9[1] [a] [b]) stipulated:

> If in the case of any area in Great Britain outside Greater London the Minister considers it expedient for the purpose of securing the provision of a properly integrated and efficient system of public passenger transport to meet the needs of that area, then . . . the Minister may by order designate that area for the purposes of this part of the Act by such name as may be specified in the order and shall by that order provide for the establishment of . . . a Passenger Transport Authority . . . (and) a Passenger Transport Executive

These selected regions would be known as "designated areas." The minister subsequently designated the areas of:

1. South-East Lancashire–North-East Cheshire (SELNEC) of greater Manchester
2. Merseyside (greater Liverpool)
3. West Midlands (greater Birmingham)
4. Tyneside (greater Newcastle-upon-Tyne)
5. Glasgow Area

LOCAL GOVERNMENT ACT 1972

By the Local Government Act of 1972, which reorganized local governments throughout England and Wales, effective in 1974, one category recognized was that of the metropolitan county. The act stipulated that each "metropolitan county shall become a passenger transport area for the purposes of... the Transport Act 1968, and the Passenger Transport Authority for that area shall be the county council" (sec. 202[1]). The act added the other element in the two-tier structure for transportation, providing that, "in relation to each metropolitan county the Secretary of State shall... make provision for the establishment of a Passenger Transport Executive" (sec. 202[4]).

This act adds two more Executives for: (1) South Yorkshire Metropolitan County; and (2) West Yorkshire Metropolitan County. The metropolitan counties, for the most part, would have the same boundaries as the designated areas, and, therefore, the Executive, serving the Passenger Transport Authority in the interim period until the metropolitan counties should come into existence, simply would be transferred from the Authority to the metropolitan county: "The Secretary of State may by order... provide that the Passenger Transport Executive for an existing passenger transport area shall become the Executive for the relevant metropolitan county" (Part IX, sec. 202[5][a]). This was expected to occur on April 1, 1974, for England, and sometime the following year for the Glasgow "West" region of Scotland. In Scotland the term, metropolitan county, was not to be used, but a large region had been selected as the "designated area" centering on Glasgow, and would become the areawide governing body. The government explained that "(o)nly a regional authority covering the whole area will have the broad perspective and the essential resources of finance, manpower and land to cope with them effectively" (Secretary of Scotland, 1971: 16).

The final picture then, authorizes metropolitan counties as the Authority for transportation in the area, each with a Passenger Transport Executive, and a region, for the Glasgow area, with its Passenger Transport Executive. These, in all would include the metropolitan areas centering on London, Manchester, Liverpool, Birmingham, Newcastle-upon-Tyne, Sheffield, Bradford and Leeds, and Glasgow.

The interim Passenger Transport Authorities, "filling in" for the metropolitan county until it should be created—or, preparing the way for it—were to have members appointed by the councils of the local governments within the area, as the minister would designate, and not more than one-sixth of the total appointed directly by the minister "from among persons appearing to him to have special knowledge or experience which would be of value to the Authority in the exercise of their functions" (Schedule 5, part I sec. [1]). The minister would name one of the members as its chairman. The selection of members to be appointed by the local governments within the area could be apportioned according to the weighting of the rates (taxes) paid. The Tyneside Authority, by way of illustration of its size, had 19 members and 17 alternates; the Merseyside Authority, 27 members and 25 alternates; the West Midlands, 27 members; and SELNEC, 29 members. The Executives were to have a director general and "not less than two nor more than eight other members, appointed by the Authority after consultation with the Director General" (Transport Act 1968, Part II 9[1][b]). Members serving as councilmen of any constituent local government were ineligible for appointment to the Executive. The principal task of the first year for the Authority and the Executive was to be that, for one thing, of the preparation of a "statement setting out in general terms the policies which the Authority and the Executive intend to follow, and any action they have taken or propose to take" (Transport Act 1968, Part II, sec. 18[1]). One of the main sections of this statement was to be the nature of any agreements the Executive had made with the railways or with the National Bus Company (or Scottish Group) in its area. This was to be one of its most difficult assignments, as here a local metropolitan area was directed to coordinate local transportation with the activities of national undertakings, railway and bus. The Joint Policy Statement issued by the Tyneside Authority and Executive (1970: 17) in September of 1970, for example, singled out this confusion:

Although we will eventually have extensive powers to secure or promote the provision of a properly integrated and efficient system of public passenger transport, the Executive's use of them is likely to be conditioned by the fact that operationally it does not dominate the area. A large proportion of the bus services is operated by the National Bus Company and rail services are provided entirely by British Rail. Thus local transport on Tyneside is heavily dependent on two organisations whose policy and terms of reference are determined at national level.

The Railways Board annual report for the year ending December 31, 1971(9), could point to two achievements in cooperation with the Executives: the starting of work on an inner rail loop connecting central Liverpool with the Wirral section; and the development of a plan with the SELNEC Executive for a tunnel under central Manchester, linking the Victoria and Piccadilly stations. By January of 1973, British Rail had signed a £3 million a year contract with the West Midlands Executive to provide commuter services in the Birmingham area, and a £4.5 million a year contract with SELNEC for similar service in the Greater Manchester area. Negotiations were proceeding with the Tyneside, Merseyside, and Glasgow Executives. The central government subsidized the Executives heavily for such railway contracts, as well as similar arrangements with the bus companies. The Executives otherwise were supposed to depend on fares and local rates (taxes) to keep their transport services budget in balance. Assessments for additional taxes are to be made by the Authority to constituent units in proportion to the amount of their rates (taxes) in the total of rates for the area:

> Any such precept shall be so issued as to require the levying in each rating area [constituent area] falling wholly or partly within the designated area of a rate of such amount in the pound as will produce an amount bearing to the aggregate amount required by the Authority the same proportion as the product of a rate of one penny in the pound for so much of that rating area as falls within the designated area bears to the product of such a rate for the whole of the designated area [Transport Act 1968, Part II, sec. 13(2)].

A segment of the designated area may have special services provided for which only the people therein who benefit most from that service will be assessed.

The Executives are to have considerable freedom in their day-by-day operations. However, for any policy matters they must gain the approval of the Authority (or, subsequently the metropolitan county):

The Executive for a designated area shall submit to the Authority and obtain the Authority's approval of—

a. any proposal for a major reorganisation of any transport services provided within or to and from that area;

b. all annual or other estimates of income and expenditure prepared by the Executive or any subsidiary of theirs;

c. any proposal for the development or extension of any services or facilities provided by the Executive or any subsidiary of theirs or provided in pursuance of arrangements with the Executive which involves a substantial outlay on capital account;

d. any agreement proposed to be entered into by the Executive . . . with the Railways Board for the provision by the Board of any railway passenger services within, or to and from, that area . . .

The Executive shall obtain the approval of the Authority—

a. before making or authorising or consenting to the making of, any alteration in the general level of charges for the transport services or facilities provided by the Executive or any subsidiary of theirs [Transport Act 1968, Part II, sec. 15].

Within two years from the date of the establishment of the Executive, the Executive was charged with the publication of proposals "for the development of the passenger transport system." This was to take cognizance of any local government's plans (Transport Act 1968, Part II, sec. 18[2]). In all respects, therefore, the Passenger Transport Executives were to be professional operating special-purpose agencies, implementing the policy and comprehensive plans of regional general-purpose government. This was a major shift in emphasis in the development of the special-government concept—far more than the British public recognized. "The inception of a greater Glasgow Passenger Transport Authority on October 1," cautioned the Edinburgh *Scotsman* (1972b), "seems likely to be a low-key affair, but it is an event of profound long-term significance for all who live and work in and around Glasgow." Residents of London continued to direct most of their complaints to London Transport, but seemed to be beginning to realize that the main responsibility for defects and deficiencies ultimately rests now with the Greater London Council.

NEW AMERICAN
PLANNING EMPHASIS

The full significance of the change in relative roles of general-purpose and special-purpose agencies for transportation in Great Britain could not be appreciated unless one could understand the confusion in the United States over these very same interrelationships. A purely operational special authority has been very rare in America. The New York City Transit Authority, which had no capital budget at all, but was totally dependent on New York City for its capital construction, was one such operational special authority. However, even in its operations, it was so restricted that its fares could not meet its daily overhead. The Tennessee Valley Authority was solely operational in its early days, when its capital budget for the building of dams and other facilities was chargeable to the whole nation, through the congressional understanding that a weak section of the country anywhere served only to draw down the entire people, and the additional thought that the increased production in the Tennessee Valley made possible by the TVA would add to the gross national product. For the most part, however, the United States had conceived of the special authority as a method by which local governments could borrow money that they otherwise could not do under the restrictive debt ceilings imposed by the states. As the prime borrowers of the money, they came to have the responsibility for determining how it would be spent, and, thereby, almost inadvertently, became the planners for metropolitan areas where they were most used. Their borrowing proclivities tended to overshadow their operational potentialities.

As the British were launching their new approach, in which the overall policy making and planning would be the responsibility of the general-purpose governments, accountable to the electorate, and the special-purpose governments would serve as highly concentrated professional specialists to implement the general government's will, the Americans were beginning to cast eyes in the same direction. The change had come through the sporadic suggestions that perhaps the obligation of contract under the revenue-bond guarantees could be interpreted in another way. Instead of invariably favoring the overprotected bondholder, the thought was beginning to occur, as it had in the United Kingdom, that special governments lie somewhere in between the private and public sectors and they may lean, or be forced to lean, in either direction. The British, from the beginning, had favored their public posture; the Americans, their private possibilities. The latter focus had meant, however, the neglect of the deficit modes of a function, such as transportation, and the elevation of the revenue-producing modes, such as those for the automobile. The sheer breakdown of the commuter railroads, upon which so many Americans depended daily, and the growing concern for the environmental pollution by the car, began to make visible the lack of balance in the modes that prevailed. The immediate outcome was the inception of a new type of special agency, the Metropolitan Transportation Authority, capable of uniting the mass transit functions so that they could, at least, attempt to compete with the private automobile. The next step—that taken by the British in the stripping of their special mass transit authorities of their policy-making and comprehensive-planning prerogatives, has not yet caught hold in America to the extent that it could become crystallized as a political issue.

Signs of concern, under the American system of federalism have come from various parts of the country. In the 1970s disconnected indications could be discerned here and there. Most important, perhaps, was a change in attitude on the part of the federal government. The influential Advisory Commission on Intergovernmental Relations, representing all levels of government in the country, and advising the Congress, began to take a critical look at the disparate federal interest in the special agencies as against the general-purpose elected governments. This preference for dealing with the less complex special units by the Congress and administration, it will be recalled, had had its genesis in the desire to stimulate special public authorities by the New Deal program under President Franklin Roosevelt in 1934. In its annual report of January 1970, the Advisory Commission recommended that the states take a serious look at the problem of special districts within their borders, "making them harder to form and easier to consolidate or eliminate, increasing their 'visibility' and political accountability, and requiring them to coordinate their operations with those of counties and municipalities." It urged the federal government to begin "tidying up the local government landscape by modifying Federal categorical aid programs that encourage special districts" (Advisory Commission on Intergovernmental Relations, 1970: 15).

In a practical implementation of such a viewpoint, the federal administrative agencies began to insist that comprehensive planning rest with areawide general-purpose governments, rather than the special public authorities, even the MTAs. The problem was to find any regional general-purpose governments that had any real meaning and possibilities for implementing their suggestions. Very few could be found. Reliance, instead, was on councils of government, which, at the best, are voluntary associations of local government officials. At least, they are primarily general-purpose, and accountable to the electorate. Under the federal government's spur of the carrot and the stick (federal funds), the Massachusetts Bay Transportation Authority signed an agreement with the Metropolitan Area Planning Council of the Boston area in 1971. The terms provided the following role for the general-purpose planning council:

> Assure that mass transit development programming for the Boston metropolitan area is consistent with overall metropolitan development objectives;
>
> Participate in both ongoing and new major study efforts dealing with metropolitan mass transit and transportation planning;
>
> Collect and analyze data on the impact of the MBTA South Shore extension project;
>
> Assist the MBTA in the preparation of "environmental impact statements" required for all applications for federal transit assistance submitted by the authority;
>
> Evaluate, as an independent third party, transit development projects proposed by the authority, and
>
> Focus on the relationships between transit operations and development proposals in the fields of open space/recreation, conservation, solid waste disposal, water/sewer, housing, and municipal revenue-producing capabilities [National Civic Review, 1971].

The next year, 1972, the directors of the Southeastern Pennsylvania Transportation Authority (SEPTA) also approved an agreement with the regional planning agency of its area, in the Delaware River Valley. SEPTA would continue to conduct transportation planning for its functions, involving as they do, the City of Philadelphia and four counties, but these plans henceforth would have to conform to the much more comprehensive plans of the Delaware Valley Regional Planning Commission. It will be recalled that SEPTA boundaries had confined it to the Philadelphia side of the Delaware River, whereas the metropolitan area had spilled over into New Jersey on the other side. This relationship of SEPTA with the Delaware Valley Regional Planning Commission had

been brought about through a threat by Secretary of Transportation of the United States, John A. Volpe, to cut off
federal transit funds to the area. Secretary Volpe exerted a
similar influence in the actions of the Metropolitan Atlanta
Rapid Transit Authority (MARTA) at the same time. He
announced a grant of $3.2 million for aiding MARTA's
proposed rapid-transit system, but said that the money would
be given to the Atlanta Regional Commission, which would
then make it available to MARTA. "This arrangement,"
according to Secretary Volpe, "is the result of mutual state
and local agency agreements which require all transit planning funds to be channeled through the Atlanta Regional
Commission" (B. Jones, 1972).

Lacking regional general-purpose governments, America
was experimenting with various general-purpose voluntary
associations to give the comprehensive overview for planning
into which the activities of the Metropolitan Transportation
Authorities, now concerned with mass transit, and with its
coordination, could fit. It was a far cry from the British
sweeping reorganization of general-purpose governments,
which had made it possible to delineate more clearly the
relative responsibilities of the general and special governments. The ready expediency of the continued proliferation
of special-purpose authorities each to attempt to meet, individually, one part of the emergency, and the myth of none
of them "costing the taxpayer anything" had made unnecessary in the United States the hard-headed type of thinking
that must come in a reappraisal of the relative responsibilities
of modern government. The British remained one step ahead
of America in its desire to work out these proportions.

Chapter 8

SUMMARY OBSERVATIONS

One way to differentiate the special-purpose governments in the United Kingdom from those in the United States is to refer to the British special agencies as "public" and the American as "quasi-public." In both countries, the special units borrow characteristics from both the public and private sectors. The "quasi" prefix affixed to them in the United States is defined in legal terminology as a word "used to mark a resemblance, and which supposes a difference between the two objects" (Bouvier, 1946: 1008). The British special governments have shown, throughout their development, a decided public responsibility, whereas the American have shaded more toward their private posture. In both countries, they have functioned, however, with a sense of independence that readily distinguishes them as agencies other than those found in the more conventional, general-purpose governments. Proponents of them in the United Kingdom and in the United States, indeed, have singled out their combination of public and private characteristics as peculiar attributes. Professor A. H. Hanson stated that the aim of the British public corporation "is to provide an organizational form through which the reconciliation of commercial freedom with public control may best be facilitated" (Hanson and Walles, 1970: 174). President Franklin D. Roosevelt, who championed their use in the United States, referred to the special public authority as "a corporation clothed with the power of Government but possessed of the flexibility and initiative of a private enterprise," in his message to Congress, April 10, 1933, in support of his proposal for the formation of the Tennessee Valley Authority.

One clear explanation of this distinction between the public orientation of the British public corporation and the "quasi-public" emphasis of the American special public authority lies in the fact that many of the British agencies—almost all of the modern ones—came as vehicles for the nationalized industries, and the American authorities came in large numbers under the New Deal program of general welfare within the free-enterprise system. Be that as it may, the fact is that although in both countries the special public government is expected to be self-sufficient, the British have not cut off their public corporations so decisively from the general-purpose governments as to force them into an alliance with the private investment world as their principal source of support. The American special public authorities, on the other hand, developed so independently of conventional governments as to enable them to be exploited as means to circumvent restrictions, both constitutional and statutory, on public borrowing. This role, encouraged by the federal government, was directed against debt ceilings set by the states, and it was in the states, rather than on the national level, that the great proliferation of the special governments has occurred.

The difference here is a subtle one, as special-purpose governments, by their nature, serve in ambivalent ways. It is perceived most clearly in a comparison of the lack of influence of the stockholders of the British public corporations in the affairs of those organizations when set against the dominant impact of the bondholders of the special public authorities in the United States. In both countries, the obligation of contract of governmental units is supported equally, but in the case of the American special governments the bondholders' liens have been accepted as paramount, even over those of the general public. British special governments shade their priorities toward public concerns, and, quite secondarily, toward the investment segment of society. The comparison could be overdrawn, as the public in both the United Kingdom and the United States complain of the remoteness of special agencies from responsiveness to the people, but it must not be overlooked. Many of the other characteristics of the special governments in Britain and America are predetermined by the difference in attitude toward their respective stockholders and bondholders. Quite apart from the public corporations for the nationalized industries, British special public governments, such as the Port of London Authority, show far less dependency on the investors in their stocks than do agencies in America, such as the Port Authority of New York and New Jersey, that place their obligations to their bondholders as their first financial responsibility. This role of private investors, which varies so markedly from Britain to America, in the special-purpose field, is a far more telling distinction than is that between the fact of these agencies representing nationalized as against free-enterprise economies. The Port of London Authority, for example, is not under the nationalized industries. It is not without overall meaning for special governments, therefore, that the "constituents" of the Port of London Authority, as referred to by the Authority itself, are "the whole nation"; "traders, industry and all who live in London"; and "the Secretary of the Environment." By contrast, it is significant that the "constituents" of the Port Authority of New York and New Jersey are considered to be "the bondholders"; "the neighbors," the "parents" (the two states), and "the facility-user." Noticeably missing in the list for the Port of London Authority are its stockholders; and noticeably first in the listing for the Port Authority of New York and New Jersey are its bondholders.

Many of the divergencies in the relative development of special-purpose governments in the United States and in the United Kingdom result from this financial factor. Of the five reasons generally given for the formation of these special agencies, four of them are common to both countries. Only this one, involving the force of the borrowing power, shows marked distinctions between the special public authorities of America, on the one hand, and the public corporations of Britain, on the other. But, so significant is this one factor that it tends to override the other four, resulting in a different concept of special-purpose government from the one English-speaking nation to the other. As described in detail earlier in the book, the four reasons commonly agreed to for the establishment of special units, in both countries, are:

1. their attraction to professional and business persons who will serve on their boards but are unwilling to engage in political campaigns for elective office
2. the so-called "business-like" efficiency of their operations required by the fact that they must finance themselves from their own resources without reliance on normal tax sources
3. their taking of highly technical public functions "out-of-politics," or, more accurately, their reframing of political influences for such functions around the special interest groups concerned
4. their capabilities of leap-frogging with their boundary lines the jurisdictional lines, of use for most of the other functions of conventional governments, in order to follow their particular function (or related functions) wherever they may lead.

The fact of the one dissimilarity, in the midst of these four similarities, accounts, in large measure, for the different courses the special public authorities have taken in Britain and America over the years, but for the fact, as well, that their movements always have had certain common characteristics.

The recent reconsideration of the excessive influence of the bonding interests on the special public authorities in the United States now has redirected the line of the American special public authority much closer to that of the British public corporation. At this point in their convergence, these unique progenies of the two English-speaking nations have much to say to each other about their common experiences. The lack of intercommunication in regard to these very unusual kinds of government between British and American officials, and, to a lesser extent, between British and American scholars, has been a serious deterrent to the most constructive employment of the special governments in the past in both countries. It was more understandable previously, however, as there was always the attitude that the economic systems of the two countries were so different, what with British nationalization of certain industries intimately associated with the public corporation, that there was little basis for comparison. Although the author discounts that factor as of genuine significance at any time, it now certainly should be laid to rest, as the American and British special authorities begin to resemble each other even in the matter of sources of borrowing and finance. There remains no plausible reason for hesitancy in the lively exchange of ideas on the little known, misunderstood, and significantly active special-purpose governments. Britain has had special agencies for at least 500 years, and America for the entire period of 180 years of its government under the federal system. In fact, by the time the word "Authority" in relation to special public authorities first was used in England, for the Port of London Authority in 1908, more than 100 of Britain's ports were being managed by special governments known as "local port trusts." The word first appeared in the United States in 1921 for the Port of New York Authority, which had taken the idea from its London prototype. The distinctions between the special-government movement in the two countries became apparent at that point. The Port of New York Authority took several divergencies from the Port of London Authority:

TABLE 3
CHRONOLOGY OF DEVELOPMENT
OF SPECIAL-PURPOSE GOVERNMENTS
IN THE UNITED KINGDOM AND UNITED STATES

United Kingdom	United States
1. Special units trace back 500 years.	1. Special units trace back 180 years.

2. Port of London Authority (1908):
   a. oriented to the river
   b. functional representation
   c. responsibility to minister of transport
   d. lack of stockholder influence
	2. Port of New York Authority (1921):
	   a. oriented to a port district
	   b. generalist representation
	   c. veto power of governors of two states
	   d. dominance of bondholders

3. Publication of Lord Morrison's *Socialisation and Transport* to establish public corporation in Britain, 1933.	3. President Roosevelt's encouragement of special public authorities, to establish them in the states, 1934.
4. Creation of British Transport Commission and executives, centralizing special-government movement in Britain, 1947.	4. Creation of special public authorities for automobile facilities, decentralizing them to municipalities, 1940s.
5. Creation of London Transport Board, with policy-making role, intermodal, regional, but with clear lines to minister of transport, 1962.	5. Creation, in six metropolitan areas of USA, of metropolitan transportation authorities, with policy-making roles, intermodal, regional, with certain closer ties to state governors, 1964 to date.
6. Creation of passenger transport authorities and passenger transport executives, to decentralize special governments somewhat and to separate policy making and implementation or operations, 1968.	6. Beginning of emphasis by federal government of general-purpose local governments as recipients of planning grants, rather than special governments (late 1960s, early 1970s).
7. Provision for designation of metropolitan counties, or regions, with these becoming the passenger transport authorities, and with each having passenger transport executives under them, 1972.	7. No such provisions.

1. it oriented itself to a "port district," which included far more inward territory than had the Port of London's restriction to the Thames River, itself, and involved in that district many more functions directly and indirectly related to port activities than had the London Authority

2. it chose its commissioners as generalists, able to represent mostly the business and financial interests of the port district, at large, where the Port of London Authority had selected its board on a functional basis, from among the principal users of the port

3. it set up a structure of accountability that relied heavily on a veto power that could be exercised by either the governor of New York or the governor of New Jersey

4. the Port of New York Authority tied itself to its bondholders, who were to have first lien on its income, thereby dictating that the Authority undertake mostly those functions that would be profitable. Mass transit was not among the surplus-producing modes of transportation, although it was of prime importance in the port district, and so was largely ignored.

The worldwide depression of the late 1920s and the 1930s served to crystallize the importance of the special government movement in both the United Kingdom and the United States. The principal impetus to the centralization of these ad hoc governments in the United Kingdom for the handling of the nationalized industries under the organization known as the public corporation came in 1933 when Herbert Morrison (later Lord Morrison of Lambeth) developed both the philosophical concept, and the practical application, in regard to a proposal for the coordination of transportation in London. The act of Parliament that resulted, although not wholly in accord with Morrison's conceptualization, was the first special-purpose government for the intermodal and regional attack on the transportation problem. The fact that in the course of the prolonged debate on the bill, all three political parties (Conservative, Labour, and Liberal) accepted the basic precepts of the public corporation, gave it meaning far beyond that of a mere vehicle for socialization.

At almost the same time in the United States, the New Deal administration of President Franklin D. Roosevelt was moving into the special public authority method empirically, but without any overall philosophy as to its use. The American leader eschewed the *national* (federal) government corporation, used by the British, and, instead, in 1934, wrote to the governors of the *states* to urge them to enable the municipalities to borrow money from the New Deal federal government through the establishment of local special public authorities that would be free of the kinds of restrictions that were prohibiting the general-purpose local governments from availing themselves of the federal public funds. These units were to be considered expediencies, for the present emergency, rather than, as in the United Kingdom, permanent entities for the management of the nationalized industries. Geared, as the president's proposals were, to the local governments, the special public authorities appeared throughout the United States with boundaries coterminous with those of existing municipalities. In addition, each was to handle just one special mode of a function. The British idea to meet the Depression involved the use of the special public corporation for transportation as a permanent organization for the nationalized industries, and as intermodal and regional. In the United States, on the contrary, the special public authorities were to be a temporary expediency, whose facilities were to revert to the general-purpose governments when the bonds, with interest, would be paid off. They were to handle only one mode of transportation, which would have to be a profit-making one, and they often were confined to the same boundaries as those of the municipality. By the time of the Census of Governments of 1967, the statistics revealed that only 2,300 of the total of 21,264 special governments extended beyond the jurisdiction of one county, and only 453 of them were taking on more than one function. British and American special-purpose governments were moving in opposite directions.

These special agencies in Britain and in America moved further apart in the late 1940s and the 1950s. The British

Transport Commission of 1947 centralized powers over transportation, using the newly formed "Executives" with little more than clerical responsibilities for carrying out the commission's directives. Concomitantly, the American special public authorities were being spawned in all directions, particularly to accommodate the surge of the automobile, whose tolls would make possible the amortization of the bonded indebtness of the authority. Self-sufficient as they thus were, the local special public authorities in America were decentralized, and became the "borrowing machines" for local government. As such, they came to plan the development of capital construction around their specializations which, by force of their commitment to private bonding, had to be capable of producing income beyond their expenses. This meant, in most instances, the automobile facilities. At this point, the special governments of Britain and America were taking different paths, with those in the United Kingdom serving merely as non-policy-making units for implementing the decisions of the British Transport Commission, and those in America assuming increasing decision-making roles, limited only by the essentiality of showing a profit to maintain their ratings in the private bond market. Centralization characterized the special development in Britain, and decentralization, that in America. The Transport Act of 1962 moved the British special-purpose governments again into a policy-making position, eliminating the impotent "Executives." The London Transport Board that began operation on January 1, 1963, under this legislation, had real power over mass transportation in London, but with a clear sense of responsibility to the minister. Its jurisdiction was intermodal within the mass transport field, regional over a broad area extending far beyond the city, and planning as well as operational. It could borrow money either from the minister or from "any other person." The kind of policy-making planning function the London Transport Board was to perform, in addition to its operating responsibilities, resembled the power of the local special public authorities in the United States. What the American authorities lacked, however, that the new British

Authority was granted were the intermodal and regional type jurisdictions that extended the London Transport Board's aegis over mass transit, in general, and in an extensive geographic area. Lacking, too, in the United States, was a clear line of responsibility of the special authority to a high executive officer, which the British board had with the minister. In the early 1960s, therefore, special public authorities were being used in both the United States and in London, with real powers over transportation, one limited by the fact that the automobile would pay the necessary tolls to amortize its facilities, and the other, in England, serving mass transit, at the expense of attention to roads.

In the middle 1960s, there began to appear in a few metropolitan centers of the United States, a new-type special public authority, known, commonly, as a Metropolitan Transportation Authority. The first two were created to serve the Boston and Philadelphia metropolitan areas in 1964, and subsequent ones arose in Detroit, Washington, D.C., New York, and Atlanta. A State Task Force proposed a Metropolitan Regional Agency for the Chicago metropolitan counties. These were, in all instances, intermodal for mass transportation, and regional for the core city and its surrounding commuter towns or counties. The greatest change over the former-type special public authority, that had prevailed in America since the 1930s, was that these MTAs no longer were chained to dependency on the surplus-producing automobile toll, but now were to be charged with the responsibilities for mass transit. To assume these deficit functions, the MTAs would have to have additional sources of income, and these were to come from a variety of taxes, such as those on cigarettes, gasoline, sales, and the like. Striking similarities are apparent between the London Transport Board and the new MTAs in America. They all were policy-making, special-purpose units for mass transit. They were intermodal within the mass transit area and were regional. The MTAs were more decentralized to the metropolitan areas than was the London Transport Board, but even the American agencies were showing more interrelationships with a high executive officer of general-purpose government (usually the governor of the state) through the fact that the state was to help finance their deficit undertakings.

The American special-purpose authorities traditionally had been decentralized. As a matter of fact, one argument frequently made on their behalf had been that they reflected the American's predilection for pluralism, where government power would be dispersed so that no one center of power would arise as a monopoly. British special governments, on the other hand, had been related to the minister of the appropriate department in the centralized government, and the British, instead of having the kind of confidence that the American citizens had felt in the decentralized units near them, instead had relied on their relationships with the minister. The first change in the British centralization of control over special governments came with the Transport Act of 1968, in which the entire nexus was moved down one step nearer the metropolitan area. The act provided for the assumption by the Council of Greater London of the responsibilities for mass transport, and for the establishment of a Transport Executive, which would be the operational arm of the Greater Council for transportation. Instead of the combine of the Minister of Transport and the London Transport Board, the new organizational structure was stepped down to the combine of the Greater London Council and its Transport Executive. This was an advance toward decentralization, and at the same time, toward the placing of policy making and comprehensive planning for transportation in the hands of the general-purpose elected officials of the Greater Council. The new Executive was to be a special-purpose government, as it was designated as "a body corporate with perpetual succession and a common seal."

London had been organized as a metropolitan government, through its two-tier structure, since 1965, but no other conurbations had been so designed. The Transport Act of 1968, however, anticipated the possible extension of metropolitan forms of government about other major cities. In the meantime, until that should happen, the act provided for the establishment of a Passenger Transport Authority and a Passenger Transport Executive for each of the so-called "designated areas." The areas subsequently designated were those of greater Manchester (South-East Lancashire–North-East Cheshire); greater Liverpool (Merseyside); greater Birmingham (West Midlands); greater Newcastle-upon-Tyne (Tyneside); and the Glasgow area. The Authority, in each instance, would operate, in the interim, as a regional transportation policy organization, and its Executive would serve as its operating arm. The Local Government Act of 1972, which provided for the reorganization of local governments throughout England and Wales arranged for the formation of metropolitan counties, and, in Scotland, of large regions. These metropolitan counties and one region were to become the Transport Authorities, taking over from the temporary Authorities, and each was to have its own Transport Executive. Added to the areas listed above were the newly named metropolitan counties of South Yorkshire and West Yorkshire. Beginning with these new arrangements, effective in 1974 and 1975, Transport Passenger Executives will be the operational special governments in the metropolitan counties, as now in Greater London, as well as in the region of Glasgow. The counties and region, being general-purpose governments of elected officials, will assume the responsibilities for policy making and comprehensive planning for transportation, and the Executives serve under them to implement their provisions.

Operational special authorities of the nature envisioned by the new Executives in Great Britain almost are unknown in the United States where the special public authorities have been created primarily for borrowing for capital construction. However, by the 1970s there were indications that general-purpose governments were to be recognized increasingly by the federal government for its planning grants, rather than the special-purpose units, as heretofore. There has been no change in America in the official provisions for the special public authorities for transportation, but the federal government was beginning to make it clear that the general-purpose governments were to be favored with the assignment of funds for overall planning purposes.

Planning, of course, is a continuous process running through all government functions, and it cannot be sharply differentiated from the operations of that same activity. There can be, however, an emphasis on the one aspect or the other. The general-purpose government seems better suited to perform the comprehensive planning and policy making for a major function, such as transportation, and the highly professional special purpose authority, consisting usually of appointed experts to carry out the plans and policies. In Britain, this kind of distinction now has been identified, and is being put into effect with the assignment of policy-making roles in transportation to the metropolitan counties and the Glasgow region, and the provision for Transport Passenger Executives for operational activities under the general-purpose governments. The emphasis, in both the United Kingdom and the United States had become blurred in recent years, as, almost by default in the absence of regional governments of elected officials, the special agencies simply had come to assume the policy-making and planning functions for transportation. They, alone, had had the capabilities of crossing existing governmental boundary lines that had lost their meaning for modern transportation needs. And they, in the United States, had become the units of government able to borrow the large funds necessary for capital construction, and, by dint of that capability, had become the planning agencies for governments, particularly in metropolitan areas. Further thought will indicate that special governments, obsessed as they are with their responsibilities for a single function, are in the most unfavorable position to undertake comprehensive planning, which consists of the determination of priorities of varied needs and functions. Much of the criticism of special-purpose governments in both Britain and America was caused by the assumption by them of these duties that they were totally inadequate to perform. Their prospects as highly specialized operational units appear much brighter. They are able to bring to bear on a highly technical function of government, in all its modes, a total concentration of effort by trained specialists. In Britain, they now have been turned in this direction; in America, there have been certain indications that the thought of such a role is beginning to crystallize to the point that it could, at some time, be enacted into legislation. This means, therefore, that consideration must be given to this whole new concept of the special purpose government in both countries. Their new potentialities as skilled expertise units will need attention and guidance, as, collectively, it represents a new force in British and American democracies. The problems posed throughout the years, vis-à-vis their interrelationships with the general-purpose governments, and recounted in this book, take on new significance as the special governments now stand in a new relationship to the general governments. The older questions simply are reframed: how should their boards be comprised, and on what system of representation; to whom should they be accountable; what now is to be their interrelationships with the executive, either minister or governor; what will be their political impact as it centers now, even more than before, on groups of special interests in society; what is to be their degree of influence on the planning processes now to be conducted primarily by the general-purpose governments; how will their operational expenses be met; what will be their dealings with the labor unions, as the costs of labor continue increasingly to constitute the bulk of the operating budgets; what will be their medium for recognizing the activities of other special-purpose operating units for other functions; and a host of such concerns. Their role will be defined more clearly than in the past. But the ambivalence of their posture in government will persist, as that kind of flexibility appears to be their raison d'etre. We know surprisingly little about the methods for integrating experts into the governmental process. And, when the experts are segregated in semiautonomous units so that they can function without interference from the normal system of governmental checks and balances, they could, conceivably, become a more serious force for fragmentation than before. The experiences of the past, as detailed in this book, therefore should offer some guidance, as both the United Kingdom and, perhaps, the United States, confront a new period of special-purpose government. On the strength of past performance in both countries, the potentialities of their operating contributions seem so to outweigh those of their prior planning and policy-making activities as to suggest that this recent development may well hold the key to their most appropriate place in democratic governments. The fact of their persistence throughout all the changes in the two forms of democracy over the many years, and the undeniably refreshing characteristics that they have lent to the rigidities of local governments, have indicated to the few scholars and practitioners who have studied them that they must have a place somewhere in government. As they have not been at their best in either country in the planning functions, there is a genuine feeling of anticipation about their importance to the operational side of government. It may well be there that special-purpose governments will be able to display their true capabilities.

REFERENCES

ADRIAN, C. R. (1967) State and Local Governments. 2nd ed. New York: McGraw-Hill.

––– (1961) "Metropology: Folklore and Field Research." Public Administration Rev. 21, 2 (Spring): 148-151.

Advisory Commission on Intergovernmental Relations (1970) Eleventh Annual Report, January 31. Washington, D.C.: Government Printing Office.

––– (1964a) Impact of Federal Urban Development Programs on Local Government Organization and Planning. Prepared in Cooperation with the Subcommittee on Intergovernmental Relations of the Committee on Government Operations, United States Senate. Washington, D.C.: Government Printing Office.

––– (1964b) The Problem of Special Districts in American Government. Washington, D.C.: Government Printing Office.

––– (1961) State Constitutional and Statutory Restrictions on Local Government Debt. Washington, D.C.: Government Printing Office.

The American County (1970) "City-County Consolidations, Separations, and Federations." Volume 35 (November): 12-13, 16-17 30-31.

ANDERSON, W. (1942) The Units of Government in the United State Chicago: Public Administration Service.

ATKINSON, B. (1971) "The Big Boys Against Prink Hill." The Ne York Times (August 5).

BANFIELD, E. C. (1961) "The Political Implications of Metropolit Growth." Daedalus 90 (Winter): 61-78.

BARKER, T. C. and M. ROBBINS (1963) A History of Londc Transport. Volume 1, The Nineteenth Century. London: Geor¿ Allen & Unwin.

BAWDEN, L. A. H. (1962) "Some Landward Links with the Docks P.L.A. Monthly 37 (August): 199-202.

BAYLY, L. (1934) Letter to Halsey Powell, July 1. On file, Franklin C Roosevelt Library, Hyde Park, New York.

BIGGER, R., E. A. IVERSON, J. N. JAMISON, J. D. KITCHEN, E. F. STANIFORD (1958) County Government in California. Bureau of Governmental Research, University of California, Los Angeles. Sacramento: County Supervisors Association of California.

BIRD, F. L. (1949) A Study of the Port of New York Authority. New York: Dun & Bradstreet.

BOLLENS, J. C. (1957) Special District Government in the United States. Berkeley: Univ. of California Press.

Bond Buyer (1965) Special Convention Issue no. 1 (June 7): 22.

Bouvier's Law Dictionary (1946) Baldwin Students Ed. Cleveland: Banks-Baldwin Law Publishing Co.

British Airports Authority (1972) Report and Accounts 1971/1972. London: British Airports Authority.

British Railways Board (1972) Annual Report and Statement of Accounts for the Year Ended 31 December 1971. London: Her Majesty's Stationery Office.

California, State. Assembly Interim Committee on Municipal and County Government (1961) Special District Problems in the State of California. Assembly Interim Committee Reports 1959-1961, 6: 15.

Central Office of Information, Reference Division (1972) Britain 1972. London: Her Majesty's Stationery Office.

Commissioner of Police of the Metropolis (1972) Report . . . for the Year 1971. London: Her Majesty's Stationery Office.

Committee of Inquiry into the Major Ports of Great Britain (1962) Report. London: Her Majesty's Stationery Office. Cmnd. 1824.

Council of State Governments (1953) Public Authorities in the States. A Report to the Governors' Conference. Chicago: Council of State Governments.

CROSS, C. A. (1971) Principles of Local Government Law. 4th ed. London: Sweet & Maxwell.

DAVIES, E. (1946) National Enterprise, The Development of the Public Corporation. London: Victor Gollancz.

DAVIS, H. A. (1935) "Borrowing Machines." National Municipal Rev. 24 (June): 328-334.

DAY, J. R. (1972) The Story of London's Underground. London: London Transport.

Department of the Environment (1972) The New Local Authorities, Management and Structure. London: Her Majesty's Stationery Office.

DRUCKER, P. (1959) "The Breakdown of Governments," quoted in Public Administration Rev. 19, 4 (Winter): 64.

Duke University School of Law (1961) "Public Authorities." Law and Contemporary Problems 26, 4.

DUPRE, J. S. (1967) "Intergovernmental Relations and the Metropolitan Area." Paper No. 5 of Centennial Study and Training Programme on Metropolitan Problems (February). Toronto: Bureau of Municipal Research.

ELLIS, E. R. (1966) The Epic of New York City. New York: Coward-McCann.

Executive Office of the President, Office of Management and Budget (1973) "Criteria Followed in Establishing Standard Metropolitan Statistical Areas," November 1971. (April 27 release.)

FAINSOD, M., L. GORDON, and J. C. PALAMOUNTAIN, JR. (1941) Government and the American Economy. New York: Norton & Co.

FESLER, J. W. (1949) Area and Administration. University: Univ. of Alabama Press.

FRANKFURTER, FELIX (1933a) Letter to President Franklin D. Roosevelt. Oxford, England (October 29). On file, Franklin D. Roosevelt Library, Hyde Park, New York.

——— (1933b) Letter to President Franklin D. Roosevelt, with enclosure of copy of J. M. Keynes' "An Open Letter to President Roosevelt." Oxford, England (December 16). On file, Franklin D. Roosevelt Library, Hyde Park, New York.

FRIEDMANN, W. [ed.] (1954) The Public Corporation, A Comparative Symposium. Comparative Law Series, University of Toronto School of Law. Volume 1. Toronto: Carswell Co.

Glasgow Herald (1973) August 25.

GORDON, L. (1938) The Public Corporation in Great Britain. London: Oxford Univ. Press.

Government Corporation Control Act, 1945. Public Law 248, 79th Congress, Chapter 557, 1st Sess.

Governor's Transportation Task Force (1973) Crisis and Solution, Public Transportation Northeastern Illinois. Chicago: Office of the Governor, State of Illinois.

GUILD, F. H. (1918) "Special Municipal Corporations." American Political Science Rev. 12 (November): 678-684.

HANSON, A. H. (1958) Public Enterprise and Economic Development. London Routledge & Kegan Paul.

——— [ed.] (1955) Public Enterprise, A Study of its Organisation and Management in Various Countries. Based on documents prepared for a United Nations Seminar held in Rangoon (March 1954). Brussels: International Institute of Administrative Sciences.

——— and M. WALLES (1970) Governing Britain, A Guidebook to Political Institutions. London: Fontana/Collins.

HAPGOOD, N. and H. MOSKOWITZ (1927) Up From the City Streets. New York: Grosset & Dunlap.

HEFFERNAN, P. (1972) "Retirement of Austin J. Tobin At New York Port Authority Could Signal Complexes' End." Weekly Bond Buyer, 178 (April 17): 19.

HERMAN, H. (1963) New York State and the Metropolitan Problem. Philadelphia: Univ. of Pennsylvania Press.

HOFSTADTER, R. (1948) The American Political Tradition and the Men Who Made It. New York: A. A. Knopf.

Illustrated London News (1972) Volume 260, 6891 (October): 53-54.

International Bridge, Tunnel, and Turnpike Association [IBTTA] (1972) Report of the Fortieth Annual Meeting. Washington, D.C.

——— (1971) Annual Revenue Traffic 1971-1970. Washington, D.C.

——— Tollways (January, 1973) Quoting Roads and Streets, October 1972; November 1972.

JAY, A. (1972) The Householder's Guide to Community Defence Against Bureaucratic Aggression, A Report on Britain's Government Machine. London: Jonathan Cape.

JONES, B. (1973) "Urban Transit and Bus Transportation," in "From the State Capitals" report (January 1).

––– (1972) "Urban Transit and Bus Transportation," in "From the State Capitals" report (November 1).

JONES, G. W. (1973) "The Local Government Act 1972 and the Redcliffe-Maud Commission." London: Political Quarterly 44, 2 (April-June): 154-166.

JONES, V. (1953) "Local Government Organization in Metropolitan Areas: Its Relation to Urban Development," in Coleman Woodbury, the Future of Cities and Urban Redevelopment. Chicago: Univ. of Chicago Press.

––– (1950) "The Withering Away of the City." Public Management 32, 12 (December).

KURSHAN, D. (1968) Letter to Robert G. Smith (December 30).

LEVITT, A. (1972) Statewide Public Authorities. Volumes I and II. New York State Comptroller's Studies on Issues in Public Service. Albany, N.Y. Office of the State Comptroller, Division of Audits and Accounts.

LILIENTHAL, D. E. (1945) TVA, Democracy on the March. New York: Pocket Books.

LINDSAY, J. V. (1966) "Transportation Administration and Transportation Council of the City of New York." City of New York, Office of the Mayor, Executive Order No. 4 (January 17).

––– (1965) "A Modern Transportation System for New York City." Campaign White Paper. New York.

Local Government Act 1972. Chapter 70. London: Her Majesty's Stationery Office.

Local Government Act 1933. 23 & 24 Geo. 5, chapter 51. London: Her Majesty's Stationery Office.

London Evening Standard (1972) November 1.

London Government Act 1972. Chapter 70. London: Her Majesty's Stationery Office.

London Government Act 1963. Chapter 33. London: Her Majesty's Stationery Office.

London Passenger Transport Act 1933. 23 & 24 Geo. 5, chapter 14. London: Her Majesty's Stationery Office.

London Transport (No. 2) Act 1971. Chapter 62. London: Her Majesty's Stationery Office.

London Transport Board (1964) Annual Report and Accounts 1963 for the Year Ended 31 December 1963. London: Her Majesty's Stationery Office.

London Transport Executive (1972) Annual Report and Accounts for the Year Ended 31 December 1971. London: London Transport Executive.

MARX, F. M. [ed.] (1959) Elements of Public Administration. 2nd ed. Englewood Cliffs, N.J.: Prentice-Hall.

MASON, M. S. (1967) "Government Means Cybernetics," part II entitled "The Resistant Executive." New York Law Journal 157, 91 (May 11): 4.

Massachusetts, The Commonwealth (1964) Acts, 1964, chapter 563.

Massachusetts Bay Transportation Authority vs. Boston Safe Deposit and Trust Company, et al. (1965), 348 Mass. 538, 205 N.E. 2nd 346 (Sup. Jud. Ct. Mass.).

MAYOR, A. and R. W. BURTON (1969) Parliament's Passport to London. New York: Corinthian Editions.

Metropolitan Transportation Authority (1972) 1971 Annual Report. New York: Public Affairs Department, Metropolitan Transportation Authority.

Metropolitan Water Board (1963) Sixtieth Annual Report Year Ended 31 March 1963. London.

Michigan, State (1967) Public and Local Acts of the Legislature of the State of Michigan, No. 204.

Ministry of Transport (1968) Transport in London. London: Her Majesty's Stationery Office. Cmnd. 3686.

MITCHELL, J. D. B. (1954) The Contracts of Public Authorities, A Comparative Study. London: London School of Economics and Political Science.

MORRISON, H. S. [Lord Morrison of Lambeth] (1964) Government and Parliament. A Survey from the Inside. 3rd ed. London: Oxford Univ. Press.

——— (1933) Socialisation and Transport. London: Constable and Co.

National Civic Review (1971) Volume 60 (November): 573-574. (1970) Volume 59 (March): 158.

National Industrial Recovery Act (1933) Public Law No. 67, 73rd Congress, 1st Sess.

National Technical Information Service, Action Plan for Improvements in Transportation Systems in Large U. S. Metropolitan Areas (1972) Prepared by the London Transport Executive Association, Springfield, Virginia.

New Jersey Supreme Court (1971) New Jersey Sports & Exposition Authority (N.J.S.A.) v. Joseph M. McCrane, Jr. etc., and Louis Montenegro, et al. 61 N.J. 1; 292 Atl.(2)545.

New Jersey Statutes Annotated (1967) and Cumulative Annual Pocket Parts. St. Paul, Minn.: West Publishing Co.

New York [Magazine] (1971) New York Commuter Special. Volume 4 (February): insert.

New York City (1952) The City of New York and The Port of New York Authority, Second Supplemental Agreement with Respect to Municipal Air Terminals (November 7).

New York State (1970) Annotated. McKinney's Consolidated Laws of New York. Public Authorities Law. Volume 1 and 2. St. Paul, Minn.: West Publishing.

––– (1970) Cumulative Annual Pocket Parts. St. Paul, Minn.: West Publishing.

––– (1966) Senate Intro. No. 4134, Assembly Intro. No. 5417; Senate Intro. 4135, Assembly Intro. 5418. (Mayor John V. Lindsay's proposal for reorganization of transportation coordination in New York City.)

New York Times (1973a) July 3; (1973b) April 30; (1972a) August 30; (1972b) March 31; (1971a) August 20; (1971b) August 5; (1971c) May 6; (1971d) April 25; (1970) March 4; (1969) November 26; (1967) April 7; (1966) February 25; (1961) January 1. Copyright © by The New York Times Company. Reprinted by permission.

O'BRIEN, T. H. (1937) British Experiments in Public Ownership and Control. A Study of the Central Electricity Board, British Broadcasting Corporation, London Passenger Transport Board. London: George Allen & Unwin.

Passenger Transport, The Weekly Newspaper of the Transit Industry (1973a) Volume 31, January 26; (1973b) Volume 31, January 19; (1972a) Volume 30, May 26; (1972b) Volume 30, February 25; (1970) Volume 28, November 6.

Pennsylvania Commonwealth, Department of Internal Affairs (1960) 1960 Pennsylvania Municipal Authorities Directory. Harrisburg.

Pennsylvania Municipal Authorities Association (1969) The Pennsylvania Municipality Authorities Act and Related Laws. Harrisburg.

PERKINS, R. B. (1966) Letter to Editor of The New York Times (February 25).

Philadelphia Daily News (1964) April 20.

Philadelphia Evening Bulletin (1970) January 29; (1964) September 16; (1961) October 3.

Port of London Act 1968. Chapter 32. London: Her Majesty's Stationery Office.

Port of London Authority (1972) Annual Report and Accounts Year Ended 31 December 1971. London.

––– Port of London (1972) Volume 47 (June): 164-166.

––– (1971) Notes on the Port of London. London.

––– (1958) Port of London. London.

––– P.L.A. Monthly (1964) Volume 39 (October/November): 311-315, 347-351; (1963) Volume 38 (January): 18-20; (1962) Volume 37 (October): 257-263.

Port of New York Authority (1968) "The Exercise of the Veto Power over the Port of New York Authority." New York. (Currently known as Port Authority of New York and New Jersey.)

––– (1967) The Port of New York Authority 1966 Annual Report. New York.

––– (1961) The Port and the Community. New York. Issued May 1956. Reprinted May 1959; November 1961.

PRESSMAN, L. (1935) Inter-Office Communication to Harry Hopkins (February 27). Federal Surplus Relief Corporation. On file, Franklin D. Roosevelt Library, Hyde Park, New York.

The Random House Dictionary of the English Language (1967). New York: Random House.

Reconstruction Finance Corporation Act (1933) Amended June 30, 1947. Washington, D.C.: United States Congress.

RHODES, G. [ed.] (1972) The New Government of London: The First Five Years. London: London School of Economics and Political Science (Weidenfield and Nicolson).

ROBSON, W. A. (1973) Letter to Robert G. Smith (December 6).

––– (1970) Justice and Administrative Law. 3rd ed. Westport, Conn.: Greenwood Publishers.

––– (1962) Nationalised Industry and Public Ownership. 2nd ed. London: George Allen & Unwin.

––– (1948) The Government and Misgovernment of London. 2nd ed. London: George Allen & Unwin.

––– (1937) Public Enterprise, Development in Social Ownership and Control in Great Britain. London: George Allen & Unwin.

––– and D. E. REGAN (1972) Great Cities of the World. 3rd ed. London: George Allen & Unwin; Beverly Hills: Sage Publications.

ROOSEVELT, F. D. (1934) Letter to Governors. On file, Franklin D. Roosevelt Library, Hyde Park, New York.

ROSENBERG, S. D. (1969) "Can the Inviolability of a Bond Indenture Withstand the Avid Hunt for New Pools of Money?" Bond Buyer, special issue (December 8): 59-63.

Royal Commission on Local Government in Greater London 1957-60 (1960) Report. London: Her Majesty's Stationery Office. Cmnd. 1164.

SAUSE, G. G. (1962) Municipal Authorities, The Pennsylvania Experience. Harrisburg: Commonwealth of Pennsylvania, Department of Internal Affairs.

Scotsman (1972a) October 13; (1972b) September 28. Edinburgh.

Secretary of State for Scotland (1971) Reform of Local Government in Scotland. London: Her Majesty's Stationery Office. Cmnd. 4583.

SELF, P. (1955) "Town Planning in the United States and Britain," number II entitled "Planning the Urban Leviathans." Town Planning Rev. 25, 4 (January).

SHARPE, L. J. (1966) "The New Government in Greater London." Public Management 48 (April): 91-99.

SMITH, R. G. (1969) Public Authorities in Urban Areas. Washington, D.C.: Research Foundation, National Association of Counties.

––– (1968) "County Service Districts and Special Districts," pp. 59-93 in Guide to County Organization and Management. Washington, D.C.: National Association of Counties.

––– (1965) "What's Good and Bad About Authorities," in Airport Operators Council Management Handbook, volume 1 (M-9-M-17). Washington, D.C. Airport Operators Council.

––– (1964) Public Authorities, Special Districts and Local Government. Washington, D.C.: Research Foundation, National Association of Counties.

Supplementary Report of the Urbanism Committee (1939) Urban Government. Volume 1. Washington, D.C.: National Resources Committee, Committee on Urbanism.

SYME, R. (1959) The Story of British Roads. 3rd ed. London: British Road Federation.

TAUBER, G. and S. KAPLAN (1966) The New York City Handbook. Garden City: Doubleday.

Temporary State Commission on Coordination of State Activities, State of New York (1956) Staff Report on Public Authorities under New York State. Albany, N.Y.: Williams Press.

TENNYSON, E. L. (1972) "Rail Lines Prove Popular in Philadelphia Mass Transit System." Pennsylvanian 11 (April): 18.

THURSTON, J. (1937) Government Proprietary Corporations in the English-Speaking Countries. Cambridge, Mass.: Harvard Uni. Press.

Times [London] (1973) August 25; (1972a) November 12 (London Times Magazine)j (1972b) October 27; (1972c) October 8 (The Sunday Times).

TOBIN, A. J. (1953) "Authorities as a Governmental Technique." Speech before the Third Annual Institute, "The Place of Authorities in the Life of New Jersey Citizens." Sponsored by the New Jersey Council for Social Studies, and the Bureau of Governmental Research at Rutgers University (March 26).

Transport Act (1969) Chapter 35. London: Her Majesty's Stationery Office.

Transport Act (1968) Chapter 73. London: Her Majesty's Stationery Office.

Transport Act (1962) 10 & 11 Eliz. 2, chapter 46. London: Her Majesty's Stationery Office.

Transport Act (1947) 10 & 11 Geo. 6, chapter 49. London: Her Majesty's Stationery Office.

Treasury and Department of Trade and Industry (1972) Nationalized Industries Relations with the Public. London: Her Majesty's Stationery Office.

Triborough Bridge and Tunnel Authority (1966) Statements Presented at the Joint Public Hearings of the Senate and Assembly Rules Committees in Opposition to the Proposed Bills on Consolidation of Various Transportation Functions within the City of New York, Albany (March 10-11).

Tyneside Passenger Transport Authority and Tyneside Passenger Transport Executive (1970) Joint Policy Statement. Newcastle-upon-Tyne.

United States Congress, House of Representatives Committee on the Judiciary, Subcommittee No. 5, 86th Congress, 2nd Sess. (1960) Hearings, November 28, 29, 30; December 1 and 2. Serial No. 24, Part I, Part 2.

United States Supreme Court (1973) Salyer Land Co. v. Tulare Lake Basin Water Storage District. 410 U.S.

WEBB, S. and B. (1922) Statutory Authorities for Special Purposes, with a Summary of the Development of Local Government Structure. English Local Government Volume 4. New impression, 1963. Hamden, Conn.: Archon Books.

——— (1913) The Story of the King's Highway. English Local Government Volume 5. New Impression, 1963. Hamden, Conn.: Archon Books.

Weekly Bond Buyer (1965) 171 (September 7): 4.

WELLER, J. L. (1969) The New Haven Railroad, Its Rise and Fall. New York: Hastings House.

WHITE, L. D. (1955) Introduction to the Study of Public Administration. 4th ed. New York: Macmillan.

——— (1951) The Jeffersonians. New York: Macmillan.

WINDERS, J. J. (1973) "Tax-Exempt Financing for Pollution Control Soars to $819.6 Million in Year's First Half." Money Manager (July 9).

WOOD, R. C. (1961) 1400 Governments. Cambridge, Mass.: Harvard Univ. Press.

INDEX

ABOUT THE AUTHOR

ROBERT G. SMITH is Pfeiffer Professor of Political Science at Drew University. He is the author of *Public Authorities, Special Districts and Local Government* (1964) and *Public Authorities in Urban Areas* (1969), and many book chapters and journal articles about metropolitan government and politics. Professor Smith has also served as a consultant to government agencies such as the City of New York, the State of Illinois, and the State of New Jersey. Currently a consultant to the Research Foundation of National Association of Counties and the Advisory Commission on Intergovernmental Relations, he has recently completed a national study of coordination of transportation by special purpose government in United States metropolitan areas for the latter.